THE GREAT EFFICACY OF SIMPLE FAITH IN
THE ATONEMENT OF CHRIST,

EXEMPLIFIED IN

A MEMOIR

OF

MR. WILLIAM CARVOSSO,

SIXTY YEARS A CLASS-LEADER IN THE WES-
LEYAN METHODIST, CONNEXION,

WRITTEN BY HIMSELF,

AND

EDITED BY HIS SON;

———•———

*" He staggered not at the promise of God through unbelief;
but was strong in faith, giving glory to God."*

———

NEW-YORK:

PUBLISHED BY T. MASON AND G. LANE,

For the Methodist Episcopal Church, at the Conference Office,
200 Mulberry-street.

———

J. Collord, Printer.
1837.

TO THE

MEMBERS AND FRIENDS OF THE WESLEYAN

METHODIST SOCIETIES IN CORNWALL,

AMONG WHOM ARE SO EXTENSIVELY CHERISHED

THE PRINCIPLES OF VITAL CHRISTIANITY,

This Brief Memorial

OF THE CHRISTIAN EXPERIENCE AND USEFUL LIFE

OF ONE WHO ARDENTLY DESIRED,

AND DILIGENTLY LABOURED,

TO PROMOTE THEIR SPIRITUAL INTERESTS,

IS MOST AFFECTIONATELY AND RESPECTFULLY

DEDICATED BY

THE EDITOR.

PREFACE.

"THE observations of good old Mr. Carvosso have been read by myself and others, with that awful reverence which is due to the directions of one, who—having himself found the way, and being about to enter the kingdom of blessedness—is anxious to direct the multitudes who would arrive at the same place. Every syllable has a force, and comes with an irresistible authority:—The whole is emphatic, clear, and scriptural."—This is an extract from a letter, written by the late eminent Counsellor Drew, of Jamaica, to his sister; at whose request my father had written to him; and of whom an interesting account will be found in a subsequent part of this volume.

I have no knowledge of the contents of the letter which was written to Mr. Drew, but doubt not that multiplied observations, of the same kind and quality, will be found in the ensuing pages; and if they be read by persons whose minds are as simple and well-disposed as his was, there is every reason to believe they will be received as clear and scriptural—felt to have force and authority—and be pronounced good to the use of edifying. Indeed, if the opinion on this subject be correct, which is contained in a letter addressed to the Editor, by a very judicious friend, there is a numerous class of readers who are prepared to feel a greater interest in this little work, than could be felt by Mr. Drew and such as never saw my father's face in the flesh. The respected writer says "I am glad you are about to publish a Memoir of your late excellent father; I hope to receive much comfort and benefit from its perusal—as I doubt not thousands more will; especially those who had the happiness of his acquaintance: The recollection of the man will render the Memoir doubly interesting. Of the many favours of Divine Providence, which demand my daily acknowledgment, his friendship, which I enjoyed so many years, stands in the foremost rank." Another intelligent friend, who well knew him, remarked to me, "If ever there was a man whose piety, and extraordinary usefulness, in that sphere of life in which he moved, deserved a biographical record, your late venerable father is the person."

With such statements, it would be easy to swell these introductory pages. But while the Editor deems it unnecessary further to trouble the reader with suffrages of this kind, he has considered those not uncalled for; to justify the part he has taken, in bringing the volume before the public,—to bespeak the candid attention of the stranger,—and also to remind the Christian reader that, as he is about to tread hallowed ground, it is meet he should do it with that awful reverence which is only found in a devotional frame of mind. This is the more necessary, as the accumulation of strong meat which

will be found in many of these pages, cannot be
used by any, so as to grow thereby, until it be
sanctified by prayer to Him whose special grace
alone conveys the requisite power to feed on
Christ in the heart by faith.

The subject of this Memoir was a Methodist
—a warm, simple-hearted, old Wesleyan Methodist; and, therefore, nothing more or less
than Methodism, in the old way, must be looked
for here. Be it his fault or his excellence, my
father was a passionate admirer of Mr. Wesley.
Having been twenty years a member of the
united society, before the death of that great
man and great minister of Christ; he was often
one of those who followed him from place to
place, and mingled among the overwhelming
crowds, that hung upon his lips when he visited
these parts. A thousand times, with streaming
eyes, he would bless God for sending Mr Wesley into Cornwall. The doctrines taught by
him, he regarded as the pure truth of God; and
received them with his whole spirit and soul.
Mr. Wesley's Sermons and Hymn-Book were
prized by him, perhaps, as highly as any earthly
things ought to be. Their very existence was
to him a continued subject of adoring gratitude.

Present, free, and full salvation, by simple
faith in the atonement, formed the theme on
which he dwelt with delight, and almost without intermission; more particularly during the
last twenty-five years of his lengthened pilgrimage. In receiving the salvation of the Gospel,
he had no opinion of delays, exceptions, or

limits. To the spiritually diseased, of every class, his constant cry was, "Come; for all things are now ready." He saw, in the strong commanding light of faith, Christ present, able, willing to save unto the uttermost; and therefore, when he exclaimed,—

> "Believe, and all your sin's forgiven;
> Only believe, and yours is heaven!"

it often produced an effect peculiarly his own. In no man's lips, whom I have heard speak on matters of faith, did it ever appear to me that the word "believe" meant so much as in his. When others said to the penitent, "You must believe," the words often appeared without force, and almost without meaning; but no sooner did he utter those, or similar words, than the wisdom of God was manifest, and Gospel truth, spoken in simplicity, frequently seemed like a leaver that moved the world. Hence the multitudes of captive souls who found almost instant liberty when they fell into his hands.

To some who had no personal knowledge of his character,—having never heard the wisdom and the spirit with which he spake of faith in the blood of Christ,—it may appear strange, and perhaps scarcely credible, that so many persons, variously instructed and informed, and often long groaning under spiritual bondage, should find the joy of salvation, on their being introduced into his presence but a few minutes only: The sorrowful soul being brought out of darkness into marvellous light, simply by the

usc of two or three right words. In some
degree to account for this, it should be borne in
mind, 1. That, on these occasions, his words
came from a heart which felt the power of the
Lord was present to heal. His falling tears,
his lifted hands, his affecting emphasis, and
every lineament of his countenance, declared
THAT to the sorrowful spirit whom he addressed, and powerfully enforced the truth contained
in his burning words. 2 His faith, no doubt,
brought a degree of gracious aid to the helpless
soul. To what extent our faith may be regarded while we seek the salvation of others, we
have no means of ascertaining; but that it
sometimes has an important bearing on the subject, is evident from the case of the man who
was brought to Christ, sick of the palsy. Of
the man's own faith, we hear nothing; but of
his four benevolent friends, who used such extraordinary exertions to bring him to Jesus Christ,
it is written, " When Jesus saw their faith, he said
to the sick of the palsy, Son, thy sins are forgiven
thee " Now, when a broken-hearted penitent
was introduced to my father, and he heard him
inquire, amidst the flowing of humble, contrite
tears, " What must I do to be saved ? " he un-
hesitatingly pointed him to the Lamb of God ;
confidently believing that he could and would
save the soul that lay thirsting for salvation at
the footstool of the mercy-seat : And is not
" Jesus Christ the same yesterday, to-day, and
for ever ? " 3. On the first exercise or act of
faith by which the sinner comes to Christ, it is

well known that the subject of this Memoir was apt to teach. He was most fruitful in expedients and illustrations, to help the understanding and the confidence of the seeking soul. A young man, a member of our society, one of much intelligence, and more than ordinary strength of mind, who has since died in faith, observed to me one day in his affliction, " Until I saw your excellent father, it seemed to me I never met with any one whose exposition of faith came within the reach of my understanding; but his remarks on the nature of that important grace were clear and forcible in an extraordinary degree, commending themselves to my reason, as well as to my heart and conscience : And," he added, "suffer me to say, If his papers shall fall into your hands, you will be guilty of an act of injustice to the world, if you do not give them to the public."

His illustrations, which told so remarkably, were commonly of the most simple kind. Entering into the house of a poor man, known to him to be deeply and sorrowfully concerned for the salvation of his soul, he found him blowing the fire, to assist in preparing the ordinary meal. My father said to him, "John, if you had half as much faith in Jesus Christ as you have in those bellows, you would be set at liberty in a moment." This at once brought the subject of faith in Christ within the man's reach ; in an instant he saw—he felt—he believed—and was saved from all his sins and sorrows It was in this way he would seize on any thing open to

the senses, and in one way or other render it
subservient to his great object, the bringing of
the soul to Jesus: And his deeply spiritual mind,
clear conceptions of the subject, and great simplicity of soul, rendered this mode of instruction
highly interesting and profitable.

He would often put the person who was
eagerly inquiring after Christ, to read an ap-
propriate Scripture, or verse of a hymn; telling
him, that he must try to read for himself. If,
at the first reading, his heart did not take hold of
the truth, he would be required to read over
the portion more carefully, again and again.
In this way he has helped many a poor mourner over the bar of unbelief. Closely connected
with this method of instruction, he had another,
which was equally successful: At some ap-
posite turn of expression, he would stop short
the sorrowful and heavy-laden reader, look him
in the face, with the feelings of a devoutly melting heart visible in his eyes, show him what
was contained in, and his right to, what his lips
had uttered; and then, in the most persuasive
and affectionate manner, inquire if he did not
perceive the meaning, and believe the gracious
truth, contained in the words which had now
dropped from his own lips. Thus many, ere
they were aware, felt themselves gently borne
from the fearful precipice of unbelief, and set
down amidst the ocean of redeeming love. Of
this I have an instance before me, detailed in a
letter from one of my father's correspondents:
The writer says of him, " He went with me to

see an old couple, whom I was in the habit of visiting once a week. While we were there, a woman, who was a near neighbour, came in; your dear father, who was always ready for such work, asked her, I think, if she loved God. She said, ' Yes; but there is something I still want.' He said, ' Come, and sit down by me, and I will tell you all about it.' She sat down accordingly, and he soon discovered she did not know her sins were pardoned. He told her, 'You may receive this blessing now.' He then took our Hymn-Book, opened to the thirty-sixth hymn, and put her to read the fourth verse. When she had read, ' Thy debt is paid,' he put his thumb on the words which followed, looked her in the face, and inquired, if she thought it *was paid?* She burst into a flood of tears, and was made happy from that moment. This is many years ago, but his dear name is as precious to her as ever; and, I may add, she is still a consistent member of the society.'

There is another way in which he was sometimes made a very great blessing to the sincere seekers of Gospel salvation; it was, by clearly and familiarly pointing out to them the error into which they occasionally fell, of undervaluing, and overlooking, the good work which God had already wrought in them; and thus, by a voluntary humility, adding to their own difficulties in the work of faith. Another extract, from the letter above referred to, will afford an interesting and profitable illustration of this remark: After detailing the unsuccessful pains which he, and certain of his friends, had taken to obtain the blessing of perfect love, the writer proceeds to state, " About this time your father had visited some neighbouring places, but I had not seen him. But, one day, brother B. called on me, and, in his quaint manner, said, 'Brother T., you will not be with him five minutes, before you will be hot all over.' My expectations were raised; and at last he arrived, and took up his abode under my roof. One memorable night, my friends being present with me, he was conversing with us on the blessing of perfect love. He, like a wise master builder, having examined our spiritual attainments, discovered that we were in possession of the essential properties of that happy state, but without the joyful witness thereof. Therefore, he no longer held up the thing in prospect before us, but declared us in possession of it; and charged us with the error of asking for what God had already given. 'Now,' said he, 'it is rather your business to give thanks and rejoice.' To illustrate and impress on us his view of the subject, he took up a hymn-book which lay before us on the table. 'Suppose,' says he, 'one of you ask me for this book. Well, there it is: I give it to you;' putting it at the same time into the hands of one of our little company. 'Now,' he observed will it not be manifest folly in you, to continue asking me for the book, when you have it already in your possession?' This simple method helped us to the act of faith; we believed, the sacred fire

kindled within, and presently, we were all in a
blaze of love, shouting and praising God together; and, what is matter of greatest praise, the
savour of the good then received we retain to
this day."

As to the true nature, the object, and the
fruits of faith, he never misled the inquirer by
new and strange notions, but uniformly kept in
the good old way. With him the immediate
and constant fruits of full Christian faith, were,
" Pardon, and holiness, and heaven;" the object
of this faith, " Christ crucified;" and as to the
nature of it, he ever maintained that the power
to believe was from God, that the act of believing
was necessarily ours; and that the former was
received, and the latter performed, only in the
spirit of prayer. St. Paul's definition of faith,
" Now faith is the substance of things hoped for,
the evidence of things not seen," Heb. xi 1, he
greatly admired, and often quoted; and the
marvellous effects of faith detailed in that chapter
were much his theme in life and in death. Faith
subdued all his evils, repaired all his breaches,
supported and solaced him under all his trials
and sorrows, made the fulness of Christ all his
own, and empowered him with an ability to become an immense blessing to multitudes; hence
the prominence which he gave to it in his public
addresses, his private conversations, and spiritual letters; and hence, also, the bold relief in
which it will be found the grace of faith stands
in the subsequent narrative. Should there be
any who call for a defence of this peculiarity

in the book, we may refer them for such a de-fence to the example contained in the teaching of Jesus Christ and the apostles.

Of all the Wesleyan tenets, none was received by my father more heartily than the doctrine of Christian Perfection. He saw it with the eyes that compiled the Wesleyan Hymn-Book, and, throughout his long Christian career, he held it to be just as important as Mr. Wesley himself did, when he said, " It is the grand depositum which God has given to the people called Me-thodists; and chiefly to propagate this, it ap-pears, God raised them up." " Where it is not preached, there is seldom any remarkable bles-sing of God; and, consequently, little addition to the society, or little life in the members of it. Speak, and spare not Let not regard to any man induce you to betray the truth of God. Till you press believers to expect full salvation *now*, you must not look for any revival." " That point—that we may be saved from all sin in this life—can hardly ever be insisted upon in preaching or prayer without a particular bles-sing. Honest J B firmly believes this doctrine: but I wish, when opportunity serves, you would encourage him, 1. To preach Christian perfec-tion constantly, strongly, explicitly: 2. Explicitly to assert and prove, that it may be received now: And, 3. That it is to be received by simple faith * Into all this pious ardour for " perfect holiness of heart by faith, now," my father en-

* Wesley's Works; Vol. xii. p. 254; Vol. xiii. pp. 9, 49.

tered with the full tide of feeling and of conviction. It was no matter of speculation with him.
He had felt his want of such a blessing as is
understood by the words Christian perfection,
entire sanctification, or perfect love. Unaided
by human teaching, he searched the Scriptures,
and found that God had clearly promised it:
by the prayer of faith he applied to the throne
of grace for it; and the Spirit of holiness, with
glorious power and demonstration, revealed it in
his heart. Hence, neither men nor devils,
could shake his faith in the verity of this doctrine; nor could his tongue, or humble pen, be
silent in recommending it to all believers with
whom he had intercourse; and his success in
this forms one of the most striking features of
his brief history.

From his distinct profession on this point, together with the large developement of his experience contained in this volume, some little
instruction perhaps may be gained on the practical bearings of the doctrine. As far as his
views and experience go, we learn, 1. That
perfect love admits of a direct and satisfactory
testimony from the Spirit, as to the time when
God accomplishes the great work within us.
2. That faith alone is the condition and instrument of its application. 3. That it does not
make man independent of the atonement; but on
the contrary increases the believers consciousness of its necessity, and inestimable worth;
inasmuch as the holiness of God, the purity
and extent of the law the sinfulness of sin, and

the defects of our lives, are better understood.
4. That a present profession of enjoyment of the
blessing is not responsible for failures, past, or
to come.   He that can now say, " In me verily
is the love of God perfected," may have often
grieved the Spirit, since he first knew this great
salvation by experience, and may again cast
away his confidence, and feel a return of the
carnal mind; for he stands only one moment
at a time, and that moment by a faith whose
life depends on our constancy in watching unto
prayer.   5. That in the time of temptation
when the soul is stripped of the joyous witness
of the blessing, it is our privilege and duty to
go at once to the atoning sacrifice, and exercise
a bold and firm reliance on Christ, for present
and full salvation; and that this faith brings
that blessed inward witness, the absence of
which was a little before so sensibly felt.
6. That when the believer has sustained a spiritual loss, and is conscious he has given way
to sin, on the first perception of it, he should
humbly, but instantly, fly to the blood that
makes the wounded whole, resting therein and
agonizing in prayer, till the soul be again
completely restored   7. That although the'
enjoyment of perfect love does not admit of outward or inward sin, properly so called, yet it
admits of a strong conviction of the presence of
numberless short-comings and infirmities; and
requires a vivid perception of the evil of our
fallen nature, the aggravation of sins that are
past, and the judgment for which they are con-

tinually calling, should we be found one moment separate from the blood of sprinkling.

As Mousehole is so often mentioned in the
ensuing pages, it will doubtless be an object of
interest to some readers; and, therefore, a brief
notice of it here may not be unacceptable.   It
lies about three miles south-west of Penzance,
on the shore of Mount's Bay.   Prior to the
reign of Queen Elizabeth, when it was burned
by the Spaniards, history informs us, it was a
town of considerable notoriety.   It is very plea-
santly situated; and, at present, bears the character of a compact, interesting village; containing about one thousand inhabitants, whose sub-
sistance is derived almost entirely from fishing.
Upwards of fifty years the Methodists have had
there a numerous society; which has uniformly
borne a very high character for its Christian
simplicity, and intelligent, fervent, and stable
piety.   Its number was small, not exceeding
twenty, when my father, sixty-four years ago,
first united himself to it.   Their place of worship was then a small room in a dwelling house.
Soon afterwards they removed into a disagree-
able place, used as a cellar for curing fish.   After
awhile, they fitted up for public worship a large
upper room, the beams of which gave way,
with a tremendous crash, the first time the
congregation assembled in it.   My father was
present on the occasion: No lives were lost by
the accident.   Their first chapel was built in
1783, at the time the Rev. Joseph Taylor, sen.,
travelled in Cornwall; whose labours were much

blessed at Mousehole, as well as in other parts of the county. In 1813 this chapel was greatly enlarged. But still being too limited in its dimensions to contain the congregation, this gave place to a much larger one, in 1833.

For such a place, this chapel is a noble-looking building, is beautifully situated, will contain about eight hundred hearers, and is remarkably well attended. The number of the society is at present about three hundred.*

* During the same period, the interests of religion in the county, as connected with Methodism, has progressed in a similar manner. At the Conference before my father joined the Society, the space now included in the Cornish district, (about two-thirds of the superficies of the county,) contained two circuits, seven preachers, and two thousand three hundred and eleven members. At that time there were no schools, and but few chapels or local preachers. At the Conference which preceded my father's death, there were within the same limits, thirteen circuits, twenty-five preachers, eighteen thousand one hundred and twenty-two members in society, and about nineteen thousand children in our Sunday-schools, two hundred and ninety local preachers, two hundred and twenty chapels, and, as nearly as can be estimated, about fifty-five thousand hearers.

Within the same period, the Methodist Connexion throughout the world has increased with equal rapidity. In the year 1770, the total number of Methodist preachers was one hundred, and the total number of members, twenty-nine thousand four hundred and six. In 1834, the total number of preachers was three thousand seven hundred and seventy; and the total amount of members in the different parts of the globe, one million five hundred and fifty-eight. "Let no man glory in man: He that glorieth, let him glory in the Lord.".

In the perusal of the following personal narrative, it should be borne in mind, that, as an Author, my father laboured under peculiar disadvantages; such, indeed, I apprehend, as cannot be easily paralleled in the history of literature. Here is the singular instance of a man writing a volume for the instruction of the world, and raising himself into very extensive notoriety and esteem by his epistolary correspondence; who, at the advanced age of sixty-five, had never written a single sentence! At this period the utmost performance of his pen was to mark his class-book, or class-paper; and, on a rare occasion, when circumstances required something of the kind, to put together, with much effort, the letters of the alphabet which composed his name. As he used with much regularity to mark his class-paper, when he returned from meeting, and commonly filled up the ruled interstices with the letter P, I remember my mother used now and then humorously to rally him about the extent of his penmanship; telling him, the utmost he could do was to make P's. To this circumstance, however, by rendering him somewhat familiar with the use of a pen, I am inclined to believe, we are, in a great degree, indebted for the benefit which he has conferred on others, by his subsequent rather voluminous writing. In page 276 allusion is made to the circumstance which first called forth the use of his pen. From that hour an avenue of new pleasure and usefulness was open to his active and benevolent mind;

and now thousands of closely written pages in his hand-writing attest how piously and dili-gently he improved it. He, indeed, presents the remarkable phenomenon of a person who, with great diligence, toiled in business above half a century, acquired a sufficiency to retire with credit and comfort to himself; and who, with his pen, filled up volumes, and wrote hundreds of letters; and yet I believe not a page or a letter was ever written by him on any other topic than experimental and practical godliness! Surely this is one way of showing how fully he " counted all things but loss for the excellency of the knowledge of Christ Jesus his Lord."

After this statement respecting the origin of the book, it is presumed with some degree of confidence, that the literary reader's indulgence will not be asked in vain. The more impor-tant part of writing a free and perspicuous communication of his thoughts, my father readily mastered; yet, from the great simplicity of his mind, and the fervour of his soul, he was generally drawn out too eagerly to grasp at things, to pay much attention to orthography, or the arrangement of words in a sentence; Still, such was the obvious improvement which he made, in every department of writing, during the first few years after he commenced what may be inoffensively termed his literary life, that I think it likely, had any one attempted to give him, at seventy-five, only a very few lessons on the subject, he would have readily learned to write with considerable correctness. In the mechanical part of the art of writing, he excell-ed most men of his standing in life. I have before me a letter on a post sheet, which was addressed to me; it contains upwards of two hundred lines, or more matter than is con-tained in ten of the printed pages of this book; and yet so carefully is the whole written, and so distinctly are the letters formed, that it is just as legible, and can be read with as much ease, as a plain letter from a clever school-boy.

As my father's letters were so numerous, and mostly so lengthy, and have in general been so carefully preserved by his affectionate correspondents, it would have been very easy to produce a volume two or three times the size of the present. The few which are inserted will serve as a specimen of his pious exer-tions in the epistolary way. Should any of his friends be disappointed at not finding their letters here, after they had kindly forwarded them for the use of the Editor, his apology is, he feared to swell the book to such a magnitude as would necessarily make its price too great for a numerous class of persons, to whom it will probably be most useful; and by whom it is likely to be most highly prized.

In preparing the manuscripts for publication, the Editor has felt it to be highly important to refrain as much as possible from altering the language; that the narrator may, in his own words, tell his own simple, affecting story. Where necessary retrenchments and corrections

have required a few verbal alterations, there
has been no interference with the obvious
meaning of the writer.

The Editor cannot conclude his work,—in
which he has felt unwonted pleasure and profit,
—without expressing his hope, that this little
volume, however unpretending and defective in
a literary point of view, will prove a blessing
unto many. The memoir of such a man cannot be read by the well-disposed, without feeling something of the sacred unction which
followed him from place to place, from house
to house, and from one class to another; and
which rested upon him in his secret intercourse
with God. His personal friends will drop a
tear over many of the incidents which he has
recorded; and calling to mind how often the
holy fire warmed their hearts, when he was
present, to join in their devotions, they will feel
a momentary return of the vital joys connected
with the many happy opportunities now passed
into the rear of time. To his own children in
the faith, no doubt, this record will yield something more than a momentary pleasure: His
own pious and telling narrative; his instructions, admonitions, and prayers, followed by his
triumphant death, will attract and impel them
toward that heavenly rest, where they expect
soon to meet again their beloved father in the
Gospel. And as to such as have been unfaithful in improving the grace which they once
professed to receive through his instrumentality,
I am inclined to hope and to believe that some

of them will be hereby again quickened, and restored to the liberty and enjoyment of the salvation of God. With respect to the thousands of the unsaved, whom he personally and earnestly warned and admonished, it is likely it will fall into the hands of many of them; and I pray God that the perusal of it may bring their vows to their remembrance, and rivet on their consciences the solemn and important truths which their ears once heard from his thrilling voice. The pious reader, who personally knew him not, will doubtless soon recognise a kindred spirit, and " glorify God in him."

———

WHEN the writer of the following narrative had delivered his papers into the hands of the Editor, he requested that, if it should be deemed proper to publish them, the profits of the publication might be given to promote the spread of the kingdom of Christ in the earth. It is therefore proposed, that if any profit accrue to the publisher by this edition, it shall be appropriated to the funds of the Wesleyan-Methodist Missionary Society. 2. The Editor would take this opportunity of observing, that if any of his father's friends should find, on perusing the Memoir, that such interesting incidents are omitted as they think it would be profitable to publish, he would be happy to receive from them such accounts in writing; that they may be inserted, should a second edition be called for. 3. The portrait is intended to represent him in his usual animated conversation with one who is seeking " instruction in righteous-ness." It was drawn by a friend at - Helston; partly from recollection and partly from sketches and miniatures previously taken, and is deemed a good likeness. The autograph and the text of Scripture are a *fac simile*, or accurate specimen, of his hand-writing. For the gratification of such personal friends and others, as may desire to possess the portrait separately from the volume, and in its most perfect state, a few fine proof impressions, on large India paper, have been taken off, and may be had of the publisher, at 1*s*, each.

Redruth, July 16*th*, 1835.   B. C.

MEMOIR

OF

MR. WILLIAM CARVOSSO.

CHAPTER I.

WHEN I have lately reflected on the forbearance of God, in sparing me while I lived without him, amidst innumerable sins and provocations, more than twenty years; and have also considered the amazing displays of his mercy and love, during nearly half a century, since I first fled as a poor penitent sinner to Jesus Christ for pardon and salvation; I have felt an ardent desire to write down something of his kind dealings towards me; and more especially so since my dear son requested me to do it. Convinced in my own mind it is a duty so to do, I now sit down to make the attempt. I can appeal to THEE, O thou Searcher of hearts, that in this matter I aim at nothing but thy glory; and my earnest prayer is, that to what I write thou wouldst give thy blessing for thy own name's sake. Amen.

I WAS born March 11, 1750, near Mousehole, in the parish of Paul, county of Cornwall. Of my father I knew but little. He went to sea, in a trading vessel, when I was very young, and was afterwards taken by a press-gang, and put on board a man-of-war. He continued in the king's service many years, and died in Greenwich hospital. My mother was a churchwoman, and one I trust who feared God, and found her way to heaven. We were four brothers and one sister. I was the youngest of the family, and till I was ten years of age lived with my mother; who during this time, carefully taught me to read. A respectable farmer, of the same parish, now requested me to come and live with him; to this I cheerfully consented. After awhile my master became very earnest about having an indenture for me; and, just at this time, my father happening to come into Plymouth, he went up to him, and got me bound till I was eighteen years of age. Three years after this my master died; but, as I was treated with great kindness, I remained in the family eleven years During this time, I was borne down by the prevailing sins of the age; such as cock-fighting, wrestling, card-playing, and Sabbath-breaking; and though I cannot recollect that during this period I heard a sermon by a Methodist preacher, yet I was a regular attendant at my parish church

When I reflect on these years of my life, I cannot but praise God for his kind providence over me while I knew him not. How often am I constrained to say,—

" Through hidden dangers, toils, and death,
Thou, Lord, hast gently clear'd my way!"

Twice I was near being drowned; once, when a child, by falling into a river; once by attempting to cross over Hayle, on horseback, when the tide was too high: This was a very narrow escape. On another occasion I was thrown from a horse; and taken up for dead.

In the year 1771 the Lord was pleased, in his mercy, to convert my sister; and having tasted that the Lord was gracious, she came from Gwinear, a distance of twelve miles, to tell us of the happy news, and to warn us to flee from the wrath to come. On entering my mother's house on the Sabbath morning, I was not a little surprised to find my sister on her knees praying with my mother and brothers. After she had concluded, she soon began to inquire what preparation I was making for eternity. I was quite at a loss for an answer. She then asked me if I attended the preaching of the Methodists. I told her I did not. Upon this she particularly requested me to go that night. "And be sure," says she, "you hear for yourself."* As the evening drew on, I felt a very strong desire to go to the preaching, which was at Newlyn, in a room on the Maddern side of the river. As soon as I entered the place, I steadfastly fixed my eyes on the preacher, who was Mr. Thomas

* In the same fervent spirit in which this exellent woman commenced her Christian career, she continued to the end. Her subsequent life evinced that she could *suffer*, as well as *do*, the will of her Master. She was "a burning and a shining light;" and finished her course in the triumph of faith, after she had "walked in the fear of the Lord and in the comfort of the Holy Ghost" about eighteen years.—ED.

Hanson. His text was, "We are ambassadors for Christ, as though God did beseech you by us: we pray you in Christ's stead, be ye reconciled to God." The word quickly reached my heart; the scales fell off from my eyes; and I saw and felt I was in "the gall of bitterness, and in the bond of iniquity." I had such a sight of the damning nature of sin, and what I had done against God, that I was afraid the earth would have opened and swallowed me up. I then made a solemn promise to the Lord, that if he would spare me I would serve him all my days. I now gave up my sins, and all my old companions, at a stroke; and at once determined, if I could see any one going to heaven, I would join him. For myself I was determined to go to heaven, cost what it would. That night I had a hard struggle with satan, about praying before I went into bed. He appeared as if he was by me, and laboured to terrify me with his presence, and the cross of the duty; but the Lord helped me against the temptation, by applying that portion of Scripture, "Let your light so shine before men that they may see your good works," &c. Satan instantly fled, and I fell on my knees. It would be too tedious to mention every thing that passed, and all my inward struggles, before I found the Lord. I suffered much for many days, but about the space of eight hours before I received the pardon of sin, I might say with David, "The pains of hell gat hold upon me;" and the adversary of my soul harassed me with this temptation,

"The day of grace is passed; it is now too late."
I had no one to instruct or encourage me, no
one to point me to Christ; I knew nothing of
the way of faith, nor had I been at a class-meeting. I remember, however, that in the midst of
the conflict, I said, in answer to the powerful
suggestions of the devil, "I am determined,
whether I am saved or lost, that, while I have
breath, I will never cease crying for mercy."
The very moment I formed this resolution in
my heart, Christ appeared within, and God pardoned all my sins, and set my soul at liberty.
The Spirit itself now bore witness with my spirit
that I was a child of God. This was about
nine o'clock at night, May 7, 1771; and never
shall I forget that happy hour.

From experience I now well knew that satan
was a "roaring lion," but I was not yet aware
of his being able to "transform himself into an
angel of light" He now told me, I must not
declare what I had experienced; that if I did, I
should at once fall into condemnation. I was
caught in the snare, and without the least hesitation I said, "Then I will take care not to
mention it." For two days I kept it from my
brother, who lived in the same family, and was
labouring under the same distress of mind as
that from which I had been delivered. But
overhearing some friends at Mousehole, after
they came out of a meeting, talk on the subject
of their knowing their sins forgiven, I was
drawn to join in the conversation, and told them
of what I had felt. The delusion under which

I laboured now vanished, and I at once saw the matter in a scripture light: That "no man lighteth a candle and putteth it under a bushel," but, that as with the heart man believeth unto righteousness, so " with the mouth confession is made unto salvation "

Here I would remark, how wonderful is God's method of saving sinners, and spreading the knowledge of his grace! My sister was converted at the distance of many miles from us; but, in the fulness of her heart, she came that distance to tell us what great things the Lord had done for her, and to invite us to partake of the same salvation. The Lord was pleased to bless her visit, and make it instrumental in bringing my brother Benedict and myself to the knowledge of the truth.

My brother and I both joined the society at Mousehole at the same time. At this period the society there was very small, consisting of one class only. In this class the principal persons, whose names I can recollect, were John Harvey and his wife, (in whose house both the class-meeting and preaching were held,) Jacob George and his wife, Joseph Beaden and his wife, John Yeomen and his two daughters, and Richard Wright, who afterwards became a travelling preacher, and was one of the first who went to America.

In the same happy frame of mind, which God brought me into at my conversion, I went on for the space of three months, not expecting any more conflicts; but, O, how greatly

was I mistaken! I was a young recruit, and
knew not of the warfare I had to engage in.
But I was soon taught that I had only enlisted
as a soldier to fight for King Jesus, and that
I had not only to contend with satan and the
world from without, but with inward enemies
also; which now began to make no small stir.
Having never conversed with any one who
enjoyed purity of heart, nor read any of Mr.
Wesley's works, I was at a loss both with respect to the nature, and the way to obtain the
blessing of full salvation. From my first setting
out in the way to heaven, I determined to be a
Bible Christian; and though I had not much
time for reading many books, yet I blessed God,
I had his own word, the Bible, and could look
into it This gave me a very clear map of the
way to heaven, and told me that " without
holiness no man could see the Lord." It is
impossible for me to describe what I suffered
from "an evil heart of unbelief" My heart
appeared to me as a small garden with a large
stump of a tree in it, which had been recently
cut down level with the ground, and a little
loose earth strewed over it. Seeing something
shooting up I did not like, on attempting to
pluck it up, I discovered the deadly remains of
the carnal mind, and what a work must be done
before I could be "meet for the inheritance of
the saints in light." My inward nature appeared so black and sinful, that I felt it impossible to rest in that state. Some, perhaps, will
imagine that this may have arisen from the

want of the knowledge of forgiveness. That
could not be the case, for I never had one doubt
of my acceptance; the witness was so clear, that
satan himself knew it was in vain to attack me
from that quarter.   I had ever kept in remembrance,—

> ' The blessed hour, when from above
> I first received the pledge of love."

What I now wanted was "inward holiness;" and
for this I prayed and searched the Scriptures.
Among the number of promises, which I found
in the Bible, that gave me to see it was my privilege to be saved from all sin, my mind was
particularly directed to Ezek. xxxvi. 25–27:
"Then will I sprinkle clean water upon you,
and ye shall be clean : from all your filthiness,
and from all your idols, will I cleanse you.   A
new heart also will I give you, and a new spirit
will I put within you : And I will take away
the stony heart out of your flesh, and I will give
you an heart of flesh.   And I will put my
Spirit within you, and cause you to walk in my
statutes, and ye shall keep my judgments, and
do them."   This is the great and precious promise of the eternal Jehovah, and I laid hold of
it, determined not to stop short of my privilege;
for I saw clearly the will of God was my
sanctification.   The more I examined the Scriptures, the more I was convinced that without
holiness there could be no heaven.   Many were
the hard struggles which I had with unbelief,
and satan told me that if I ever should get it, I

should never be able to retain it; but keeping close to the word of God, with earnest prayer and supplication, the Lord gave me to see that nothing short of it would do in a dying hour and the judgment-day. Seeing this, it was my constant cry to God that he would cleanse my heart from all sin, and make me holy, for the sake of Jesus Christ. I well remember returning one night from a meeting, with my mind greatly distressed from a want of the blessing: I turned into a lonely barn to wrestle with God in secret prayer. While kneeling on the threshing floor, agonizing for the great salvation, this promise was applied to my mind, " Thou art all fair, my love; there is no spot in thee." But, like poor Thomas, I was afraid to believe, lest I should deceive myself. O what a dreadful enemy is unbelief! Thomas was under its wretched influence only eight days before Jesus appeared to him; but I was a fortnight after this groaning for deliverance, and saying, " O wretched man that I am, who shall deliver me from the body of this death ?" I yielded to unbelief, instead of looking to Jesus, and believing on him for the blessing; not having then clearly discovered that the witness of the Spirit of God's gift, not my act, but given to all who exercise faith in Jesus and the promise made through him. At length, one evening, while engaged in a prayer-meeting, the great deliverance came. I began to exercise faith, by believing " I shall have the blessing now." Just at that moment a heavenly influence filled the room; and no sooner had I uttered or spoken the words from my heart, "I shall have the blessing now," than refining fire went "through my heart,—illuminated my soul,—scattered its life through every part, and sanctified the whole." I then received the full witness of the Spirit that the blood of Jesus had cleansed me from all sin. I cried out, "This is what I wanted! I have now got a new heart." I was emptied of self and sin, and filled with God. I felt I was nothing, and Christ was all in all. Him I now cheerfully received in all his offices; my Prophet to teach me, my Priest to atone for me, my King to reign over me.

> " Amazing love! how can it be
> That thou, my Lord, shouldst die for me !"

O what boundless, boundless happiness there is in Christ, and all for such a poor sinner as I am! This happy change took place in my soul March 13, 1772

Soon after this, Mr. Wesley's pamphlet on Christian Perfection was put into my hand. I do not know that I had ever seen any of his works before. On reading this little work, I was filled with amazement, to think that a man I had never seen could read my heart in such a manner. This tended greatly to establish me in the truth of the Gospel.

About three years after I became a member of the socity, I was requested to take the charge of a little class ; to which I submitted in the fear of God. I had been a leader about four or five

years, when I was convinced it was my duty to
alter my condition in life, by exchanging the
state of a single, for that of a married, man.   In
this matter I ever believed I was divinely directed; for God gave me a wife who proved a help-
meet for me all the days of her life.   In matters temporal and spiritual, I always found her
a lasting blessing to me.

. On entering into the marriage-state, I took a
small farm near Mousehole, and engagaed myself on the seine in the summer, during the
pilchard season.   Though our accommodations
were humble, for some years the preachers
lodged with us   But I never found the sea to
agree with me, and at length I earnestly prayed
that God would direct my steps, and fix me in
some place where I might support myself and
family wholly on the land; and soon he condescended to grant me the desire of my heart.
For this I hope I shall praise him in time and
to all eternity.

Unsolicited, and in a manner which I did not
expect, my way was opened to take a farm in
the parish of Gluvias, near Ponsanooth.   And
here, at Christmas, 1788, I brought a beloved wife
and two children, and before the end of a year
came round we had another son.   In entering
on our new sphere of life, with little capital, we
had many unpleasant things to encounter; but
the Lord was with us, and brought us through
all.

Here I found my outward religious privileges
were widely different from what they were at

Mousehole; it was like being brought from the
land of Goshen into a dry and barren wilderness.   There was no chapel in the neighbourhood; but at a farm-house, about three quarters
of a mile distant, we had preaching once a fortnight.   Here was a little class, feeble and des-
titute enough; for it had no leader, (he having
been removed some time before,) and not one of
the members could even assist in holding a
prayer-meeting.   When I beheld these few
poor sheep in the wilderness without a shepherd, I began to discover the reason why God
had brought me from the distance of twenty-six
miles, and fixed me in this place.

I took the charge of the little class, and went
on for some years without seeing much good
done.   At length, two pious men came into
the neighbourhood for a short time to work, and
I was led, in rather a singular manner, and
without knowing their characters, to give them
lodging at my house.   With their help, a
prayer-meeting was now commenced; and
about this time, I saw it my duty, though the
Lord had given me but one talent, to attempt in
the prayer-meetings to give a word of exhortation.   I saw sinners perishing without repentance, and the Lord seemed to say to me, " Their
blood will I require at thy hands " With fear and
trembling I opened my mouth to beseech them
to flee from the wrath to come.   And soon after,
to our great joy, it pleased the Lord to convince
and convert a few souls, and add them to our
little number.

It was about this time that the Lord condescended to hear prayer, and convert my two
elder children. Returning one night from the
quarterly-meeting love-feast at Redruth, in company with a pious friend, he told me he had the
unspeakable happiness the night before to witness the conversion of his young daughter while
he held her in his arms. I informed him I had
two children who were getting up to mature
age, but I was grieved to say I had not yet seen
any marks of a work of God upon their minds.
His reply I shall never forget:—"Brother,"
says he, "has not God promised to pour his
Spirit upon thy seed, and his blessing upon thy
offspring?" The words went through me in
an unaccountable manner; they seemed to take
hold of my heart · I felt as if I had not done my
duty, and resolved to make a new effort in
prayer. I had always prayed for my children ·
but now I grasped the promise with the hand
of faith, and retired daily at special seasons to
put the Lord to his word. I said nothing of
what I felt, or did, to any one but the Searcher
of hearts, with whom I wrestled in an agony of
prayer. About a fortnight after I had been
thus engaged with God, being at work in the
field, I received a message from my wife, informing me that I was wanted within. When
I entered the house, my wife told me, " Grace is
above stairs, apparently distressed for something;
but nothing can be got from her, but that she
must see father." Judge of my feelings, when
I found my daughter a weeping penitent at the

feet of Jesus. On seeing me she exclaimed,
"O father, I am afraid I shall go to hell!"
The answer of my full heart was, " No, glory
be to God, I am not afraid of that now." She
said she had felt the load of sin about a fortnight,
and that now she longed to find Christ. I
pointed her to the true Physician, and she soon
found rest through faith in the atoning blood.
My eldest son had hitherto been utterly careless
about the things of God, and associated with
youths of a similar disposition of mind; but
now he became the subject of a manifest
change; he cast off his old companions; and
one Sunday afternoon, just before I was going
to meet my class, he came to me with a sorrowful mind, and expressed his desire to go with
me to the class-meeting. He did go, and that
day cast in his lot with the people of God; and,
blessed be his holy name, they both continue
to this day.

The society had now considerably increased,
and the barren wilderness began to rejoice. We
had two large classes, but no one had yet arisen
to assist me as a leader. We had now preaching
twice a week, and the place where we assembled
became too small for the congregation, and
there was also much uncertainty about our being able to occupy it much longer: I therefore
saw it my duty to do my utmost to get a little
chapel erected, before the Lord should remove
me from them. After much labour and anxiety,
a suitable spot was procured for the purpose.
To build the chapel was a great work for us;

but by labour, giving what we could, and begging of those whom the Lord inclined to help us, we at length saw the blessed work accomplished And now that I beheld the desire of my heart given me, O how did I rejoice and exult in the God of my salvation !

The work of the Lord prospered more and more in the society; and I now began to feel a particular concern for the salvation of my younger son I laid hold by faith on the same promise which I had before done, when pleading for my other children, and went to the same place to call upon my God in his behalf One day while I was wrestling with God in mighty prayer for him, these words were applied with power to my mind : " There shall not a hoof be left behind " I could pray no more ; my prayer was lost in praises ; in shouts of joy and, " Glory, glory, glory ! the Lord will save all my family !" While I am writing this, the silent tears flow down from my eyes.——His life was quite moral, I could not reprove him for any outward sin. In his leisure hours his delight was in studying different branches of useful knowledge ; but this though good in its place, was not religion ; I knew his heart was yet estranged from God. After the answer I had in prayer, I waited some time, hoping to see the change effected in him as it was in his sister and brother; but was not taking place according to my expectations, I felt my mind deeply impressed with the duty of taking the first opportunity of opening my mind to him, and talking closely to him about

eternal things. I accordingly came to him on
one occasion when he was, as usual, engaged
with his books; and with my heart deeply
affected, I asked him if it was not time for him
to enter upon a life of religion I told him
"with tears," that I then felt my body was failing,
and that if any thing would distress my mind
in a dying hour, it would be the thought of
closing my eyes in death before I saw him converted to God This effort the Lord was pleas-
to bless· the truth took hold of his heart; he
went with me to the class-meeting, and soon
obtained the knowledge of salvation by the remission of his sins. This was a matter of great
joy and rejoicing to me and my dear wife;
we had now the unspeakable happiness of seeing
all our dear children converted to God, and
travelling in the way to heaven with us

Our place of worship now again became too
strait for us; and the society and friends of
God's cause had so increaaed, that after much
deliberation it was resolved to pull down the
chapel that had been erected a few years before,
and build a much larger one on the same site,
and attach a burying-ground to it. This was
done accordingly; but I did not take so prominent a part in it as on the former occasion;
God had now raised up others to take this burden from me.

In the month of June, 1813, it pleased the
Lord to visit me with a severe and heavy trial,
by bereaving me of my dearly beloved wife.
She died of that painful disease, a cancer in the

breast. In the beginning of her complaint, two physicians were consulted; but, by reason of a difference of opinion between them, it was never cut out. For eighteen months she suffered at times indescribably; but the Lord wonderfully supported her. She bore up under her affliction in a most astonishing manner. Such were the manifestations of the Divine presence to her soul, that in the midst of her severest sufferings, she would often sweetly sing her favourite hymns; and so loud as to be heard over all the house. "The God of Abraham praise" was the hymn she much delighted in singing; especially these two verses:—

"The God of Abraham praise,
Whose all-sufficient grace
Shall guide me all my happy days
In all his ways.
He calls a worm his friend,
He calls himself my God;
And he shall save me to the end,
Through Jesus' blood.

"He by himself hath sworn,
I on his oath depend;
I shall, on eagle's wings upborne,
To heaven ascend·
I shall behold his face,
I shall his power adore,
And sing the wonders of his grace
For evermore"

One morning when distracted by pain, she said, "Do not trouble yourself about my everlasting state, for the Lord has given me such an assurance of hope, that should pain be permitted utterly to deprive me of my reason, I know I should go to heaven." A short time before she expired, she called me and my son Benjamin to her bed-side, and requested us to sing that beautiful hymn,—

" Let earth and heaven agree."

She sweetly joined with us as far as her strength would admit; and the triumph of faith and love contained in the hymn appeared the language of her heart. Just before she fell asleep in Jesus, she said, "The rest shall be glorious." I was enabled, without a murmuring thought, to offer her up unto the Lord as his own gift, in the full assurance of faith, that we should soon meet in heaven to part no more for ever. She was the first person interred in the Ponsanooth burying-ground; and I intend that my body shall be put in the same grave when I die; that we may sleep together till the great day when the "trumpet shall sound, and the dead shall be raised incorruptible;" and *we, and I trust all our dear children with us*, shall fly up and be for ever with the Lord.*

Soon after this, in the beginning of the year 1814, a great and glorious revival broke out at Redruth, and spread to various parts of Cornwall. It was such a revival as my eyes never saw before. I call it "a glorious revival," for such it proved to my own soul; my faith was

* See a farther account of my mother in the Wesleyan Methodist Magazine for 1814.—EDIT.

so increased to see the mighty power of God displayed in convincing and converting such vast
multitudes. For this great and merciful visitation, numbers will praise God to all eternity. It
has been my privilege to witness the happy
deaths of many who were brought to the knowledge of the truth at this time. At Ponsanooth we
partook largely of the general good. The society, which, twenty-five years before, consisted
-of one small and feeble class, now became a
society of near two hundred members, divided
into eleven classes. Three of these came under
my care, and one of them was committed to my
younger son, who had for some time before
acted as a local preacher.

[† Of all the various revivals of religion, of
which Cornwall has been so remarkable a
scene since Methodism was first planted in it,
the revival of which my father here speaks is
by many considered the most striking and interesting. It is therefore now generally distinguished by the epithet of "the *great* revival."
It commenced in the month of February, at a
prayer-meeting in this town, (Redruth;) when
eight persons found peace with God. The night
following, at another prayer-meeting, many
more were powerfully seized with convictions
for sin, and, after much wrestling and impor-
tunity in prayer, they found refuge in the
Saviour. From this time, serious concern be-

† These and all subsequent remarks in the narrative included within [ ], brackets, are inserted
by the Editor.

came very general; and, in the course of the following week, many hundreds in the town and neighbourhood, who had before been living in neglect of their souls, were brought into deep distress about their spiritual interests, and multitudes of them were enabled with much soundness of speech to testify that they had experienced remission of sins. About a week after this extraordinary work commenced, the rumour of it drew me to the scene, and I spent the greater part of one night with the people in the chapel The pungency of the "penitential pain," the extent of the distress, the fervour of devotion, the number of happy young converts whose countenances were beaming with joy, far exceeded any thing of the kind I have yet witnessed. The heavenly flame was soon carried to the various societies in the circuit; and in those different places, similar scenes were presented to the wondering beholders. At Tuckingmill, the effect was so simultaneous, general, and powerful, that the meeting which commenced in the chapel on Sunday the 27th, could not be broken up, but continued without intermission, till the Friday morning following. It rapidly extended to the neighbouring circuits; and, in the course of a few weeks only, more than five thousand of the ignorant, trifling, and immoral world became seriously concerned about eternal things, united themselves to religious society, and exhibited in their external demeanour all that is beautiful in the early blossoms of piety and virtue. It is true that very many of these "heirs of promise," ere long, fell away, and returned to their old practices; but it is also true, that, to this day, multitudes of them are found steadfast in the ways of God, and that hundreds, if not thousands, of them have "died in faith," testifying with their latest breath that they had not "received the grace of God in vain." In promoting this great and "glorious work," as my father calls it, he was a very active and useful agent; and I believe thereby partook of an abundant increase of spiritual life and strength; which had a happy effect on all the subsequent movements of his life]

My daughter and elder son being married, I had now none of my family with me but my son Benjamin; to whom I was united in love and affection more than I can express. But, lo and behold! the time was now come when I must give up *my Benjamin* to the Lord. I was present at the quarterly meeting, held at Redruth, March, 1814, when Mr Truscott, then Superintendent of the Circuit, proposed to the meeting that he should be recommended to the ensuing Conference, to be employed as a travelling preacher. This was passed unanimously, for I did not dare to oppose it, being quite convinced it was of the Lord; for I had reason to think, even from circumstances connected with his childhood, that God had destined him for the ministry. ● He passed the district-meeting; and, being accepted by the Conference, he was appointed the first year to Plymouth-Dock (now

Devonport) circuit.   When the time came for
parting, we mingled our tears together, but
resigned ourselves to the will of the Lord.

[To do justice to my father, it is necessary to
insert the following extract from his FIRST LET-
TER; which was written to me, and by which
I was much surprized, affected, and comforted;
surprised,—because I had never before known
him to attempt to communicate his thoughts by
writing; *affected*,—at the proof of his tender
parental affection; and *comforted*,—by his faith,
and the pious and consoling observations which
the letter contains.   This letter was the more
welcome to me, because it came at a time when
my mind was greatly dejected, by the natural
discouragements attendant on entering into the
ministry.   The writing is very legible; but,
contrasted with his letters written a few years
afterwards, it is, in every way, very inferior.
It is dated a fortnight after I left home.   The
leader who was appointed to my class, was his
own son in the Gospel, having been awakened
under an exhortation, which he gave in a
neighbouring society a few years before.
Brother Grose was an eminently pious class-
leader, and a very dear friend both to my father
and myself.   To his affectionate, persevering,
and powerful prayers, I was much indebted for
some years.   This man of God, whose name I
delight to record, lived and died in the triumph
of faith and hope.]

My dear Son,   *November* 8, 1814.

"I received your letter with joy, and am thankful for the kindness which the people manifest towards you. May the Lord make you a blessing to their souls! I am confident God will be with you, from what I have felt in my own mind. The Friday morning after you left me, while engaged in prayer to God for you, he so filled my soul with his love, that I have been happy ever since. I am resigned to God's will, and it is sweet indeed; so that I would not have you be distressed in mind about me. O may God fill you with faith and love, and a burning zeal for his glory and the good of souls! All things will be pleasant, while Christ is precious to you. Always remember, that without him we can do nothing. May he be your Prophet, Priest, and King! See you preach him in all his offices. I am ready to say,—

> 'O for a trumpet voice,
>   On all the world to call;
> To bid their hearts rejoice
>   In him who died for all!'

O may you be enabled to feed the church of God, which he hath purchased with his own blood! Remember, Christ says, 'Feed my lambs;' these must be fed with the sincere milk of the word. He also says, 'Feed my sheep;' press them on to greater degrees of faith and holiness. Soul-work is important work; on

this account I feel for you; and my prayer to
God, daily and hourly, is, that he may be with
you, and make his word spirit and life; and
send it home to every heart and every conscience. O may you feel for sinners on the
brink of ruin, and may you have the pleasure of
hearing them cry for mercy, and of pointing
them to the wounds of a crucified Saviour: and
may Jesus be present to bind up their broken
hearts! Tell them that he is a medicine for
their every wound, and that 'all—all they want
is there.' You know the great end of preaching is to save souls; but if you should not see
the seed immediately spring up, wait with
patience: it may not produce the worse crop.
Pray that it may take root downwards, and then
it will spring up in due time.

> ' O for a firm and lasting faith,
> To credit all the Almighty saith!'

And may he give you all the wisdom and grace
to fit you for the work! Mr. Truscott dined
with me on Sunday; he gives his kind love to
you, and would be glad to have a line from you.
He told me he would write to you again. By
the decision of the leaders' meeting, John Rich-
ards is fixed to be the leader of your class.
Much prayer is offered up for you by preachers
and people. Brother Grose says he is always
happy when praying for you; he gives his kind
love to you. The spelling is bad, but I hope
you will find out my meaning"

[Before we proceed with the narrative, an extract from his *second* letter to me may not be unacceptable to the reader. It further shows, not only his sympathy, but his ability, to instruct and succour those who needed his aid.]

"*December* 13, 1814.
"MY DEAR AND LOVING SON,

"YOUR long-expected letter came safe to hand, and I was glad to hear that my letter was made a blessing to your soul; but was sorry to find your mind any ways weighed down Suppose we are not vessels of gold or silver, you know the eathenware ought not to be despised. Remember the precious Jesus with his towel and bason, and learn of him, to be meek and lowly of heart, and you shall find rest to your soul: and let me tell you, *I* can find no other way Besides, more has been done by the ram's horn, than by the silver trumpet. A good man observes, 'Every one cannot be excellent, yet may be useful. An iron key may unlock the door of golden treasures. Yea, iron can do some things that gold cannot.' O what a wretched enemy self is to the poor pilgrim! How close it sticks! and may I not say, it is a dreadful murderer? The great lesson is to learn obedience to the will of God We are the clay, and he is the potter. It will take some time to learn this lesson as we ought. I am not yet half perfect in it. How reasonable that we should be tried! I never saw this so clear as I have of late; while waves and storms have

gone over my head; and my strength, and
health, and friends, are departed from me.   But
while I am left alone, God is with me, and I
can say,—

> ' On this my steadfast soul relies,
>   Father, thy mercy never dies.'

What I feel for you, none knows but God and
my own soul.   A few days ago, while I was
going to see one of my class, who is sick, I was
praying for you, as I went along the road, and
God gave me a precious promise for you, and
assured me his grace was sufficient for you.
At this my soul leaped for joy within me, and
streams of gratitude flowed from my heart to
God on your account.   O! how strong was
my faith for you at that time!   My dear son,
hang on Christ alone; then you will be safe,
and he will make crooked paths straight, and
rough places smooth."

For many months after my son left me to enter
upon his great and important work, being quite
alone on my farm and the prices of all articles
of produce being in a very fluctuating state, I was
at times much perplexed as to the course I
ought to take for the future.   At seasons I was
much weighed down, and could only find comfort in looking from my outward circumstances.
At times, the Lord greatly comforted me by his
precious promises, and I was much blessed in
labouring to make myself useful to souls.   I
had no desire to seek riches; yet if I were as-

sured it was the path of duty to continue a little
longer in business, I was willing to submit,
though I scarcely knew how I should get
through.   In this state of things, I spread my
case before the Lord, and earnestly sought direction from above. He saw my motive was to please
Him, and he condescended to direct me.   One
evening, while sitting alone, and considering
whether I ought to give up my farm and free
myself from the cares of the world, these words
came with power to my mind: "Behold, I have
set before thee an open door." I immediately
considered it the voice of the Lord, and my heart
replied, "Then I will at once go out of the
world, and retire from all its cares." From
this moment I saw my way clear; I was entirely freed from the world, and resolved to give up
my few remaining days wholly to the service
and glory of God. When my friends, belonging
to the society at Ponsanooth, heard of my determination, sorrow filled their hearts, and it was
with the greatest difficulty they could bring their
minds at all to submit to it.   On laying the
matter before the preachers and the leaders'
meeting, it was thought best for me to continue
as the nominal leader of my three classes, and
to visit them as often as I could; three other
leaders, or assistant leaders, being appointed, to
take charge of them in my absence.   Thus it
has continued to the present time.

[As we have now seen the subject of these
memoirs close his worldly affairs, and retire
from the bustle and anxieties of business, before

we follow him in the important movements of his new career, in the leisure of life, we may profitably spend a few remarks on such traits of his business-character as are most worthy of notice and imitation. Here he operated within a narrow sphere, for which reason his example is better calculated to teach ; as the world's happiness depends on managing well a little, rather than much.

[He was an example of industry; both as a servant, and as a man pursuing his own business. While he acted under an employer, his diligence and trustiness in every department of his duty commended him from his early youth to his master's special esteem and confidence. Whatever was committed to his care, so far as the diligence of his hand or the fidelity of his heart was concerned, was in good keeping ; often, indeed, far better than in the owner's own hands. As a religious servant, or a servant professing godliness, he " adorned the doctrine of God his Saviour in all things." In his own affairs, after he settled on a farm, his industry was proverbial. He began with little, and got on " by the sweat of his brow." To him, however, this was no slavery ; for he went forth with cheerful feet, and grateful delight, to " labour truly to get his own living, and to do his duty, in that state of life in which it had pleased God to call him." His industrious hands soon produced a striking change on his farm. When he entered on it, it was a mere desert; on which his neighbours prophesied he would soon starve; but, within a

few years, it became a favourite spot, exhibiting
the happy effects of good management and diligent culture. As he could not bear sloth in
himself, neither would he bear it in others;
hence, as a master, when occasion required, he
would, with stinging, stirring words, move on
those about him

[His punctuality, also, deserves imitation.—
Whether he was to make a payment, or
perform any other duty, the thing must not
only be done, but it must be done, if possible,
in the earliest part of the time allotted Never,
perhaps, did a man more practically adhere
to the ancient maxim of "taking time by the
forelock" From what HE had to do, no business which belonged to *other* men could detain
him a moment No one waited for him; for
he could no more rob men of their time than of
their money. In their dealings with him, dis-
appointment was an evil over which none had
to mourn. The work which should be done
to-day was never put off till to-morrow; nor
what should be attended to in the morning, left
undone till evening He seemed always to feel
the force of these words; "Whatsoever thy
hand findeth to do, do it with thy might:" And,
as far as his influence could extend, he endeavoured to make others as prompt as himself.
One of his oft-repeated and well-remembered
aphorisms was, "Make haste, for you will find
the time all busy" How well had it been for
the honour and interest of religion, if this practical regard to punctuality had been more ob-

served, both by servants and by men of business.

[In his views and habits he was unambitious and anti-speculative. " Mind not high things," was a precept to which he strictly adhered; and hence, no one could ever draw him aside to embark either in vain politics, or in airy schemes to advance his worldly interests.— With great simplicity he aimed at duty and heaven. He sought nothing more than a moderate competency of this world's good; for this he quietly, honestly, and manfully struggled; with this God blessed him; and, in the possession of it, he had the wisdom to live as contentedly and happily as most men. After the Lord had prospered the labour of his hands, he was not wanting in opportunity to enlarge his borders; but all his needs were supplied, and he had little inclination to burden himself with the unnecessary throes of the world. He neither desired the benefits, nor would he partake in the miseries, of speculation. No one could ever induce him to take a share in a mine. Some of his friends pressed him vehemently; but feeling that such undertakings were not to him the path of duty, his uniform answer was, " I am not called to engage in such matters." For his faithful adherence to this principle, he felt himself amply rewarded at last. Not long before he quitted his farm, one of his most intimate friends came to see him, bringing with him a mining agent, and they used every argument in their power to induce him to venture; but

he declined having any thing to do with their
flattering schemes, "because it was not his
business to venture beyond 'a plough deep'"
Like many other affairs of the kind, the mine
in question soon turned out badly; and in his
last sickness, while gratefully enumerating the
mercies of Him who had watched over him
all his life long to do him good, my father observed to me, with some emotion, that had he
suffered himself to be prevailed on in that
instance, he should have been stripped of all
the little fruits of his industry at a stroke, and
reduced to indigence all the remainder of his
days. What a number of Christian families
would have been saved from the ruinous snares
of riches; and how many more from the
overwelming trials of disappointments and failures, had there been the same stern adherence
to the path of duty, as that which is here exemplified in the subject of these memoirs !

Another commendable trait in this branch of
my father's character was, his carrying religion
into the world, and at the same time keeping the
world out of religion. " Not slothful in business; fervent in spirit, serving the Lord." On
this text his life has supplied me with a better
comment than any other I have yet seen: and
as such I have frequently quoted it. He certainly was not one of those who called upon
God for help, without " setting their shoulder to
the wheel;" for some who have seen him so
earnest at the wheel, have, I apprehend, been
under a degree of temptation to question whe-

ther he had not forgotten the other part of his duty, or at least whether he had a proper confidence in it; but assuredly, while he attended to the one, he did not leave the other undone. Like the people under the direction of Nehemiah, he had "a mind to work," and at the same time he adopted their practice, and "made his prayer to his God" As he would sometimes pounce on the slothful and make them spring, so would he with much earnestness admonish professors of religion on the importance of their engaging " in every thing with prayer and supplication;" asking of God "those things which are requisite and necessary, as well for the body as the soul" When he entered on his farm, he could not stock it without going into debt: This was a burden and a grief unto his soul; and while he rose early, wrought late, and ate the bread of carefulness, I have heard him say how fervently he pleaded with God to bring him into those happy circumstances in which he should " owe no man any thing " "While," says he, " I have followed my cattle to the watering, my heart has been earnestly engaged with God, praying for his blessing on my temporal affairs, and telling him how happy and how grateful I should be, if he would condescend to give me my little stock free from debt." Upon fit opportunities he would endeavour to bring religion before worldly men; hence in buying and selling, there was often something put in of the merchandize of a higher order I have often admired, how naturally and readily he would slip from the world into religion; at the same time keeping both in their place. But while he sought thus carefully to bring religion into the world, he took equal care to prevent the world from treading on the boundaries of religion. In his attention to the means of grace, he moved with the regulaiity of clockwork. Seldom could either company, or fatigue, or employment keep him from visiting the place of public worship, from five to seven times a week; though the distance was about a mile from his residence to the chapel. By pushing on the work a little in the former part of the day, he would find time even in the bustle of harvest, to break off from labour, so that all hands, if they were inclined, might attend preaching or meeting at night. Often when urging on others who profess religion, and are pretty much occupied with the world, the importance and practibility of their regular attention to week-night services, I have been led to mention his example as a happy illustration of the thing I wished to recommend.]

CHAPTER II.

I now went to live with my daughter, at Dowstall, in the parish of Mylor, about three miles distant from Ponsanooth. Since I have given up the world, my peace has flowed as a river, and my joys have abounded like Jordan's swelling stream.

"All glory and honour to Jesus alone."

O! what a salvation is that which Jesus has pur chased for poor sinners! It is a full, free, and present salvation; a salvation from all sin, its guilt, its power, and its very in-being; and a salvation into all the glorious image of God. And this salvation is attained by simple faith. O, how great are the privileges of believers! Not only are they cleansed from sin, but are become the children of God;—heirs of God, and joint-heirs with Christ. "All are yours, and ye are Christ's."

"O for a thousand tongues to sing
My dear Redeemer's praise;
The glories of my God and King,
The triumphs of his grace!"

Many circumstances have occurred in my life, besides those already mentioned, in which it has pleased the Lord to make me useful, both to his own people and to sinners. The first that now strikes me is this;—Returning one Sabbath-day from worship, I happened to look behind me, when I saw a neighbour of mine coming. It was immediately impressed upon my mind that I must speak to him about his soul. So I stopped till he came up with me. I then spoke freely to him about his future state; but I soon found death and eternity were subjects he had thought little about, for he was asleep in his sins. I began to preach the law to him, and often, while speaking, lifted up my heart to God to bless what I said. I asked him, if he was willing to die in his present state. He acknowledged he was not. I then earnestly requested him, that, as he was now labouring under indisposition, as soon as he should reach his house, he would go into his chamber and fall down upon his knees, and implore that mercy of which he stood so much in need. Blessed be God, he took the warning; for he went home, and instantly retired for prayer. The Lord gave him to see and feel that he was a poor lost sinner. He soon obtained an interest in the blood of Christ, lived for some time a striking witness of the power of Divine grace, and died happy in God.

At another time, while giving a word of exhortation, the Lord was pleased to bless my feeble endeavours, in awakening another poor sinner. He has now stood fast in the faith for many years, and is become a class-leader. No tongue can express the gratitude to the Lord, which my heart has felt on account of these things: To think that the Eternal Jehovah should use such a worm as I am, to effect such a great and glorious work! I trust to praise him for it to all eternity. And, O, how is my faith hereby strengthened to go forward in my humble endeavours to do good!

In the latter part of the year 1815, when I was going to see my son, then travelling in the Liskeard circuit, when I came to Teague's Gate, between Grampound and St. Austell, a young female, about eighteen or nineteen years of age, came out to take the toll. She was a stranger to me; but, the moment I saw her, I felt such a love for her soul, and such a concern for her salvation, that I thought I could have died for her, if that would bring her to the Lord, and be the means of saving her soul. But as soon as I had delivered to her the toll, she instantly retired, and I had no opportunity of speaking to her. When I had proceeded a few steps from the gate, I stopped my horse and lifted up my heart to God; for I was at a loss what to do; whether to go forward, or turn back to enquire into the state of her mind. While I reflected for a moment, it was impressed upon my mind I should see her again when I returned. So I proceeded on my journey; but, during the eleven days that intervened, she was seldon absent from my thoughts, when on my knees before God in secret. On my return, a little before I came to the gate, I resolved before the Searcher of hearts, that, if she should again come out, I would not deliver her the money till I had made some enquiry into the state of her mind. As soon as I saw her come out, my heart said—"Surely the Lord has a hand in this matter!" As soon as we came near to each other, to open the way for a conversation, I said to her.—" Can you be happy in this lonely place?" But I soon found she was a stranger to happiness, for she was an unawakened sinner, without God and without hope in the world. While talking to her for a short time, her mother, over-hearing the conversation, came to the door. On seeing her, she slipped from me and went in. On this account, I felt sorry, as I had not said to her all I intended. I immediately alighted, went in after her, and found the Lord had touched her heart, for she was bitterly weeping. At the sight of this, I soon wept also. Her father was present, a pious man and a class-leader, but unknown to me: He requested me to pray with her. The Lord poured his Spirit upon us, and my soul seemed overwhelmed with the Divine presence. After prayer, her father said he had often wished his daughter to go with him to class-meeting, but he could never induce her to do it. I urged her to promise me that she would go that night; for I learned that was the night of the class-meeting. She felt the cross, and seemed reluctant to take it up. But I continued to urge my plea. She wept much, and my own mind was much affected; at length, I was constrained, by the love I felt for her soul, to say,—"I cannot let you go unless you will promise me that you will to-night go with your father." She paused for a moment, and then said, "I will go with him." I now turned my attention to her sister, who was present, and also a stranger to Divine things. She was already much affected by the conversation which had taken place; and I felt considerable hope that I should not in her case find a very difficult conquest. Accordingly, she soon promised me that that night she would go with her sister, and join the people of God. After this, I heard nothing of them for four months.

5

About that time, Liskeard friends having requested me to pay them another visit, I had again to pass through Teague's Gate. When I came near, I laboured to conceal my countenance as much as possible, by leaning forwards on the neck of the horse. But the moment Jane saw me she knew me, and exclaimed, "You were sent here to save my soul." I said, "It is the Lord that did it, and you must give the glory to him." Her sister hearing my voice, ran out with heaven sparkling in her eyes, and shouting aloud the praises of the Most High "Come in, come in !" was their language. I went in, and they told me, they both went to class-meeting that night according to their promise ; "and now," said they, "we are both happy." Their father assured me there was now no need to urge them to go to class-meeting, for they were anxious to go at every opportunity About eighteen months after this, it pleased God to remove Jane to a better world. She held fast the beginning of her confidence, and died in sure and certain hope of eternal glory. A short time after her death, I called to see the family, and said to Robert, her elder brother, "You must now go and fill up your sister's place in the church." Jonathan, the younger brother, being present, burst into tears, and from that time gave his' heart to the Lord. He continued steadfast in the ways of the Lord three years, and then died happy in a Saviour's love. About twelve months after the death of Jonathan, I called once more on the family; and finding Robert still unconverted, I felt a longing desire for his salvation When he came in, I requested the other members of the family to leave the room. I then asked him what objection he had to give his heart to God The silent tear soon began to flow; and before we parted he promised he would give himself to the Lord, and go with his father to class-meeting. Five years he walked in wisdom's ways, and then finished his course with joy. O how do these things humble my soul in the dust! With a heart deeply affected with my nothingness, I sweetly fall at the feet of Jesus,—

"And the Lover of sinners adore."

Yes, I will give all honour to my precious Jesus alone. His love is as a fire in my heart while I am writing, constraining me to cry out,—

"O how precious! O how precious!
Is the sound of Jesus' name."

But I must leave this delightful subject, and go on to record more of his wondrous works

Can I forget the happy seasons, and manifestations of the power of God, which I have witnessed at Bicton-Mill, with my brother Body and his family? No, never by me can these things be forgotten; particulary while at one time conversing with his eldest daughter, Mary. She had for some time known her acceptance in Christ, but now she said, "I want to be cleansed from inbred sin, and to love God with all my heart." I told her, "The will of God is your sanctification; and God himself has expressly said, 'I will sprinkle clean water upon you, and ye shall be clean: A new heart also will I give you, and a new spirit will I put within you.' Here," said I, "the eternal God speaks to you. Take him at his word; and, at once 'reckon yourself to be dead indeed unto sin, and alive unto God, through Jesus Christ." She obeyed the command; and, through an act of faith in the atonement, entered into the glorious rest of the people of God:—

> " A rest where all our soul's desire
>   Is fix'd on things above ;
> Where fear, and sin, and grief expire,
>   Cast out by perfect love."

She now told me she felt the blood of Christ had cleansed her from all sin. I corresponded with her for some years. She was a burning and a shining light; but the Lord did not leave her long a member of his church below. A short time before she was taken ill, she said to her sister, " I dreamed last night I was with you and others in a prayer-meeting. It was a blessed time, and we were all happy in God. But it seemed to me I was suspended in the air, above you all." She died in the faith, leaving a blessed testimony behind her that she is gone to glory.

The first time I visited Cal'ington, a friend

asked me to take a walk before meeting. We called on Mr. Jope, and I fell into conversation with his daughter Nancy, on the necessity of preparing to meet God, and the danger of delaying such an important work. After I left her, her spiritual state so lay on my mind, that I could sleep but little during the whole night. In the morning, I felt it a duty impressed on my mind to see her again before I left Callington. It was not a little cross "to flesh and blood," but I saw I must do it. .So I went to her, and delivered my own soul. She wept much, promised to give herself to God, and to unite with his people. The next time I came into that neighbourhood, I found her at a friend's house where I took tea; she was then concerned for her soul, but in a state of bondage, and quite unacquainted with the plan of salvation I spoke to her of Jesus Christ, and of the punishment which he had borne in his own body on her account; and shewed her that now there was nothing wanting but faith on her part. Afterwards, in an exhortation at the. chapel, I offered, in my simple way, Christ as a full, free, and present Saviour, able and willing to save unto the uttermost. When I came out of the meeting, she caught hold of my arm, and said in the fulness of her heart, "I am happy: I am happy. These words were applied to my mind,—

    ' Thy debt's discharged,—thy ransom's paid;
      My Father must forgive ; '

and I instantly believed, and received the pardon

of my sins." She has since been ranked among my much-esteemed correspondents.

I have sometimes had seasons of remarkable visitation from the presence of the Lord. I well remember on one occasion, while paying a visit to my Camborne friends, I was one night in bed, so filled—so overpowered with the glory of God, that, had there been a thousand suns shining at noon-day, the brightness of that Di vine glory would have eclipsed the whole! I was constrained to shout aloud for joy. It was the overwhelming power of saving grace. Now it was that I again received the impress of the seal, and the earnest of the Spirit, in my heart. Beholding as in a glass the glory of the Lord, I was changed into the same image from glory to glory by the Spirit of the Lord. Language fails in giving but a faint description of what I then experienced. I can never forget it in time, nor to all eternity. Many years before, perhaps not fewer than thirty, I was sealed by the Spirit in a somewhat similar manner. While walking one day between Mousehole and Newlyn, I was drawn to turn aside from the public road, and under the canopy of heaven kneel down to prayer. I had not long been engaged with God, before I was so visited from above, and overpowered by the Divine glory, that my shouting could be heard at a distance. It was a weight of glory that I seemed incapable of bearing in the body, and I therefore cried out, (perhaps unwisely,) "Lord, stay thine hand!" In this glorious baptism, these words came to my heart with indescribable power, " I have sealed thee unto the day of redemption "

Giving glory to my God, I can say to the present moment, I feel the blood of Jesus Christ cleanseth me from all sin. I am become a living temple, glorious all within. I can now love God with all my heart, with all my mind, and with all my strength. My inward heaven of joy and peace was, I think, never so great as of late. O Lord, help me to make some suitable return of love and gratitude! O stupendous redeeming grace! Feelingly can I sing this verse,—

" O Love, thou bottomless abyss !
   My sins are swallow'd up in thee ;
Cover'd is my unrighteousness,
   Nor spot of guilt remains on me,
While Jesus' blood through earth and skies,
Mercy, free, boundless mercy, cries ! "

[In recording some of the preceding incidents, my father has anticipated the time. It appears, that, in some instances, after he had made the first record, subsequent occurences led him to make additions. This is particularly the case in the interesting account of Mr. Robert Jose's family, at Teague's Gate. My father, having now finished his recollections, proceeds with his narrative in the form of a journal.]

JAN. 10th, 1817.—I have just returned from visiting the friends at Mabe. At the monthly meeting the Lord was with us of a truth. The testimonies which some bore to the gracious efficacy of the all-cleansing blood of Jesus Christ made my heart leap for joy Such humbling views had I of myself, such poverty of spirit as I never felt before. These are profitable seasons, when the soul is emptied of self, and filled with the Divine fulness. Glory be to God, my evidence was never brighter, my faith never stronger, than now.

> " Thee I can love, and thee alone,
>   With pure delight and inward bliss ;
> To know thou tak'st me for thine own,
>   O what a happiness is this ! "

JAN 14th.—O how precious is the word of God to my soul! especially the promises of full salvation, the truth of which I have happily experienced for many years ; nor have I at proper times shunned to declare what God has done for my soul. Not all the powers of darkness have been able to baffle me out of the reality and truth of this glorious doctrine. It does really appear to me, it would be one of my greatest sins to deny this work of the Spirit of God in my soul. I do not mean to say, that I have not often, by my unfaithfulness, grieved the Spirit of God, since I first obtained the great blessing of " a clean heart ; " but when my garment has been spotted by sin, I have remembered that I have " an Advocate with the Father," and through his prevalent intercession, and the efficacy of that open fountain which washes whiter than snow, I have felt my soul mercifully restored to the joys of full salvation.

[What a mercy it is that the salvation of God is as *free*, as it is *full!* "If thou, Lord, shouldst mark iniquities, O Lord, who shall stand?" The subject of this memoir generally lived in the Spirit throughout his long pilgrimage, yet he needed an Advocate and an open fountain It was only by the blood of Jesus he could daily enter the holiest place. He did enter with humble boldness; but it was by simple faith in that blood which cleanses from all sin. Indeed, I never knew any man who expressed such an abiding conviction of the necessity of Christ's continued intercession; nor have I known any one who appeared uniformly to possess such a grateful sense of the Divine goodness and mercy herein manifested to the subjects of the new covenant. On this ground he would very frequently remark, that, as "an heir of God through Christ," he considered himself in circumstances which more loudly called for praise and thanksgiving to the beneficent Creator, than if he had been placed with Adam in Paradise]

FEB. 2d —I am just returned from a visit to the friends at Sparnock In meeting the class I had a precious time, my soul was like a watered garden. The next morning, a friend asked me to visit a woman who was sick, and offered to accompany me. When we arrived at the house, we were informed she was very ill. I went up stairs, and found her, to all human

appearance, on the borders of eternity. Finding
that she had been three years a member of the
society, and knew nothing of salvation by the
remission of her sins,I felt no little concern for
the salvation of her soul. I asked her for
what end Jesus Christ came into the world.
She replied, "To save sinners." I then told
her, that Jesus Christ was the same yesterday,
to-day and for ever; and that he would never
be more willing to save her than he was at that
moment. I explained to her the plan of salvation, and showed her, it was "to him that
worketh not, but believeth on Him who justi-
fieth the ungodly, that his faith is counted for
righteousness." "And now," said I, "it is a duty
which God requires of you to believe in Jesus
Christ, and in the truth of his promises." While
I was thus speaking to her, she was seized in
a strange manner; and it appeared to me, and
those present, that she was dying. But in a
moment or two she lifted up her hands and eyes
to heaven, and cried out, "Glory be to God, I
am healed,—I am healed!" And for some considerable time she kept on repeating, "The
Lord has healed me, body and soul." The news
of this was soon conveyed to her neighbours,
who rushed into the chamber in such crowds
that I was afraid the beams would give way.
But she continued saying, "The Lord has
healed my body and my soul." We then kneeled
down to praise the Lord for what he had done;
and, while engaged in prayer, two of those who
came in were awakened, and began to cry for

mercy. With these distressed souls I was occupied four hours before I could leave the place.
The next day, Mr. Sibly, from Truro, came
there to preach, and dined with us at the friend's
house where I lodged; when the friend who
had been with me the preceding day related the
circumstance to him. Having expressed a
desire to see the woman, I went with him to
the house; and, to our very great astonishment,
we found her down stairs, sitting by the fire.
Several of her neighbours came in to behold
the wonderful works of God. Mr. S. then
required, whether she was the person who had
been so very ill. She replied, "I am, Sir."
"Well, what has the Lord done for you? Has
he pardoned your sins?" She answered, "Yes,
he has pardoned my sins" "How long have
you been a member of the society?" "Three
years" "And do you not think you might have
known it sooner?" "Yes," she replied, "in
six days, had any person shown me the way."
I visited her several times after this, and found
her not only happy in God, but confirmed in her
restoration to health. I have seen many of the
mighty works of the Lord, both in convincing and
converting sinners, but never before saw the body
healed as well as the soul. But has not Jesus the
same power now as in the days of his flesh?
Can he not as easily cure the body now as when
he said to the man, "Arise, take up thy bed and
walk;" or when he touched Peter's wife's
mother, and healed her of the fever under which
she was suffering? O for more faith! Amen.

This was the beginning of a glorious work in that neighbourhood, for which I believe many will bless God in eternity. The same evening, one of the family at whose house I was kindly entertained was deeply distressed for her soul. Four hours she continued on her knees crying earnestly to God; at length the desire of her heart was granted, and she was not ashamed to declare that she knew that God, for Christ's sake, had forgiven her sins. Hearing this, another young woman, a member of the society, but a stranger to the witness of the Spirit, sought me out, and came to converse with me. I was in the house where the Lord had wrought the two-fold miracle of mercy. At first she was much affected, but then, through shame, the dreadful sin of unbelief crept in, and nothing I could afterwards say seemed to affect her mind. I perceived what had taken hold of her, and when she accompanied me into another friend's house, I said to her, "Joanna, you would have been set at liberty just now, had you not been ashamed." She replied "I was tempted to be ashamed of you." I then told her, that till she had overcome that enemy she could not find liberty. She at once rose up, and adding courage to her faith, she cried out, "I will believe, I will believe" And according to her faith it was done unto her. Overwhelmed with joy, she shouted aloud the praises of God. After we had joined in prayer, to give glory to her Deliverer, I accompanied her to her class; where her testimony set all her classmates on fire with Divine love. Nor did she stop here, but hastened home to tell her kindred what great things the Lord had done for her. Her sister had retired; but, under the constraining love of Christ, she ran up stairs to her bedside. And no sooner had she communicated the tidings, than her sister was cut to the heart, and began to cry for mercy. Nor would she rest till, accompanied by her father and sister, she came, through the darkness of the night, to the house where I was. The doors were bolted, and the family and I were retiring to rest. A knock was heard at the door, and no sooner was it opened than she entered, crying, " What must I do to be saved ?" After some time she returned back again with her load of guilt. The next day I visited her, and while engaged with her in prayer, the Lord was pleased to burst her bonds, and fill her soul with joy unspeakable. For these things, O my God, may I never forget to praise thee ! How delightsome a work it is to be thus employed in fishing for souls ! And, blessed be God, I am not permitted to say, '· I toil and catch nothing.''

APRIL 25th.—After an absence of four weeks, I am now returned from a visit to my Mousehole friends. I rejoiced to see my old friends and companions, but was sorry to find that some, in whose welfare I felt much interest, had grown weary in well-doing. Constrained by love, I went immediately in pursuit of the wanderers. When I came where one of them was, my bowels yearned over her. O what

amazing difference did I discover in her! No
running now with joy to show her love and
affection, as in days past! But, for me to look
at this, I knew, was not the right way to restore her. I was not with her long before the
silent tear began to flow. She laboured hard
to conceal from me her feelings; but this she
could not do, for I had fixed my eyes steadfastly on her. O how did my heart rejoice
when I saw any marks of contrition! Before I
left her, I got her promise that she would again
return to the Lord. I then went in search of
the other; and, glory be to God, I obtained the
desire of my heart. On Sunday I had them
both at class-meeting with me. No tongue can
express, no heart can conceive, the joy arising
from such a sight as this! Blessed be God, they
have been steadfast ever since. O Lord, keep
them unto the end! After I left Mousehole, I
staid at Penzance four days. The first night I
met brother Boase's class; three entered into
the liberty of perfect love. The next night I
attempted to meet a class, but I was prevented
by the number of people who crowded into the
room. It was an extraordinary time; many
were filled and overpowered with the love of
God. I breakfasted at my dear friend, Mrs.
Vivian's; seldom has grace made a greater
change in any one than in her. She is a burning and a shining light, and has been so for
many years. It was while I was meeting a
class at Camborne that she received power to
believe unto full salvation. Since that, the

Lord has made her a blessing to many; to his great name be all the glory! for, all the good that is done in the world, I know, the Lord himself doeth it. On my way back, I called for the first time on Mr. Glasson, sen., at Breage. Here I saw the power of God displayed in convincing and converting many sinners. Several backsliders were restored, and four laid hold on the blessing of perfect love. One person came from the distance of six miles to converse with me on the subject, and it pleased the Lord to visit her from above, and give her the desire of her heart. The Searcher of hearts knows, I mention not these things for any other purpose, than that the riches of his grace may be magnified: While I record them, my soul sinks in the dust before Him; and I feel that Christ is all in all. Reflecting on what I have recently witnessed, I see more clearly than I ever did in my life, the importance and excellency of faith. How has my soul of late been blessed in reading our Hymns; and how clear is Mr. Wesley on this point!—

> " To him that in thy name believes,
>   Eternal life with thee is given,
> Into himself he all receives,
>   Pardon, and holiness, and heaven."

I often think I shall praise God to all eternity for his raising him up, and sending him into Cornwall. His Hymn-Book contains a body of divinity. When conversing with penitents, and offering them a present salvation, through faith alone in the blood of Christ, how often has God owned this verse, and set their souls at liberty!—

> " Believe on Him that died for thee ;
> And, sure as He hath died,
> Thy debt is paid, thy soul is free,
> And thou art justified."

JUNE —Being pressed to visit the friends at Breage again, I have been over a second time, and spent some weeks with them. I rejoiced to find so much good resulted from my former visit; and I hope on this occasion I did not spend my time in vain with them. At a meeting one night, the power of God descended amongst us as a mighty rushing wind; and one present was filled with the Spirit in a very remarkable manner. At the request of the friends I visited Porthleven. I went from house to house, and reasoned with the people about righteousness, and a judgment to come; and I invited several to come to a class-meeting which was to be held the next day. At that meeting the Lord poured out his convincing Spirit, and four were deeply awakened. After a long and affecting struggle, Christ appeared to the distressed, and set their souls at liberty. O that men would praise the Lord for his goodness, and for his wonderful works to the children of men!

I went to Ponsanooth; and, while meeting one of the classes, we had a very gracious visitation from above. One who had been for four years seeking the Lord, after a severe struggle with unbelief, was enabled to believe with her heart unto righteousness, and boldly testified that she had received forgiveness of sins. Two others at the same time entered into the rest of full sanctification. At this time the language of my heart is,—

> " Stretch my faith's capacity
> Wider and yet wider still : '
> Then with all that is in thee
> My soul for ever fill."

Glory be to to God for precious faith ; it makes his fulness all my own! O what hath Jesus done for my soul? He hath already bestowed on me the exceeding riches of His grace, and will soon bestow the riches of His glory too. I shall soon see him as he is; for when Christ, who is my life, shall appear, I shall appear with him in glory, and shall be like him for ever. O the blessings of the cross of Christ conferred on me, who am unworthy of the least of all his mercies! My precious Immanuel! since the day of my espousals to thee, now more than forty-six years ago, how hast thou, by ten thousand thousand benefits, endeared thyself to me; yet can I never be satisfied till I possess thy full vision, and have in heaven the complete enjoyment of thyself:—

> " Through all eternity to thee
> A grateful song I'll raise,
> But, O Eternity's too short,
> To utter all thy praise !"

AUGUST 1st.—In meeting the classes at

Ponsanooth, we had good times; our souls were watered with showers of Divine grace, and our hopes began to revive, that, after our days of mourning, the Lord would again soon pour out his Spirit upon us O Lord, hasten it for thy name's sake! O what a necessity have I seen of late, of adding courage to my faith; yea, and temperance, patience, godliness, &c. I want to be always abounding in these things, and to have more and more of the image of God stamped upon my soul.

3d.—My soul is always happy when I write on the subject of the love of God in Christ Jesus to perishing sinners. It kindles a fire that makes all within me rejoice. I want this fire to be always burning upon the altar of my heart, going forth to God in flames of love, and joy, and praise. Lord, I want a fresh baptism of thy Spirit, a deeper plunge into the crimson flood, in order to rise more and more into all the life of God. I am ready to say with Mr. Bramwell, "O for a noble ambition to obtain one of the first seats in glory!—A constant evangelical striving to have the most abundant entrance ministered into the kingdom of God."

5th.—This morning I have been meditating on the dreadful evil of sin. It was sin that caused angels to become devils; and it was sin that caused Adam to be driven out of paradise; by sin he lost the favour and image of God, and brought death into the world with all our woe! I see it was a manifestation of God's

just displeasure against sin, when he swept off
a whole world at one stroke. But, O my
blessed Saviour! when I turn my thoughts for
a moment to reflect on what thou hast done and
suffered to redeem the ruined race, I have still
a clearer discovery of its dreadful evil.   When
I behold thee at Pilate's bar with thy sacred
body "all one wound," and follow thee to
Calvary, and see thee "stretched on yonder
tree," fainting and "crushed beneath my load,"
crying out, "My God, my God, why has thou
forsaken me?"   I see the exceeding sinfulness
of sin, and am constrained to say,—

> " O Lamb of God, was ever pain,
>   Was ever love like thine?"

SEPT. 5th.—I am now returned from a third
visit to my Breage friends.   Many of them are
full of faith and love, standing fast in the liberty
wherewith Christ has made them free.   I was
with them twelve days.   In meeting the class
of Mr. Glasson, sen., he bore testimony to the
efficacy of the blood of Christ in cleansing his
heart from all sin. On that and other occasions,
several more bore a similar testimony, all referring to the same unworthy instrumentality.
O my God, the work is thine, and thou shalt
have the glory!

Nov. 13th.—After an absence of three weeks
in visiting different societies, I am, through
mercy, again returned to my home.   Two
weeks I spent with my son in the St. Austell
circuit.   On my way back, I called to see my

Sparnock friends, met the classes, visited from house to house, and had the happiness of seeing two poor backsliders restored. May they never turn again to folly!

Feb. 18th, 1818.—Since the above date, I have been on a tour of ten weeks among the churches. The first two weeks I spent at Camborne. I met all their classes. The friends were exceedingly kind, and the Lord blessed me among them. I lodged at Capt. J. Vivian's, where I was very kindly entertained. Mrs V., feeling a particular interest in the spiritual welfare of her servant girl requested me to speak to her about her soul. At first I could find no access; she was shy and reserved. At length the Lord softened her heart, and I had the happiness of seeing—

> " The humble contrite tears,
> Which from repentance flow."

I invited her to class-meeting; the Lord met with her there, and she covenanted with him to give him her whole heart. It is now some time since this took place, and she is still steady in the ways of God. May He save her eternally, for Christ's sake. Amen? I visited Wall, and was much blessed among the friends there. After spending a few days with my warm friends at Breage, I proceeded to Mousehole, where I rejoiced to see the mighty works of God displayed in convincing and converting sinners. I intended to stay only one week; but the work of the Lord broke out among them, and the friends would not let me go. In my usual way, I went preaching from house to house, and I believe God never blessed my feeble efforts more than at this time. In one house I found a poor penitent, to whose broken heart the Lord revealed his pardoning mercy. We fell on our knees, to give glory to God for what he had done. And now a brother of her who was the subject of the happy change, being present, fell on the floor, and cried aloud for mercy in an astonishing manner; and before I left the house the Lord also set his soul at liberty. In another house, while relating this circumstance, the arrow of truth reached the heart of a poor backslider, and she trembled as in the presence of God. The next morning, I found her weeping for her ingratitude, and now made willing to return to her offended God. The following Sunday, I met her at the class-meeting; may I also have the pleasure of meeting her in heaven! There was a gracious work among the children in the Sunday school. None but those who have witnessed such a revival can form any idea of it. Some of them seemed as deeply convinced of sin as if they had been forty years of age; and, after they had found peace, could give as clear an account of the work of grace on their minds as if they had been in the good way seven years. But it will require great care to rear these tender plants.

March 11th.—As I was going to Mabe chapel with Mr. N. Earle, he said to me, " There goes another backslider !" I stepped forward, took

him by the arm, and said, " What harm did
Jesus ever do you, that you should turn your
back upon him ?" I then entreated him to return
again to the Lord. He promised me he would ;
and accordingly came to the class-meeting,
bringing another poor wanderer with him.
While I was praying, the power of God descended; and he and his penitent companion
were cut to the heart, and wept aloud for their
sins. They continued in fervent prayer for the
space of three hours, when the Lord was pleas-
sed to bestow on them a gracious sense of his
pardoning mercy. Lodging at Mr. E 's, I felt
impressed with a sense of duty to speak to one
of the same village about her soul I asked
her if she ever prayed ; she frankly told me she
had not; and when I urged her to begin, she
said she knew not how. I told her, prayer did
not consist altogether in words, but in the desire
of the heart; and requested her to kneel by her
bed-side that night before she slept, and say, in
the language of the publican, " God be merciful
to me a sinner !" She promised me she would.
I called again the next morning, to inquire if
she had performed her promise. She assured
me she had, and that she had also, in the same
manner, prayed that morning. The happy
result of this was, the next Sabbath she was
deeply awakened in her own house, and I received a message to come and visit her. When
I came, it was to me a very affecting sight indeed, to see the streaming tears, and to hear her
penitential cries. Soon the Lord Jesus revealed

his pardoning mercy to her soul; and, blessed
be God! she has now been steadfast for many
years. May she stand to the end!

12th.—This day I enter on the sixty-ninth
year of my age. And now, while I take a sur-
vey of God's dealings with me, and tender mercies towards me, I clearly discover goodness
and mercy have followed me all the days of my
life. I have been encompassed on every side.
Surely. I may say,—

> " When in the slippery paths of youth,
>   With heedless steps I ran;
>   His arm unseen convey'd me safe,
>   And led me up to man."

How applicable are these words to me! While
living in ignorance and rebellion against my
God, he protected me, he bore with me, and
kindly continued to strive till I gave him my
heart; and, since that period,—

> " Through hidden dangers, toils, and death,
>   Has gently clear'd my way ;
>   And through the pleasing snares of vice,
>   More to be fear'd than they."

O! where shall my wondering soul begin to
praise him! Eternity—eternity itself will be
too short to praise thee, O my God!

April 29th.—A respected friend at Probus
sent me a letter, requesting me to pay the
friends a visit. I went accordingly, and staid
with them four weeks. Several who had,
through unbelief, lost the witness of sanctifica-

tion, were enabled again to lay hold on the
blessing. One morning, while I with a friend
was visiting the sick, I fell into conversation
with a woman who happened to come into one
of the houses which we had entered. I ques-
tioned her concerning her soul, and soon found
her utterly dark, and insensible to spiritual
things. I spoke to her faithfully of righteousness, death, and judgment; and, like Felix, she
trembled. The next day I called on her, and
found the truths delivered to her the day before
had taken hold of her conscience. " I have
been," said she, "a vile sinner against God for
forty years. Till I saw you, yesterday, I had
been all my days asleep in sin." Seeing that
she was wounded by the sword of the Spirit, and
now wanted the Comforter, I told her that, not-
withstanding all her guilt and sin, I had good
news to tell her. "Jesus," said I, "is now ready,
willing, waiting to save you." This was news
so good, that she could not at first believe it. I
then said, "Are you willing to give up all
your sins, to give God your whole heart, and
to serve him all your days?" With a full
heart she said, "Yes, I am." Then said I,
"Now is the accepted time with God; He
needs no price, no worthiness, no delay. All
that Christ requires is, that you feel your want
of him." We knelt with her at a throne of
grace, wrestled for her in mighty prayer; and
the Lord heard, and set the captive free. With
streaming eyes, and hands and heart uplifted to
heaven, she cried, "Glory be to God, the dead's

alive, the lost is found!" Before she rose from her knees, she prayed for her husband in a striking and uncommon manner. As soon as he came home, she told him what God had done for her soul. This produced a blessed effect upon him; from that time he gave his heart to God, and set out with his wife in the way to heaven. [After the lapse of, apparently, some years, my father interlines his Journal, and says,] Blessed be God, I hear she is now gone home to glory!

MAY 7th.—This is a day which I shall have to remember to all eternity. On this day, forty-seven years ago, the Lord pardoned all my sins. And, glory be to his name! the last year has been the best of the whole! I do find that "the path of the just is as the shining light, that shineth more and more unto the perfect day." I may now say with Bunyan, "I have got into that land where the sun shines night and day." I thank thee, O my God, for this heaven, this element of love and joy, in which my soul now lives. But I am not yet landed on the eternal shore; still I live in an enemy's country, But thou, O Lord, who hast kept me hitherto, wilt keep me unto the end; thou has told me thou wilt never leave me, nor forsake me, and that thy grace is sufficient for me. I rely on thy word, cast all my care on thee, and believe that henceforth as my days so shall my strength be.

14th.—My soul more and more longs for Zion's prosperity. Not only do I desire to see sinners convinced and converted to God, but I want to see the work of grace deepening in the hearts of God's children; I want them to be saved from all the carnal mind, and to enjoy the blessing of perfect love. How few they are, comparatively speaking, who have entered into this glorious liberty! I find, by conversing with professors, that many who truly desire this inestimable privilege are prevented from laying hold of it by setting it too high. It is nothing more or less than simply loving God with all the heart. Blessed be God, I do enjoy this great salvation!

20th —I have just received a letter from a class-leader, who thus speaks:—" With gratitude I inform you of the dealings of the Lord with us here. I bless God, I still know and feel that through the blood of atonement I am cleansed from all sin. In all my temptations, my Saviour

'——— keeps me to prove
His utmost salvation, his fulness of love.'

My dear wife also is enabled to hold fast her confidence in Jesus as her full Saviour. At times, I believe, she holds with a trembling hand; and, by permitting the enemy of her peace to approach too near, she loses part of the happiness which she might enjoy. My class prospers; it is now the delight of my soul to meet this little band of undaunted Christian warriors. Be assured we have not forgotten you: for we have reason to bless God that you ever held out to us the freeness of a full salvation.

Go on still, and shun not to declare the whole
counsel of God. When you have a few days
to spare, we shall be glad to see you."

SEP. 8th.—" Keep me little and unknown,
        Loved and prized by God alone."

Never was I so truly happy in increasing union
with the Father, Son, and Spirit. Yea, in the
night season of late, I have been constrained to
say with David, " He maketh me lie down in
green pastures : he leadeth me beside the still
waters. He restoreth my soul ; he leadeth me
in paths of righteousness for his name's
sake." Of late, truly, my peace has flowed as
a river. I am not speaking of rapturous joy.
No : it is rather,—

    " The speechless awe that dares not move,
      And all the silent heaven of love."

OCT. 22d.—I am now returned from a tour
of six weeks among different societies. At
Mousehole I was glad to meet so many of my
old friends and companions still fighting the
good fight of faith. With several of them I
have now been united in Christian fellowship
more than forty-seven years. God was pleased
again to bless my conversation to some of the
feeble of the flock ; and I discovered more clearly than ever the common mistake of many who
are sincere. They say, " I wish I was so happy as I was once; " without having the least
conception of the excellency of faith as the in-

strument and condition of their salvation. God
has made known the Gospel-plan in these
words : " By grace are ye saved through faith."
We are saved by simple faith; or by believing
in Jesus from moment to moment. It is "to
him that believeth," (not *has* believed, nor *shall*
believe,) that righteousness is imputed. This
is true, whether of pardon or purity; for both
are received and retained only by faith in the
blood of Christ. While at Breage, I called
one day on my esteemed friend Mrs. L. ; and
following an impulse of duty on my mind, I
was led to converse closely with her servant-
maid about her soul. She was living without
God in the world, and unprepared for eternity.
I asked her if she was willing to die in her present state. She frankly said she was not. Then
said I, "Suppose God should now suddenly remove you to the world of spirits; what would
become of you?" With this solemn question
it pleased God to fasten the Spirit of conviction
on her heart. She now promised to yield herself to God, and begin to pray. That night I
was glad to meet her at the class. The next
morning I walked a mile to have some further
conversation with her. It now appeared she
had begun to pray in secret, and was determined
to serve the Lord. While I was conversing
with her, she burst into tears, crying out, "O
what a sinner I am, what a sinner I am!"
I then led her to the mercy of God in Christ
Jesus; showing her the covenant-blood, and
what she wanted to make her happy. Soon the

Saviour condescended to visit her broken heart, and turn her sorrow into joy; nor was her profession as "the early cloud and morning dew;" she has now walked for some years in the good way. At the house of another friend, I found one who was weary and heavy laden with sin. I opened the Bible, and pointed her to the promises, and to him "by whose stripes we are healed." While I was thus in the act of exhorting her to believe in the Lord Jesus Christ, her darkness was suddenly turned into day. I put down these things, because I have been of late more than ever convinced that it is the will of God that his mercies and dealings with his children should not be lost, but, as far as practicable, committed to writing, and retained in grateful memory.

Feb 11th, 1819.—O what sweet communion have I this night had with my blessed Jesus! And how many precious promises have been applied to my mind! such as these, "Thy Maker is thy husband, the Lord of hosts is his name." "They shall never perish; neither shall any pluck them out of my hand." At these refreshing seasons, how easy it is to plunge into the fountain that cleanses from all sin! But I can truly say,—

> "I loathe myself when God I see,
>   And into nothing fall;
> Content if thou exalted be,
>   And Christ be all in all."

13th.—This morning the Lord shined into

my heart by his Holy Spirit, and gave me to
see what is implied in the believer's being " an
heir of God, and a joint heir with Jesus Christ."
Such was my faith, I could easily claim all that
God hath in earth and heaven as my own.   I
clearly discover it is by these believing views,
that the soul is changed from glory into glory,—

" Till in heaven we take our place,
    Till we cast our crowns before Him,
  Lost in wonder, love, and praise."

It is by believing, or by faith, that we are enabled to see the true nature and emptiness of all
the things of this world, and that we see they
were never intended for our rest or portion. By
faith we see, that at last a smiling or frowning
world amounts to nothing; we see the soul's
wants, and miseries, and cure; we see Christ
and heaven near; we triumph over all our foes,
. and lay hold on eternal life.

15th.—While possessing the delightful en
joyments which are noticed above, and speaking
of the excellency of faith, I had little thought of
the trial that was at hand, and the call I should
speedily have to exercise strong faith. I received a letter from my dear son Benjamin,
dated Camelford, February 13th, stating that he
had just received a letter from the Missionary
Committee in London, in which they expressed
a wish for him to enter on the work of a Foreign
Mission; he also expressed the sense of duty
which he felt in his own mind in reference to
the great undertaking, and desired to know

what I thought of it, and stating that he could not feel himself at liberty to become a Missionary, without my consent. At reading this, I was greatly affected; indeed I was for some time overwhelmed, and incapable of giving him any answer. I knew his mind had been exercised on the subject long before; but when he mentioned it to me, I could not bear to entertain the thought, and therefore begged him not to think of any thing of the kind till I should be removed hence. My love for him was great; perhaps Jonathan's love for David was not greater. I was not only his father after the flesh, but likewise in the Gospel also. Of this he often made public acknowledgment. But now I saw he was apparently called of God to leave me, and I knew not how I could give him up to such an undertaking. The object was a burden to my mind indescribable. But on one occasion soon after, while I was in secret, pondering over the painful subject, thinking of the separation, and of the various privations and dangers attending such a work, just at the moment when nature shrunk back, and I felt as if I could not consent to make the sacrifice, I seemed suddenly surrounded by the Divine presence, and a voice said to me, "I gave my Son to die for thee; and canst thou not give thy son to go an errand for me? I will bring him to thee again." I cried out, "Take him, Lord take him!" The Lord conquered me by his dying love; and never did I offer any thing to God more willingly. Indeed it appeared to me at that time, that, if I had a thousand sons, I would cheerfully have given them all up to God for such a work. Nor have I since changed my views, or had one uneasy thought about him. At the time when I felt the wonderful deliverance, and the Father of mercies himself condescended to reason with me, it seemed, for the moment, I could not tell whether I was in the body or out of the body. Time appeared only a moment compared with that eternity, which was opened to my mind; and it was in the full assurance of faith I offered him up, believing that, if I should see him no more in time, we should quickly meet in heaven; seeing the Lord told me he would bring him to me again. When the time came for his departure to New South Wales, and I accompanied him and his dear wife to the coach, and took my final leave of him, I was so supported above myself, that I was perfectly calm and recollected. It seemed to me, if I ever found the all-sufficiency of grace, it was on that trying occasion. How does a life of faith triumph over every thing that would distress the soul! I know that we shall meet again, and that the separation will be but for a short season. And even during that little season,—

> " Mountains rise and oceans roll
> To sever us in vain."

God has united us; in him we subsist as one soul, and " no power can make us twain."

"Present we still in spirit are,
And intimately nigh,
While on the wings of faith and prayer,
We each to other fly."

Here I rest the matter with tranquillity and joy, while I continue an inhabitant of this vale of tears.

[In this conquest of faith over the natural feelings of the human mind, there are some things striking in my father's case. It was instantaneous, complete, and permanent. Previous to the victory of which he speaks, whenever I ventured to mention to him the subject of my becoming a foreign Missionary, his feelings overcame him, and I was entreated not to entertain a thought of the subject while he was alive. Partly in obedience to him, I deferred engaging in the important work for some years. At length, when I could not, consistently with the duty of keeping a conscience void of offence towards God and man, put it off any longer, I stated to him my case. This so affected him, that my brother wrote me to say, he feared the contemplated separation would shorten the days of our dear parent. At hearing this I was distressed, and sought advice of some of my aged brethren, whether to relinquish or persist in my object. But soon God took the matter into his own hands, and produced the change above described. Shortly after, when I returned to see him, before I went to London to make preparatory arrangements, I found that natural affection had no more influence upon his mind, than

7

upon the mind of the Spartan mother, when her son was called to the field of warfare. As it is said, she dreaded nothing but her son's failing in duty to his country, so did my father appear to me, as if, on this subject, he was only capable of grief, by beholding me shrink back from the work. He had made the sacrifice, and he gloried in the cross! At the time when I bade him farewell, neither of us expecting to meet again below, the language of his whole deportment was only—"Go; and the Lord be with thee!" Nor did the many years of my absence produce the slightest change in his mind; for he emphatically walked by faith, and not by sight.]

CHAPTER III.

April 10th, 1820.—Giving glory to God, I can say with dear Mrs. Rogers, I am now right; and I trust Him for all that is to come; and though all weakness, ignorance, helplessness, and unworthiness, yet I have the testimony of my own conscience, and the witness of the Spirit, that I am wholly and unreservedly his: His in body, spirit, soul; for Christ is in my heart; I dwell in God, and God in me. God is love; and he is all I want for time or for eternity.

May 7th.—A day never to be forgotten by me. It was on the seventh of May my chains fell off, I was made free in Israel and became a follower of Jesus. Yes, on this day I believed

with my heart unto righteousness; on this day
I was justified by faith, and had peace with God
through our Lord Jesus Christ; on this day I
received the Spirit of adoption, and was enabled
to say, "Abba, Father;" on this day my name
was written in heaven, I was married to Christ,
and my Maker,—the Lord of Hosts,—the Holy
One of Israel,—the God of the whole earth,—
became my husband. And hast thou kept thy
poor unworthy dust forty nine years in the wilderness? Yes, glory be to God! thou hast
kept me by thy almighty power. And now I
will sing,—

"O the infinite cares, and temptations and snares,
  Thy hand has conducted me through;
O the blessings bestow'd, by a bountiful God,
  And the mercies eternally new."

8th.—This day I consider myself as entering
upon a new year, and I have covenanted afresh
with my God. Thou, O Lord, knowest all my
wants. I feel I am weaker than a bruised
reed; and, if thou leave me but a moment, I
must perish, and sink, and die. But though I
am all weakness, thou art all strength; then, O
my God help me, by faith's strong arm, to lay
hold on thee. I know thy promises are firmer
than the pillars of heaven, and thou hast said,
"I will never leave nor forsake thee." This,
Lord, is enough; in thy might will I go forward.

"Though nature's strength decay,
  And earth and hell withstand,
To Canaan's bounds I urge my way
  At thy command.

"The watery deep I pass,
With Jesus in my view;
And through the howling wilderness
My way pursue."

9th.—This morning, while meditating on
these words, " Who shall separate us from the
love of Christ? shall tribulations?" &c , what
an increase of faith did I feel! This is one of
the great and precious promises, which are
given to us that we may be made partakers of
the Divine nature. O how sweet and delightsome to my soul are these words, " The Divine
nature!" This is what man lost when Adam
fell. But, glory be to God, what I lost, and
more than what I lost in Adam, is purchased for
me again by the precious blood of Christ; for
" where sin abounded, grace did much more
abound " So that it clearly appears to me, that,
if we are not wanting to ourselves, we shall in
the end, through the super-abounding grace of
Christ, be gainers by the fall When God's
children get to heaven they will sing a note
which angels cannot: these cannot sing, " Unto
Him that loved us, and washed us from our sins
in his own blood," &c. But this will be the
theme of redeemed sinners to all eternity.

" O may I bear some humble part
In that Immortal song :"

15th.—This morning God filled my soul
with peace and joy in believing. " He that
believeth," saith Jesus, " out of his belly shall
flow rivers of living water." It is not accord-

iug to our joy, (this is the fruit and effect of
faith,) but according to our faith, that God
blesses, and saves, and accepts, and loves us.
Our love to God, his people, his precepts, all
springing from the root of faith, are so many
acts of the soul accepted through the Beloved.
Faith clears the apprehension, impresses the
affections, determines the will, and governs the
life.   In reference to God and the things of
God, it is that which supplies the want of sight.
As if the Apostle had said, Though the glory
promised to believers be yet unseen and only
hoped for, yet the true believer is as much affected with it, and influenced by its attractive
force, as if it were present before his eyes.   To
the natural man this is foolishness, he cannot
understand it.   But believers know and feel,
that "faith is the substance of things hoped for,
the evidence of things not seen."

My kind friends in the Liskeard Circuit had
given me many invitations to pay them another
visit: but, fearing my strength would not admit
of it, I had put it off from time to time.   At
length, though above my three-score years and
ten, I determined to attempt it in the name and
strength of the Lord.   Accordingly, on May
30, I set off on what proved a tour of greater
length than I had before taken.   The first society I visited was Bicton-Mill; here I spent
six days with my friend Body and his excellent
family, from whom I received tokens of kindness
and affection beyond all I can express; and
found it very profitable to commune with them

on the things of God. My next place was
Callington, where I stayed three weeks. Great
was my joy to find some steadfast, to whom
God had before made me useful. If such be
our feelings when meeting on earth, what will
be our joy to meet in heaven! I found one had
wandered from God, for whom I felt much
compassion. I sought her out, and my bowels
yearned over her.   After frequent conversations with her, the Lord again touched her
heart, and she deeply lamented her revolting
from Him. She returned to the fold, and promised she would henceforth be the Lord's.
Since this she has gone on well. Another poor
backslider, the wife of a friend, (who had for
many years been a steady member of society,) was also re-awakened, and again went
with me to the class-meeting.   I went to Dun-
ston to a monthly meeting; and from that place
I was, by the kindness of Mr. Webb, conveyed
to Wisewandron.   Of Mr. W, it may be truly
said, he has a church in his house. He has
public worship within his own dwelling; and
himself and Mrs. W., with five children and
three servants, all meet in class! Here I met
with two friends who had cast away their confidence.   I reproved them for their cowardice,
told them of the stab they had given to experimental religion, and encouraged them again to
look to the Saviour.   I have reason to believe
my conversation with them had a good effect.
Before I left they were again restored to the
joy of God's salvation, I went to Tideford to

meet a class; and here fell in with Mr. R. Geake,
who insisted on my going with him to St. Germain's; and then he told me I must consent to
visit Dock [now Devonport]. The next morning I went with him accordingly, and was
kindly received and entertained by the friends
there. On entering the house of Mr. K., he
said, "While you stay with us, you are to make
this house your home." The next day he took
me to visit a friend; several persons were in
the room which I entered, and I began at once
conversing with them about their souls. The
one to whom I more particularly addressed myself, I soon found, was a stranger to the things
of God. She expressed a wish to go to heaven, but
frankly acknowledged she was afraid to die, and
said she believed if death should arrest her in
the condition in which she then was she should
be lost. I urged her at once to give her heart
to God, and to promise me she would that night
begin to pray. She was silent for some time.
I told her, God was present and saw the thoughts
of her heart; and that I was waiting for her
answer. At length she said, "What is the use
for me to promise? I have already made promises, but have broken them all." I told her
these had been made in her own strength, but
that I wanted her to promise in the strength of
the Lord. This remark fastened on her heart
as a nail in a sure place; and to my no small
surprise, she immediately turned to me and
said, "Sir, will you pray with me now?" We
then knelt down, and I interceded with God in

her behalf The next time I saw her, she told
me, that after I left she sought a retired part of
the house, and there fell down upon her knees
and offered herself to God From that time she
sought the Lord sorrowing; and, at the end of
twenty-one days, her load of guilt was removed,
and she was enabled to rejoice in a pardoning
God. After this I met with Miss T., who was
earnestly desiring salvation; and, while I was
pointing her the way to Calvary, she was enabled to believe, and received the Spirit of adoption. I have since had a letter from her, in
which she informs me she has now become a
member of the society. At Mr. K.'s I one day
met with two who were earnestly longing to be
delivered from the plague of an evil heart of
unbelief. I showed them what was their high
privilege as believers in Jesus Christ; and,
blessed be his holy name! before we parted,
they both received the witness that they were
saved from sin. In meeting their classes I had
many blessed seasons I now went over to
Plymouth to see my old and much respected
friends, Mr and Mrs. Allen Here I remained
three weeks before they would suffer me to get
off from them. One day I fell into close conversation with Mrs. L, and found that though
she had been two years a member of the society,
she was quite a stranger to the nature of faith,
and the knowledge of remission of sins. I desired her to get me a Bible, that I might point
her to Him, " by whose stripes we are healed."
I also took our Hymn-Book, and showed her

how Gospel faith is described there. Soon the blessed light of faith shined into her heart, and she cried out, " I see my debt is paid. Jesus hath died, hath died for me." She now sent for Miss H., to whom also God graciously revealed himself, enabling her to " reckon herself dead indeed unto sin " I have now a letter before me, dated many months after this, in which she speaks very decisively of the change then wrought. She says, " Till I saw you, my dear sir, I thought there was no higher attainment for me on earth than justification; but by your instructions God showed me otherwise, for which I shall bless Him to all eternity." Surely these things are of the Lord, yet I have sometimes thought I would pass them over in silence. But when I have thought thus, I have been admonished from within not to do it, so I dared not yield to the suggestion.

While at Plymouth, I sometimes met three classes in a day; and I can truly say it is a work in which my soul delights. I love to prop the feeble, to bind up the broken-hearted, and to proclaim liberty to the captives; to be in any way employed under God, to hold forth to redeemed sinners, a full, free, and present salvation, through faith alone in the merits of our Lord Jesus Christ. I was requested to visit Causand, where I found the kindest entertainment at the house of Mrs. Luney. Often have I been led to wonder at the love and affection of the children of God toward me. Surely this also is of the Lord; for, separate from him, I am certain I have nothing to attract them. Glory to his holy name! he was with me at Causand.   Several persons felt the power of God, were stirred up to seek his face, and were enabled to believe and rejoice in a sin-pardoning Saviour.   While I was there five new members joined the society, and I have since received a letter informing me they are yet steadfast.   My next port was Saltash; among our various friends at this place, there is a blessed spirit of love, unity, and simplicity.   I was gladly received, and lodged at my excellent friend, Mr. Tasker's.   I remained here three weeks, meeting the classes and visiting the people from house to house; and some soul's were awakened and saved.   Never shall I forget a meeting we had one night at Mr. T.'s. Himself, his dear wife, and two pious young men, came together to talk about the deep things of God.   After I had pointed out to them their privilege to be pure in heart, and the way to attain it, we went to prayer, and the Lord opened the windows of heaven, and poured out such a blessing that there was scarce room to contain it.   It was some time before any thing could be uttered but, "Glory, glory, glory!"   From that period they all four bore witness that the blood of Jesus Christ had cleansed them from all sin.   I have since received a letter from one of them, informing me that they all still retain their confidence, and are going on their way rejoicing, giving glory to God.

    [The happy effects produced at the social

meeting here spoken of, were as permanent as
they were glorious. With two of the party my
father held a close correspondence till near the
time of his death; many of their numerous
letters are of no common quality. After the
lapse of ten or twelve years, I find they had all
as lively and as grateful a remembrance of this
overpowering visitation of the Holy Spirit, as
when the letter was written which my father
mentions. Two of them are local preachers;
from one of these I have just received a letter.
After giving an interesting account of the
meeting, of my father's conversation with them,
and of " the four lepers being cleansed at once,"
he adds, " In the best sense of the word we
were now new creatures; and we went forth
with an increase of both light and heat. While
the Spirit took of the things of Christ, and revealed them unto us, the love of Christ continued to fill our enlarged hearts, and prepared
us either to do or to suffer the will of God. We
became more happy and more useful ; and, what
is matter of highest praise to ' Him who hath
loved us and washed us from our sins,' we all
continue to hold fast our possessions to the present time. Our joy indeed often varies, but
we have learned that the possession of inward
holiness is retained not by joy, but by faith.
Therefore we still go on our way, singing,
with one who is gone before us,—

> " I can, I do believe in thee,
>   All things are possible to me.' "]

From Saltash I returned to St. Germain's,

and then went over to see my old friends at Polperro. While here, I heard of Mrs. M. having a
desire to see me   Her family not being friend-
ly to the Methodists, it was with some difficulty
I obtained an interview with her.   I found, by
conversing with her, that on a former visit to
Polperro, I had providentially met with her, and
had urged her to begin at once to seek God.
It now appeared from her own testimony, that
that night, before she retired to rest, she bowed
her knees in prayer.   Her soul became awakened; she slept but little during the night; and
soon after was soundly converted to God   O
Lord, thou knowest she stands on slippery
ground; but may she prove thy grace sufficient
for her! I came to Lanteglos; stayed a few days,
met the classes, and left my respected friends,
Mr. and Mrs. P., quite on stretch for heavenly
things.   While at Charlestown, a friend wished
me to converse with her daughter, who had for
some time been unwell.   I found she had a
measure of the fear of the Lord, but at first
shewed a disinclination to converse about religion.   Her reluctance, however, was at length
vanquished by a sense of heavenly love.   She
was enabled to believe in Jesus Christ; and
promised me, if God spared her life, she would
join with his people   The Lord has since
raised her up; she has fulfilled her vow, and is
now happy in the Saviour's love.

APRIL 24th, 1821 —While talking with an
old woman sixty years of age, she was soon cut
to the heart, and in a very short time the Lord
set her soul at liberty.   The change was so

great, and the transition so sudden, that language failed to express her gratitude to God. She soon ran and told her neighbours what God had done for her soul. Another woman was deeply affected at what she saw and heard, and also sought and soon found a sense of Divine mercy.

26th.—While at Breage, a friend informed me that H. M. had a great desire to see me. I went to him, and found he had been five years under the afflicting hand of Providence. He told me he wanted the assurance that he was a child of God; and then said how he had read and prayed, and had the clergyman to administer the sacrament to him, in hopes that he should thereby attain what he wanted. " But," says he, "all seems to be of no use." I replied, "No, it is not of works, lest any man should boast." I then brought the Bible to him, and opened to 1 Peter ii 24, and requested him to read for himself: " Who bore our sins in his own body on the tree, that we, being dead to sins, should live unto righteousness: with whose stripes we are healed." He looked upon me with great earnestness, and cried out, " It was faith I wanted; I could never read for myself before " At that moment the Lord set his soul at liberty, and he rejoiced with joy unspeakable and full of glory. I do not think I was with him more than half-an-hour before the happy change took place. Soon after this, he took his flight to the paradise of God.

From Breage I went to Mousehole, and while here I completed the fiftieth year of my spiritual pilgrimage. This event was rendered the more abundantly gratifying and delightful, because it took place at the spot where I commenced, and in the presence of the three who set out in the way to heaven with me.*   After the lapse of

* This is a rare and striking fact, which contains in it much of moral sublimity. That the four young men, who, at this place, set out together for the heavenly country, in 1771, should all continue from the beginning to adorn the doctrines of God their Saviour; and, after passing through the various perils, conflicts, and changes of life, should all meet together, on the same spot, in the house of worship, on their jubilee day in 1821, is a singularly delightful occurrence, which could not fail to attract notice. The Rev. J. Smith remarked to me, a few weeks ago, how much he was impressed and delighted, when, preaching at Mousehole at this time, he beheld from the pulpit the four hoary-headed veterans, who, after fifty years' hard fighting in Emmanuel's service, were all sitting together in the leaders' pew! The irreproachable and venerable Michael Wright still survives, is able regularly to attend the public ordinances, and not only meets his class and assists at the prayer-meetings, but often leads the congregational singing with a clear and excellent voice. Of my uncle, some notice will be found in a subsequent part of my father's narrative. As to the eminent and highly-respected Richard Trewavas, who was my father's particular friend, and whom I loved and revered from my childhood, I cannot forbear inserting here a brief notice of him. Like his neighbours, he was a fisherman; but his mind was of a superior order; his intelligence was considerable; his address was engaging and dignified; and his conversation highly interesting to persons of all ages, and of every class in life. He had a frankness, a generosity, a nobleness of soul, not commonly met with; and in life and death he was a pattern

half a century, here was I, my dear brother Trewavas, brother M.Wright, and my own brother
Benedict, still kept by the power of God,
through faith, with our faces Zionward.

> " O that we at last may stand,
>   With the sheep at God's right hand ;
>   Take the crown so freely given,
>   Enter in by Christ to heaven ! "

MAY 17th —Being at the house of a friend
at St. Day, I was informed of a man who had
been in deep distress of soul for three weeks.   I
·felt pity for him, and expressed a desire to see
him.   His cry was still, " Mercy, mercy, good
Lord ! " but he was almost spent out.   I direct-

of Christian piety.   His son Richard, who was one
of my earliest and dearest religious friends, was a
man of great vigour of understanding, and great
eminence in the Divine life.   To his intercessions
with God in my behalf, I owed much in my early
ministry   Though now dead nearly twenty years,
I never pass by the spot where his ashes lie, but the
sight of his tomb kindles the fervour of devotion
within me.   In deadness of the world, fervency of
spirit, vividness of spiritual apprehension, and depth
of communion with God, I have never known or
read of his superior; and, as to his final hour, seldom in the death of saints has there been such a display of Christian triumph.   A short account of the
father is inserted in the Wesleyan Methodist Magazine for 1826; and a pamphlet was published by
the Rev. R. Treffry, containing an interesting memoir of the son ; but J believe no one will be displeased to find their exalted names recorded in the
memoir of their mutual and much-loved friend.
—EDITOR.

ed his mind to the right object, by telling him
I had good news for him, that Jesus Christ
came into the world to save sinners. It was
but a short time before his cries for mercy were
turned into shouts of, "Glory, glory." The
sight of this happy change affected his wife, a
poor backslider for seven years. She became
deeply awakened, and now sought God with
great earnestness. It was a pleasing sight to
see the husband rejoicing in the Lord, and the
wife a weeping penitent at the Saviour's feet.

20th.—The following remarks of Mr. Bramwell are striking, and deserve particular notice:
—"Justification is great, to be cleansed is greater;
but what is justification, or being cleansed, compared with being taken into God? The world,
the noise of self—all is gone; and the mind
bears the full stamp of God's image. Here we
talk, and walk, and live;—doing all in him and
to him;—continual prayer, and turning all into
Christ, in every house, in every company; all
things by him, from him, and to him."—O! I
long to be more filled with God. Lord, stir
me up to be more in earnest. I want to be
more like Jesus. My soul thirsteth for thee,
O God. I see nothing will do but being continually filled with thy presence and glory. I
know all that thou hast is mine, but I want to
feel a closer union. Lord, increase my faith.
This day, while mourning in secret for my unfaithfulness, and pouring out my soul for a fresh
manifestation of Gilead's balm, Jesus spake to
me, saying, "Reach hither thy hand, and thrust

it into my side, and be not faithless, but believing." Instantly my mourning was turned to joy, and Christ again became precious.

June 25th —I have had a fresh plunge into the fountain which is opened for sin and uncleanness. My Saviour has not only washed my hands and my feet, but my head and my heart; and he hath clothed me with the garment of salvation, he hath covered me with the robe of righteousness. O, I cannot describe what I have felt; language fails to express it.

"All is too mean to speak his worth,
Too mean to set my Saviour forth."

28th.—I see it my privilege to grow in grace, and in the knowledge and love of God. This is my song at present:—"To him who hath loved me and washed me from my sins in his own blood, to him be glory for ever and ever. Amen." The greatest thing I have had of late to contend with, is vain thoughts; I feel I have need to pray that God would not suffer them to lodge within me. If not promptly resisted, these become "the little foxes that spoil the vine; for the vine hath tender grapes."

July 3rd.—I have been confined to bed four days by an inflammation in my leg. But though the Lord has afflicted my body, my mind has been in perfect peace. My soul has mounted on the wings of contemplation, and I have enjoyed sweet communion with God. His presence makes my paradise.

5th.—With one who now rests above, I can

8

say. " I generally glide very happily along the
heavenly track, having my sails swelled with
the precious gales of grace from the spicy hills
of Zion," I steer by the compass of God's holy
word, and make a straight course to the heavenly country But I feel this happy state is
attained and secured to me by faith alone. I
am called to fight against combined and multiplied enemies; but I hear the Eternal God
saying, " Fear not, be not dismayed, I am with
thee." And, blessed be God! the language of my
soul at this time is,—

> " What, though a thousand hosts engage,
>   A thousand worlds, my soul to shake :
> I have a shield shall quell their rage,
>   And drive the alien armies back;
> Portray'd, it bears a bleeding Lamb,
> I dare believe in Jesus' name."

7th —I feel the work of grace deepening in
my soul, and I have increasing life, power,
liberty, and delight in the service of God. In
meeting the class last night, at Mylor Bridge, I
felt Christ was eminently present and precious.
O Lord, make me more thankful for these bright
manifestations of thy love to my soul! I do feel
thy ways pleasant, and that in the keeping of
thy commandments there is great reward.

9th.—Glory be to God! this is a morning
without a cloud Lord, help me to praise thee !
How applicable to the feeling of my soul at this
time is this verse :—

" Thee I can love, and thee alone,
   With pure delight and inward bliss:
To know thou takest me for thine own,—
   O what a happiness is this!"

My exulting heart now exclaims, "Behold what manner of love the Father hath bestowed upon me, that I should be called a son of God," Yes, I am now a son of God, and "it doth not yet appear what I shall be, but I know that, when Christ appears, I shall be like him, for I shall see him as he is." O, my union with him is stronger than ever! Whatever concerns me for time or eternity, I can leave joyfully in his hands. Happy state, to live a life of faith in the Son of God! O may I follow the Lord every moment!

12th —I am now returned from a visit to my friends at Sparnock. I had not seen them for three years, and was happy to find so many of them with their faces Zion-ward. When here about four years ago, I met with two sisters, whose hearts had departed from God and his people for some considerable time; and the Lord was pleased to make me the happy instrument of restoring them to the joy of his salvation. I rejoiced to find them still graciously preserved, with their souls truly alive to God. It was with divine satisfaction I met them in class on Sunday morning; and there also I met with my dear sister Oats, whose body the Lord so miraculously restored at the time of her conversion. She now appeared in such a happy state of body and mind, that I was con-

strained to say, " O that men would praise the
Lord for his goodness, and for his wonderful
works to the children of men !"

16th —By waiting upon God this night in
his house, I have renewed my strength; and
on my way home I fell in with one of my
neighbours, with whom I had not before conversed about the salvation of her soul I felt
great liberty in talking to her; and I now earnestly pray that God may seal the truth upon
her conscience, so that it may be erased no more
in time or eternity.

22nd.—Glory be to God, I still enjoy that
peace which the world cannot give nor take
away. O what cause have I to praise God for
keeping my helpless soul in the safe and precious path of simple faith and humble love !
May I ever lie at his feet, and never depart from
the rule of his written word.

> " 'Tis there I would always abide,
>   And never a moment depart;
>   Conceal'd in the cleft of his side,
>   Eternally held in his heart."

O what is all that is called great and good, compared to this ! Friends, fortune, wealth, crowns,
and kingdoms; what are they? Less, far less
than nothing: They are dung and dross! O
my God, to enjoy thee is all in all! O the
depth of dying love! My soul is penetrated
with the unspeakable grace that made my God
a man of grief, a victim to justice, a dying victim
for my sins. O spotless Victim! O Lord of

life! and didst thou die for me? For me thou
didst die; my sacrifice, my God! By a letter
just received from Saltash, I have a very pleasing account of those four who were cleansed
from sin while I was praying with them. They
are all steadfast in faith and love. I advised
them to meet in band; this they continue to do,
and find it very profitable to their souls.

24th —Last night my mind was much grieved
at a prayer-meeting, to see such carelessness in
worshipping God : Sitting at the time of prayer:
How was my mind pained at this! O my God,
how desirable to see these souls converted!
Lord, hasten it for thy mercy's sake! Amen.

27th.—This morning these words of the
Psalmist were made a great blessing to my soul :
" If I forget thee, O Jerusalem, let my right hand
forget her cunning. If I do not remember thee,
let my tongue cleave to the roof of my mouth ;
if I prefer not Jerusalem above my chief joy."
I have just now been taking a retrospect of the
mercies of God towards me ; and I find I might
as well attempt to count the stars in the firmament, the drops of water in the great ocean, or
the grains of sand upon the sea-shore. But
thanks be to his great and holy name, I have
not forgotten them all. Among the multitude
of unmentioned mercies, I will here record one :
About fifty years ago, just after I was converted,
I was seized with a fever ; I then began to ex-
amine myself, and wondered where my joys and
comforts had fled. I could trust in God, though
I could not rejoice ; but this passage of Scripture

was applied to my mind : "He that believeth
on Him shall not be confounded." I received
it as from the Lord, and my peace and joy returned again. But being only a babe in Christ,
and not knowing how to live or walk by faith,
my joys soon withered again. While examining myself, these words came with such power
to my soul, and made such a deep impression
on my mind, that I have never forgotten it :
" Behold, I have graven thee upon the palms of
my hands." These words were applied to my
soul with such light, life, and power, that I
seemed to be lifted from the bed on which I lay.
I may venture to say, that a thousand and a
thousand times have I thought on these two precious promises. They have not only been a
staff in each hand to lean on during these fifty
intervening years, but they have been as two
strong pillars, on which to rest my weary soul
in satan's darkest hour.

> " And when to that bright world I rise,
> To claim my mansion in the skies;
> Above the rest this note shall swell,
> My Jesus hath done all things well."

28th.—This morning I had sweet intercourse
with the ever-blessed Trinity, and my mind was
deeply impressed with humbling views of the
infinite condescension and love of God. O
blessed free grace, free for every soul of man !
I could weep for the hardness and stupidity of
poor sinners, who know not, but neglect and
despise, so great salvation. I have been con-

fined at home nearly six weeks with an inflammation in my leg. How it will end I know not; but I leave myself in the hands of the Lord, who will do what is best for me. I see I have no reason to murmur, but great cause to be thankful for the health I have enjoyed during the last fifty years: Not one week have I been confined to my bed by a fever, a broken bone, or any other affliction.

> "In all my ways thy hand I own
> Thy ruling providence I see:
> Assist me still my course to run,
> And still direct my path to thee."

29th —The promises this day have greatly strengthened and comforted my soul; especially that favourite portion of mine, Hebrews vii. 25. O what is contained therein! This is a promise worth ten thousand worlds. Yet what are the promises without faith? It is faith alone which is the foundation of all our holiness, strength, and happiness. All must believe, or they cannot love; and love, or they cannot obey; but to those who do believe there shall be a performance of every promise.

AUGUST 5th —Brother N. Earle, of Mabe, came to Downstall, and earnestly invited me over to meet his class. As he had four servants all living without God in the world, I felt much compassion for them, and a longing desire to do them good. One of them had known something of Divine grace, and was still rather steady in his outward conduct; so I began with

him first.   I met him in the field, and had a
long conversation with him about the state of
his soul.   I invited him to come that night to
the class-meeting, and he gave me a sort of
promise that he would.   But he did not.   The
next morning I asked him the reason why he
skulked away.   He was speechless.   I reproved him smartly, and told him that though
he could deceive man, he could not deceive
God.   "Depend upon it," said I, "you must
answer for this with me at the bar of God, and
then you will see whether this is a little thing
you have done."   This seemed to come with
power to his conscience.   I then left him to his
own reflections; and went in pursuit of his
fellow-servant, and found him.   This was a
young man for whose conversion I had before
laboured hard, but could not gain my point.
I now found his mind more susceptible of good;
he promised me he would give his heart to God,
and at once commence a life of prayer.   This
greatly encouraged me to go a fishing for the
other two; for whose salvation the Lord knew
the ardent longings of my heart.   To gain their
hearts for the Lord I used all my influence.
I strove with my might to show them the impossibility of their being saved from hell, or
getting to heaven, without prayer; and urged
them to promise me to begin that night. . With
one of them I so far succeeded that the heart of
stone became dissolved by the power of God,
and she consented to be his.   I told Mr. and
Mrs. E. what had taken place, and we turned

the family worship at night into a prayer-meeting I gave them an exhortation; and, blessed be the Lord! his presence was with us. It was a season not to be forgotten. The next morning I left them, commending them to God, and praying that he would seal the truth of what I had delivered in his name, and make it a means of bringing them to repentance. The following Sunday Mr. E. came to me, and said, " You must come over and meet the class to-morrow evening, for all my servants are determined to serve God." There was no flying from me now, no shunning my presence as aforetime; no, blessed be the Lord! it was evident from their countenances a change had taken place within. Without invitation they all four came to class-meeting. The poor back-slider seemed now resolved to return to his offended God; and the other young man wept aloud from distress of soul On the whole there is a great change at present These are fair blossoms; what will be the fruit, time must show. O Lord, may they be thine when thou shalt make up thy jewels! " Then I will praise thee, then I will praise thee, in the glorious realms above."

26th.—Brother Earle sent his niece to request I would again visit his family and meet the class. I went, and much of the Divine presence attended our meeting. We published for a prayer-meeting the following evening. This was a remarkable time: two of friend E.'s servants were brought into the liberty of the children of God. One of them was the poor backslider, over whom I could not but greatly rejoice. [He has since stood his ground well, and is become a class-leader.] In visiting from house to house, I fell in with a young woman; to whom I had not spoken many words, before she was pricked in the heart, and cried for mercy, as one hanging over the pit of hell. Her master (who like too many others had wandered from God and his people) was much affected at her cries and tears, and promised he would return again to the Lord; and I was happy to find in him afterwards some pleasing indications of penitence. One day I met with two brothers, the one a class-leader, the other a backslider. The contrast of their characters greatly struck me. I spoke very closely to the unfaithful brother: I told him of his awful state, and urged him once more to turn from the road to hell. He was deeply impressed, and before I left him he promised again to turn his feet to the testimonies of the Lord. I saw him the next day, and found he had been attempting to fulfil his vow. As his wife was also a poor wanderer, he requested me to talk to her. I went to their house for that purpose, but she fled from me to her sister's. Feeling a longing desire for her salvation, I went thither; but she again got off. Poor thing! I cannot give her up. But O, if she cannot meet man, how can she stand before the Judge, and meet her God!

Sept. 2d.—How sweet is a life of faith. It

seems to me I never saw so fully the worth of
faith as at this time.   I see Gospel salvation
is—

> " Only to believers known,
>   Glorious and unspeakable."

Nothing will stand the fiery test but the righteousness of God by faith.   Without Christ all
is sand,—all are filthy rags   In the past night
I had many sweet moments in meditating on
this delightsome verse,—

> " Thy name, O God, upon my bed,
>   Dwells on my lips and fires my thoughts;
> With trembling awe, in midnight shade,
>   I muse on all thy hands have wrought."

I felt I could easily die, and that to die
would be gain.   It was not ecstacy—not rapture; but a secret stillness, an inward heaven,
—the love of God filling the whole soul
Sweet would it have been to have laid my head
upon my last pillow, and fallen asleep in Jesus.
Some days before this, my faith was severely
tried; and not without a cause   O what a
necessity there is for more self-denial!   Lord,
keep me ever watching!

19th.—Last night my soul was drawn out in
an extraordinary manner while praying to be
filled with all the fulness of God.   The language of my heart was,—

> " Fulfil, fulfil my large desires,
>   Large as infinity;
> Give, give me all my soul requires,
>   All, all that is in thee."

Jesus spake with power, and said, "All that I have is thine." My soul leaped for joy, my eyes flowed with tears, and all within me shouted, "Glory, glory to the Lord!"

> "O for a thousand tongues to sing
> My great Redeemer's praise."

In looking over the Minutes of Conference for 1821, I was pleased and profited not only on account of the many thousands which the Lord has been pleased to add to the church, but also to see the blessed spirit of union and love which subsists among the preachers. They seem determined to adopt every measure which they think will advance the Redeemer's kingdom. I was glad to find, among many others, this resolution: "We again resolve, after the example of our venerable fathers in the Gospel, with all plainness and zeal, to preach a free, present, and full salvation from sin; a salvation flowing from the mere grace of God, through the redemption which is in Christ Jesus, apprehended by the simple exercise of faith, and indispensably preparatory to a course of practical holiness. And in this great work, our only reliance for success is upon the grace of the Holy Spirit; by whose inspiration alone it is, that the Gospel in any instance is rendered the 'power of God unto salvation.'" I am more than ever persuaded that when this doctrine is preached, God will own and bless it; and that signs and wonders will be wrought in the name of Jesus.

26th.—I have just visited Ponsanooth, and am returned with a sorrowful mind, on account of the absence of that life and power of religion which I wish to see amongst them. I am constrained to say, " How is the fine gold become dim !" Lord, once more turn and be gracious, and pour out thy Spirit upon them, for thy name's sake !

OCT.—Having received repeated invitations from my Camborne friends, I resolved to pay them another visit. On my way I called to see Mr. Burgess, at Redruth, and he insisted on my remaining with him a few days. With him and his amiable and excellent family, I spent many happy hours in talking about the things of God. I staid here ten days, and met several of the classes; but was grieved to see so little of the life of religion in that place which had so long been the praise of all Cornwall. I had some profitable seasons with them, especially at their love-feast; when I was enabled very freely to lift up my voice for God, in that house where I had often before joyfully testified of the power of Jesus to save to the uttermost. At Camborne I was received with the utmost love and affection; and here the Lord was again pleased to use me as an instrument for good. After meeting Capt. Lean's class one night, two young men, who were brothers, came in to converse with me. One of them was a poor heavy-laden sinner, seeking Jesus; but he knew not how or where to find him. I began at once by telling him that

Christ had suffered in his stead, and borne his sins in his own body on the tree, and that through his stripes all that believe are healed. After an hour and half's conversation with him, he cried out,—

> "Friend of sinners, spotless Lamb,
> Thy blood was shed for me."

It was an interesting and an affecting sight, to see the heavenly joy that beamed in his countenance, to hear the effusions of his grateful heart, and to behold his brother on his knees blessing and adoring the God of salvation for what he had wrought. They quickly left us, and ran with speed to tell their dear father and mother and sister of the glorious news ; so they all rejoiced together, and gave glory and praise to Emmanuel for what he had done for their dear William. [He is now much esteemed for his fervent piety, and is a useful class-leader.] This was the beginning of good days. Soon the prayer-meetings began to increase, and the Lord poured out the Spirit of grace and supplication upon the people. At one of those meetings one evening I gave out that beautiful and favourite hymn on page 203 :—

> " Thou hidden Source of calm repose,
> Thou all-sufficient Love Divine; "

and then gave a short exhortation upon it. From the striking language of this hymn, I endeavoured to show what Christ is to the believer. While speaking, such views of the adorable Jesus

were given me as I think will never be erased
from my mind in time or eternity. Being invited one Sunday to visit a member of the society
who was very ill, I asked her if she had a satisfactory evidence of her interest in Christ. She
said, " No, nor had I ever a sense of the pardon
of my sins." When I beheld her destitution of
soul, and the evident marks that death was near
at hand, I was filled with much compassion for
her case. I began to encourage her hopes, and
offered her Christ as a ready, able, and willing
Saviour; waiting at that moment to remove her
guilty load. I showed her the atoning sacrifice,
explained to her the plan of salvation by faith,
and told her that God required an act of faith
in her to believe what Christ had done for her.
She felt the Comforter drawing near, and said,
" I never saw it in this light before." In a short
time she was enabled fully to rely on Jesus; and
now her eyes overflowed with tears, and her
heart was filled with peace and joy in believing.
She lived three weeks after this, held her confidence to the last, and finished her course with
joy. A friend invited me to come over, and
meet the classes at Tuckingmill. In speaking
to the people in one of the classes, I found a
poor, heavy-laden penitent. I laboured to encourage her; but, such were her strong cries
and tears that I thought it best to pray with
her. Her mind apparently becoming a little
more composed, I asked her how she felt. She
said, " I see I must go home and pray more."
Aware that this was a snare of satan, I replied,

" There is no necessity for that; the Lord is here and is now waiting to bless you. There is nothing wanting, but for you to believe in Jesus as your Saviour. And if he died for you, ought you not at once to believe in him, and to love him ?" The light of faith soon appeared, and her soul found liberty through the blood of the Lamb Full of the assurance of faith, she cried out, " Now I know my sins are forgiven." I lodged at Mr. S. Burrell's that night ; and, with him, the next day, I called on her, fearing lest satan might have beguiled and robbed her; but to our agreeable surprise, we found her, having laid aside her ordinary work, keeping the day holy. " I have," said she, " set apart this day to praise the Lord, for what he did for my soul yesterday." This I thought was a very pleasing testimony to the reality of the work In meeting the other classes at Tuckingmill, we had refreshing seasons from the presence of the Lord While at Camborne, I strove earnestly to show leaders and people the necessity of being cleansed from all sin, and of pressing into ful salvation ; and I had the happiness of seeing many lay hold on Christ as their perfect Saviour. In meeting Captain Leans's class one night, four plunged a second time into the all-cleansing flood They felt so much of the overwhelming power of grace, that it was some time before they had bodily strength sufficient to walk home. The time of my visit was greatly protracted beyond what I intended ; but my soul was kept as a watered garden, and my confidence in God, and in the power of his glorious Gospel, was, I believe, never stronger.

Nov 24th.—I met the class last right at Mylor Bridge, and strongly pressed believers to seek entire holiness. I was examining myself this morning, and thought I never found myself more dead to sin. O what gratitude of heart did I feel on this account! Praise the Lord, O my soul, and all that is within me bless his holy name!

28th.—I see if I would get good every where, it must be by striving to keep my outward senses under subjection to those which grace has opened in the soul. By faith I realize the presence of my great Prophet; my ear attends to that still small voice which is not heard in the hurry and tumult of our nature; my eyes gaze on the Divine perfections, displayed in the whole economy of nature and grace; and hereby I begin a life that never ends, and obtain enjoyments which shall increase to all eternity. Faith does not merely wait for Divine influence, but actually lays hold of it, as well as on every other purchased and promised blessing; yea, by simple faith, promises and Promiser are made all our own. In this school I often lament my want of proficiency, but, blessed be God! I can truly say I am desirous of learning his way more perfectly, that I may daily make sensible objects subservient to the realities which faith reveals; and giving glory to God, I think I can say I have lately mastered some profitable lessons; and hereby my soul is stirred up to

9

get fresh fire from the holy altar.   But I want
my powers to be put in quicker and stronger
motion towards Him, whose love is a sea,

> " Where all my pleasures roll;
> The circle where my passions move,
> And centre of my soul."

For some of my best thoughts on faith, I am
indebted to the excellent Memoirs and Letters
of Mrs. Rogers.

Dec. 7th.—O I want to live every moment
in dependence on the blood of Christ, and constantly expecting the fulfilment of the Divine
will in all the sanctifying influences of the Holy
Ghost in my soul ; The way into the holiest is
opened; and, blessed be my gracious Lord !
through Him, as my prevailing Advocate, my
soul has access and waits in believing expectation for all that faith beholds !

15th.—Since I wrote last, I have had severe
conflicts with the powers of darkness, but Jesus
has proved my strong tower.   O what a blessed
thing it is to have a refuge to flee to in the time
of distress !   Since the storm, it has been a
blessed calm ; all joy, all peace.   I have had
sweet communion, and a closer walk with God.
I have no footing of my own to stand upon:
this is all sand: But Christ is a rock; and,
glory be to God, I am built upon him, and all
the storms of this life, and floods of temptation
from the enemy, have not washed me off.   I
bless the Lord, I never lived more in the liberty
of the sons of God, nor felt more of the worth

of Christ, than of late. I can truly say, " I count all things but loss for the excellency of the knowledge of Christ Jesus my Lord."

"Had I Gabriel's heavenly tongue
This should ever be my song,
Earthly things are far too tame
To divert me from the Lamb."

16th —This morning my soul has been so let into God, so filled with the Divine presence, that I am lost in wonder, love, and praise. Language fails to express my feelings at this time.

"His sovereign majesty
I shall in glory see,
And to eternity love and adore."

22nd.—This day I set off with the intention of visiting my brother and friends at Mousehole; but on the road I was taken very unwell, and with great difficulty reached Breage, where I stopped at my old and much respected friends, Mr. and Mrs. Limbrey's. I got worse; and, on the night of Christmas-eve, I thought I should have died. I lay panting for life, but all was calmness and confidence within The kindness of the dear friends at whose house I remained can never be forgotten. Mrs. L.'s assiduous attention to my wants calls for my most grateful acknowledgments; I pray the Lord to reward her for her kindness. After a few days, I got a little better, and then returned home.

31st.—Glory be to God, he has again restored me to bodily strength! I feel an increasing confidence in Him, and a fresh determination to set out anew for the heavenly kingdom. O my God, assist me to fulfil my resolutions! Amen.

[In the course of the year which closes with this chapter, my father wrote me several encouraging and quickening letters I was now in the comparatively dry and barren soil of New South Wales The following extracts will serve as a specimen of his mode of address] "You must still go on, my son, sowing in hope; leaving every thing to God; knowing that 'in due time you shall reap if you faint not.' When things do not turn up just as we expected, we are apt to be discouraged; and if we do not at these times look to God, our faith will fail. He says, 'Fear not, I am with thee, be not dismayed, I am thy God; I will strengthen thee.' It is here we must look, or our faith will soon stagger. Abraham, you know, 'staggered not through unbelief, but was strong in faith, giving glory to God.' It was not the strength of the rams' horns, nor the echo of their voices who shouted, which threw down the walls of Jericho, but Joshua's faith in God. 'And the Lord said unto Joshua, See I have given into thine hand Jericho.' Then God told him what he must do; how he must compass the city, and go round about the city once. 'Thus shalt thou do six days; and the seventh day ye shall compass the city seven times.' Joshua, no doubt, went on cheerfully

in his duty; he did not say, 'Lord, will not
once do as well as seven times?' Thus when
God sends his servants to preach the Gospel,
they must take care to preach it in faith, and
persevere in the work. They are to cry aloud,
and spare not; to lift up their voice like a
trumpet, and show the people their sin.' They
must also take care that this be done in love;
not in a warm zeal of their own, or a fire of
their own kindling. This kind of fire will not
consume the stubble; it must be the fire of love,
kindled in the heart by the Holy and Blessed
Spirit of God. My prayer night and day is,
that he would help you to cast the net on the
right side, that thousands and tens of thousands
of precious souls may be gathered into the fold
of Jesus, and be eternally saved. A good man
observes, ' In order that you may see this, you
must pray hard, believe hard, and wrestle hard,
and never be discouraged.'

"Though you do not for a while make that
havoc in the devil's kingdom which you could
wish, you must keep up your courage, and continue to fire at it. See that you level all your
artillery well, and load your guns with the
heaviest shot, aiming at its very foundation. O
for more of that faith which did such wonders
of old! We want Abraham's faith, Job's
patience, Moses' meekness, John's love, Paul's
zeal; and, I am sure, we want the wisdom of
Solomon, for we have all kinds of people to
deal with. I was pleased with the remark,
that you see more clearly than ever that you

can do nothing except God be with you. Now for God to be always with us, we must be always with him. Enoch walked with God three hundred years, and had this testimony, that he pleased God: Now this walking with God is a secret reliance or dependence upon him for all we want. 'Without me,' says Christ, 'ye can do nothing;' but faith gives us to see that every thing we want is in Christ, by whom we have access by faith into this grace wherein we stand.

> ' A fountain of life and of grace,
> In Christ our Redeemer we see.' "

CHAPTER IV.

JANUARY 15th, 1822 —

> "What now is my object and aim;
> What now is my hope and desire?"

I bless God, I can say, It is to follow the Lamb whithersoever he goeth, and to aspire after the perfection of his image upon my heart. From the ground of my heart I can say, Christ was never so near, so dear, so sweet, so precious to my soul as he has been of late, and is to the present moment. My soul is in its element when I am thinking and talking about Jesus. I can say, indeed, with one of my dear friends, from whom I have just received a letter, " I am at the bottom of all, but I do feel increasing de-light in serving my Father and my God."

> "Call'd the full power of faith to prove,
> Let all my hallow'd heart be love.
> And all my spotless life be praise."

18th —Last night, while meditating upon Christ's death and passion, and his intercession at God's right hand, I had a more affecting sight of Christ crucified than I ever before had in my life. All his wounds and bruises appear-ed to my soul in such a manner as affected every nerve in my body. I thought on that verse of Mr. Wesley,

> "Five bleeding wounds he bears," &c.;

and never saw so much in it before; while a voice seems to say, "I suffered this for thee."

21st —I have found this day, what I have not unfrequently found before, that the violent storm is often near the calm. It seemed this morning as if all the powers of darkness were let loose, and determined to devour me. I kept continually calling upon God, and looking up to him, and casting my soul upon his precious atonement; being determined to hold fast my confidence, and not give way to unbelief. I found I had nothing of my own to fly to, or de-pend upon : Nothing but faith. No promise appeared all this time; nor had I any sensible enjoyment : Nothing but a sight of my weak-ness, imperfections, short-comings, and failings.

Not that I felt condemnation for any particular act. This was a conflict of a peculiar kind; for thousands of times before, when I have been violently attacked by the enemy, I have looked up to Jesus, and found him to be a strong tower. Now, naked faith was my only defence; the only weapon with which I could maintain the fight. I looked round for help, and at last I thought on our Lord being led up of the Spirit into the wilderness, to be tempted of the devil. On this the adversary began to yield: and, in a moment, Jesus appeared to my believing eyes, and spoke to me in his well-known voice: " To him that overcometh, will I grant to sit with me on my throne, even as I overcame, and am set down with my Father on his throne." In an instant my enemies were all gone, and O, how did the transcendent glories of my precious Redeemer beam forth upon my soul! and his name was sweeter than honey or the honey-comb! This conflict for the trial of my faith was but of short continuance, but quite long enough; for it was smart work on both sides while it continued. Could satan have wrested my shield from me, he would have made an easy conquest. This I was well aware of; and therefore took the more care to hold it fast, and exercise it with all the strength I had: look-ing eagerly and constantly to my Advocate. O what a necessity there is to keep close to Jesus, and to be ever on my guard, watching unto prayer !

25th.—I was never more affected in hearing

the Gospel than I have been of late; Every sermon I hear seems better than the former. I feel an increasing love to the ministers of God, and am ready to say, " How beautiful upon the mountains are the feet of him that bringeth good tidings," &c. O, I long more and more for the salvation of souls, and willingly would spend and be spent in helping the children of God on their way to glory. I think I never did feel my heart so much delighted in the work of meeting classes, as of late. My soul rejoiced last night to see a poor backslider return to the class, for whose restoration I prayed much, and with whom I had often conversed on the subject of her return to Jesus. The Lord softened her heart while she was making a humble confession of her revolting from Him, and expressing her determination to arise and once more seek his face.

FEB. 2nd.—The more I converse with sin ners, the more I discover the darkness of their fallen state. Yesterday I was talking to a man fifty years of age, and found he could not give me an answer to that simple question, " What did Jesus Christ come into the world for?" He was confessedly speechless, though living at a very small distance from a place where the Gospel is preached. O what a necessity there is to preach from house to house!

6th.—In the course of the week past, I have met six different classes, with much pleasure and profit; for, " where the Spirit of the Lord is, there is liberty." But I mourn to think there

are so very few who enjoy the full liberty of the
Gospel. Vast numbers of professors look at
purity of heart as a thing so high as to be quite
beyond their reach; and hence are indifferent
about it. Some of them think, if they get it they
shall never hold it fast. Unbelief has so far
crushed the energies of their souls, that they do
not "hunger and thirst after righteousness;"
and the necessity of the thing they seldom attempt to urge upon themselves by reflecting on
such a portion of God's word as this : " Without
holiness, no man shall see the Lord." In meeting classes, and in private conversation, during
the fifty years of my pilgrimage, and more particularly within the last eight years, I have
gained considerable knowledge of professors,
and must express my grief that the number of
the half-hearted is so large. Alas ! what multitudes are at ease in Zion, settled upon their
lees, neither hot nor cold ! But, blessed be God,
the prospect is brightening; for the number of
burning and shining lights, among preachers
and people, is on the increase. Lord, multiply
the happy number more and more abundantly!
Amen. Were "the mystery of faith" better
known, the improvement among God's professing people would be much more rapid   Many
are not defective in their sincerity, but in their
faith. It is simple because of unbelief that they
do not enter into that glorious rest which is before them, and nigh unto them. They do not
see it is their privilege to venture now on Christ
for the blessing they want, whether justification,

or sanctification, without hesitation or delay, because he hath said, " All things are now ready !
now is the accepted time, now is the day of salvation ; by grace are ye saved through faith."
An impenitent sinner, one who lives in the wilful
breach of a known law, has no object of faith
but the threatenings, which declare that he shall
have his "portion in the lake which burneth with
fire and brimstone;" but every true penitent has
Christ set before him, and is invited and urged,
and commanded to lay hold of him for pardon,
holiness, and heaven. O that the blessed
Spirit would help the infirmities of the children
of the kingdom, and give them to see their
privileges, and the way to possess them !

28th —I attended a Missionary-Meeting at
Penryn last evening, and felt more than I can
express for the poor souls that are still in heathen
darkness. But I thank God for the prospect,
that the glorious Gospel will soon be sent among
a greater number of them. On this subject
there is a blessed spirit of unity among preachers
and people. My heart says,—

" O Jesus, ride on, till all are subdued,
    Thy mercy make known, and sprinkle thy blood ;
    Display thy salvation, and teach the new song,
    To every nation, and people, and tongue."

Lord, what an easy matter it is for thee to
say to the north, " Give up;" and to the south,
" Keep not back;" to bring thy sons from far,
and thy daughters from the ends of the earth !
If thou speak the word only, Lord, a nation

shall be born in a day. Thou hast said, " The earth shall be full of the knowledge of the Lord, as the waters cover the sea." Then "the wolf shall dwell with the lamb, and the leopard shall lie down with the kid ; and the calf, and the young lion, and the fatling together, and a little child shall lead them. And the cow and the bear shall feed ; their young ones shall lie down together." O my Father, my God, what a happy world would this be ! How desirable to see it ! Thou hast said it shall come. O hasten it, for Christ's sake ! Amen and Amen.

MARCH 6.—In meeting the class last night at Garrick, my soul felt much of the inward heaven. O what a blessed light shined into my mind, while I was giving out this beautiful verse of the 393rd hymn :—

" Open my faith's interior eye,
    Display thy glory from above,
And all I am shall sink and die,
    Lost in astonishment and love."

APRIL 25th.—I paid my Camborne friends another visit, and lodged at friend Bennett's, Camborne Vean. It being his appointment to preach at Kehelland on the Sunday, he pressed me hard to go with him. I feared the walk was to long for me to undertake, but went with him, and found freedom in speaking to the people. On our way from the chapel we over-took two young women, and overheard one of them talking to the other on the subject of believing in Jesus Christ. I stepped forward, and asked her if she knew any thing of that important subject. She said she did once. I earnestly entreated her again to give her heart to God, and unite with his people once more. The following week they both came to Captain Lean's class; and, after a hard struggle in prayer for about two hours, the Lord set them both at liberty. The next Sunday several of the Camborne friends made an appointment to go to Kehelland, to hold a prayer-meeting. The news of our coming excited some curiosity among the people, so that the house was crowded within and without. The power of God descended, and many sinners were pricked in the heart; This was a drop before the shower. The Lord began a gracious work among them, and some of the most wicked and notorious sinners in the neighbourhood were awakened. Trejuthan, a spot which had remained barren and unfruitful for a number of years, now became as the garden of the Lord For some days the cloud of mercy hung over it; and so plentifully poured its precious contents on the dry ground, that the deep concern for the salvation of their souls seemed to draw off the people's attention from every other object. I went into a house one day, which I had not before entered, to inquire after a servant girl in whose spiritual welfare I felt some concern. Her mistress, I found, was unawakened. I warned her of her danger, entreated her to give her heart to God, and, before she slept that night, to commence a life of prayer. I commended them to God in prayer, and called again in a few days. I now found Mrs. E. a penitent, and used my earnest endeavours to lead her to Jesus for pardon and salvation. After awhile we united in prayer; the Lord quickly answered for himself, and filled her heart with triumphant joy. It was a pleasing sight to behold the change in this family. Here were the husband and wife, and their servant, just brought out of darkness and sin, now all rejoicing in the Lord together. I took tea one evening at brother Smith's; just before we were going to unite in prayer, one entered the room who was a stranger to me; I had no sooner opened my mouth in prayer, than he was deeply awakened, and roared from the disquietude of his soul. I think I never saw a man in my life whose anguish of spirit was greater. He was a backslider; and saw and felt his faith and ingratitude. After a severe struggle he obtained mercy, and joyfully testified that God had pardoned all his sins. Returning one night from Troon, I saw one coming behind me, and felt my mind impressed to speak to her about her soul. I staid till she came up with me, and had not spoken many words to her before she burst into tears and loud cries. Her bodily strength was so affected by the distress of her mind, it was with much difficulty we could get her to Captain Lean's. Several friends prayed with her; but she continued to groan under the weight of her guilty load. The cries and wailings of her broken heart were deeply affecting. At length the

Comforter appeared, and she cried out, "The Lord hath shaken body and soul over hell, but, blessed be his name, he hath not let me fall in!" Some time after I met her in class, and she bore a lively testimony that the Lord had pardoned and adopted her into his family. Brother W. J. requested me to visit his father-in-law. He soon began to weep and exclaim against himself as a vile sinner. It appeared, that when he was a youth of seventeen he knew something of religion, but had now long lived without God in the world. He was sensible of his state and scarcely dared to look up for pardon. I was affected to see a man sixty-three years of age in such a distressed state of mind. The tears which streamed over his aged cheeks told the contrition of his heart. I encouraged him to expect mercy from the God against whom he had sinned. I told him there was no need to despair, because Jesus Christ was an Advocate for such sinners as he was. "And now," said I, "if Jesus Christ has groaned and died to redeem you, and risen again for your justification; and is ever at the right hand of God making intercession for you; do you not think you ought to love him?" He at once saw his obligation to the blessed Saviour, and cried out, "O yes, I do, I do love Him!" At that moment the Lord revealed his pardoning mercy to his soul, and he rejoiced with joy unspeakable and full of glory; and with full hearts we knelt down to give the praise to whom it is due. I might relate many other instances of a similar nature. I believe the

Lord never condescended to own my feeble en
deavours more than he has in my visit to Camborne this time.   Great good was done in the
class-meetings, especially in Captain L.'s, in
which it was not uncommon for two or three to
find peace in an evening.   Into this class the
people so crowded for some weeks, that it could
not be regularly met at all.   As many probably
as five hundred have been at one prayer-meeting.
I continued with them four weeks ; I was then
obliged to leave them, because the exertion was
too great for my bodily strength.   Never did I
wonder more at the universal love and affection
of the people toward me.   To Jesus alone be
all the praise !

JULY 26th.—O my Saviour, what shall I do
to love and praise thee more !   I grieve that
my faith is not more active, and that my love
and gratitude do not more abound.   I wonder
at the goodness of God toward me, and sink
with shame before him.   How is it, that the
soul being of such a value,—God so great and
good,—and eternity so near at hand, I am so
little moved?   Lord, stir me up to be more in
earnest about things above !

AUG. 7th.—I feel determined more than ever
that God shall have my whole heart.   I want
to be practically conformed to the good, and acceptable, and perfect will of God, and to feel
the well of living water continually springing
up within my soul.   " I see faith and hope
must replenish and support my joys: without
their aid, my joy must quickly droop and die.

But by the aid of these important graces, the soul is ever filled with heavenly fragrance; and a fire is brought from above which devours all the stubble of inbred sin; and every plant, root and branch, which my Father has not planted. Hereby my soul shall be purified, in all its powers and faculties, even as gold is purified in the furnace. Many waters cannot quench it; many floods of temptations and trials only serve to make it burn still brighter and brighter. O how precious is this love! It is the bond of union with my heavenly Bridegroom, the pledge of my immortal crown, the foretaste of my glorious heaven above, the source of bliss through the ages of eternity. I have found, in all my experience, that in every temptation the victory much depends on resisting the first on-set. To reason for a moment is dangerous. Is the object, or gratification, forbidden? That is enough, if we truly love the Lord our God. But when we deliberate, we throw ourselves into the arms of satan. Neither ought conse-quences to be considered: God will see to these; better suffer any thing than his frown." O may I ever walk by this rule, and live to please my God alone!

8th—O what am I? abject nothingness. Yet Jehovah is mindful of me; and after pluck-ing me as a brand from the burning: after cleansing my unholy soul by the power of his Spirit, accepting the conquered rebel; yea, adopting into his family and favour the poor fugitive, he doth now reward my poor services

10

with his approving smile and continual presence; teaching me in ignorance, strengthening me in weakness, supporting me in trials, blessing my feeble endeavours and labours, fighting for me against every enemy, and making all things work together for my good. O my soul, what mercies! what boundless love!

10th —I see more and more clearly that faith is the root from which all the branches of holiness grow. Christ is the vine, and we are the branches, grafted into him by faith before we can bring forth fruit. As a branch cannot bear fruit of itself, so we cannot bring the fruit of " love, joy, peace, longsuffering, gentleness, goodness," &c., till by faith, we are united to Christ. We are not to rank faith among the other graces, but to account it the foundation of them all. Works do not go before faith, but we must believe to work aright. Faith is the gift of God in a sense highly superior to that in which our natural powers may be called his gifts. God imparts the power or grace, but he requires us to use it. He commands us to believe. My mind was never before so deeply affected with the reasonableness and importance of these views of faith. And O what a damnation does not the sinner deserve who refuses to accept

" Pardon and holiness, and heaven."
on terms so easy.
" Only believe and yours is heaven."

13th.—I awoke this morning very early, and

found my mind solemnly engaged with God. Not a cloud appeared, and my soul longed to take her flight to be for ever with the Lord. My mind has recently been pained to meet with so many who have long been professors of religion, and still know nothing of their interest in Christ. Of justification by faith, and the witness of the Spirit, they seem just as ignorant as if they had never heard a Gospel sermon in their lives.

16th —It has been matter of great joy to my soul to hear of the general revival in the Methodist Connexion during the past year; and that not less than twelve thousand members have been added to the church. O Lord do thou grant that these souls may find their way to heaven!

" Break forth into singing, ye trees of the wood,
For Jesus is bringing lost sinners to God!"

18th —This day I unexpectedly met with a Christian friend from a neighbouring society. I felt our conversation on the things of God was particularly profitable. It turned on the necessity of our retaining a clear witness of perfect love; not only on account of our own happiness, but of our usefulness also. My mind has latterly been greatly pained to see the little effect the Gospel has on the minds of the people; how few there are who seemed to hear for eternity! Lord, save them from becoming Gospel-hardened!

21st.—I have just been thinking upon my

dear son, who is now in New South Wales. To
what an amazing distance has the kind hand of
providence removed us from each other! But
a moment's reflection tells me it matters little
whether we spend our few days on earth in each
other's company, or at the distance we now are.
The evil to be dreaded is a separation that shall
never end; and this is the separation which, it is to
be feared, must take place between the branches
of many families. How awful the thought, that
husbands and wives, parents and children, should
be parted for ever! I bless the Lord, it is trans-
porting to me to look forward to that day, when
I shall meet my dear wife and all my dear
children in heaven, to be separated from them no
more to the countless ages of a blessed eternity.

23rd —I have been meditating on God's
tender mercies towards me, as manifested in
Christ Jesus; and really feel astonished that I
should spend so small a portion of my time in
praising him for such amazing benefits. O how
am I not more thankful! Lord, save me from
the sin of ingratitude!

28th —In the many waking moments of the
past night, my soul has had sweet fellowship
with the Father and with the Son Christ Jesus.
Glory be to God, I frequently find many precious promises applied to my mind when I am
lying on my bed! But this morning it was suggested to my mind,—Suppose these promises
should not come from the Spirit of God?
For a moment I felt a shrinking back, through
the temptation, to unbelief; but suddenly these

words were applied to my mind: "Reach hither thy finger, and behold my hands; and reach hither thy hand, and thrust it into my side;" and "be not faithless, but believing." In a moment the temptation was gone, and I was constrained to cry out, with Thomas, "My Lord and my God." It was a blessed season, and the witness of perfect love was again renewed to my soul. This blessed witness of the Spirit, both in justification and sanctification, is what I see the necessity of more then ever. For my own part I do not see what progress professors of religion can make without this. Did I say religion? Can they be deemed the possessors of true religion at all till they so believe as to have witness in themselves? Till they have this Gospel faith they can only be denominated "seekers of salvation" It is extremely painful for me to reflect on the multitudes who are stopping short of their inestimable privilege. But, blessed be God, I do hope the happy number of those who enjoy it is on the increase. Thou knowest, O Lord, how I long to see it. O send forth thy Spirit among the people, for thy name's sake! Amen.

29th.—This is a morning without a cloud; all is calm, and joy, and peace; nothing of rapture, but solid unutterable bliss! I cannot express what I feel; it is "joy unspeakable and full of glory;" a sinking into nothing at the feet of Christ; a feeling that he is "all in all."

"My soul on his fullness delighted I cast."

30th.—This day I went over to see my much-respected friends at Treworlas.   On my way I called to see the old blind man, to whom the Lord graciously revealed his pardoning love three years ago, while I was conversing with him.   He was then in the eighty-third year of his age.   I now found him sitting outside the door, and no sooner did he hear the sound of my voice than he knew me, though I had not spoken to him for about two years.   He still retains his confidence in his atoning Saviour; and our interview was crowned by the refreshing presence of the Lord.   I spent five days with Mr. W. and his excellent daughter, who still bears every mark of the plain, humble Christian, though living in the prospect of speedily possessing so much wealth.   What a mercy is this, having so large a share of the world, and not borne down by the torrent!   O Lord, do thou keep her henceforth and for evermore!   I found it delightfully profitable to converse with several of my old friends in that neigbourhood.   One day I fell in with a poor backslider, and earnestly entreated him to return again to the Lord.   He accordingly came to the class-meeting while I was there: and I have since reason to hope that he has returned to the Shepherd and Bishop of his soul.   Before I went, it was my earnest petition that God would give me one soul; Glory be to his name, I trust he has granted my heart's desire.

SEPT. 18th.—This day, while conversing with a poor dark sinner, about righteousness, temperance, and a judgment to come, she wept bitterly.   O Lord, seal the truth of the Gospel upon her heart; and may these impressions not be as the early cloud and morning dew!

19th.—This day, returning from Ponsanooth, I fell in with a Christian friend, and we talked freely together of the deep things of God.   She longed to be saved from all the carnal mind, but had not clear views of the nature and method of full salvation   If saved from all sin, she thought it must be impossible to feel such and such temptations.   On this account her mind was often perplexed, and she knew not how to proceed to the Canaan of God's perfect love: But it pleased the Lord, while I was conversing with her on this matter, to shine into her heart by his blessed Spirit, and enable her to go on her way rejoicing.   Just as I parted from her, I met with a man who had been overtaken in a fault, and had for some short time withdrawn from the people of God.   Of his unfaithfulness I had no suspicion till I saw he sought to shun me.   I talked to him faithfully and affectionately; he acknowledged his error, and promised to return again unto the Lord.   He has since walked steadily in the path of duty.

22nd.—The Lord keeps my soul like a watered garden, as a spring shut up to all but himself.   How sweet the moments which I have enjoyed with my God this night!   His love has been in my soul as a well of living water.

" My hope is full (O glorious hope!)
    Of immortality."

While pleading for the salvation of a poor sinner, with whom I conversed some days ago, and whose heart then appeared somewhat contrite, the answer was, " Thy prayer is heard, it shall be so." Language fails to describe what I felt.

30th.—I rode to Cury, to see Mr. W. Hendy. With this man of God, and his pious family, I was much delighted ; himself, his dear wife and three servants, all happy in God; apparently of one heart and one mind. Joining in prayer, at a friend's house, before we parted, the power of God came down in an extraordinary manner ; one young man received the blessing of a clean heart, and a young female was awakened, and wept bitterly on account of her sins. We found it difficult to part.

> " And if our fellowship below
>   In Jesus be so sweet,
> What heights of rapture shall we know
> When round his throne we meet ?"

Oct. 17th.—While I lay awake last night, my mind was suddenly impressed, as if a voice had spoken to me, that it was my privilege to converse with God. I cried out, " What, such a worm,—an unworthy worm as I am,—converse with God!" The thought caused my heart to leap for joy ; while new scenes of glory shone around me. It appeared as if I was on the suburbs of heaven. In this happy frame of mind I fell asleep, and dreamed I was in a boat, on the water ; while hoisting the sail, a gust of

wind took it, and the man at the helm cried
out, "We shall all be drowned" As the scene
appeared as vivid as if it had been real, I expected every moment to be swallowed up in the
watery deep But I felt no fear, my mind was
sweetly tranquil, expecting instant heaven.
Just then I awoke, and my heart was deeply
affected with gratitude towards God, because he
had kept me from fear in the immediate prospect of death. This vision of the night has done
my soul much good

19th.—I see it is faith that must bring me to
the very entrance into glory. Where the one
ends the other begins. It is observed of the
most renowned ancient believers, "These all
died in the faith;" their faith did not die before them Faith must bring their dying comforts; and, O how full, and how near a treasure
has it to go to! To die to this world is to be
born into another. Faith is an act of reason,
and believing is a kind of knowing; even a
knowing by the testimony of Him whom we
believe. It will, therefore, not a little strengthen
our faith, if we contemplate the perfections of
God, and the nature of our souls. If faith be
not much exercised in its victorious acts, we
shall neither know its strength, nor find it strong
when we want to use it. The life of sense is
the enemy faith has to conquer. These are
lessons of great importance; and happy are
those who, by experience, are best acquainted
with them.

21st —I see a greater necessity than ever of

living near to God, and of keeping the heart
with all diligence continually, in order to redeem
the time; without this there can be little or no
progress in the Divine life. Without watching
unto prayer, O how soon would this heavenly
fire abate in my soul! What a necessity do I
see for leaders and people to struggle hard to
keep the life of God in their souls! O what a
danger there is of becoming withered branches!
Lord, save thy people from a dead, or dry,
formal way of worship; pour out thy Spirit,
and let there be a shaking among the dry
bones!

27th.—This morning I have felt an increased
vigour of spirit, and a fresh resolution to devote
myself more fully unto the Lord, and to urge
on others the great necessity of their receiving
and retaining the witness of the Spirit. What
I mean by the witness of the Spirit, Mr. Wesley very clearly explains in his excellent sermon on this subject. "The testimony of the
Spirit," says he, "is an inward impression on
the soul, whereby the Spirit of God directly
witnesses to my spirit that I am a child of God;
that Jesus Christ hath loved me, and given himself for me; that all my sins are blotted out;
and that I, even I, am a child of God. But let
none ever presume to rest in any supposed testimony of the Spirit, which is separate from the
fruits of it."

Nov. 1st.—I now feel the infirmities of age
fast growing upon me; My memory fails me
greatly, especially in writing: I have restless

nights, and often a violent pain and much heat
in my feet; but, while I lie awake, I bless God
I do not suffer from the lashes of a guilty conscience. No, glory be to God, I can say,—

"Jesus, my all in all thou art,
    My rest in toil, my ease in pain;
The med'cine of my broken heart,
    In war my peace, in loss my gain:
My smile beneath the tyrant's frown,
In shame my glory and my crown."

13th.—I bless the Lord he is still deepening
and widening his good work in my soul. In
all my pilgrimage I never saw so much included in the word "believing" as I do now. I
clearly perceive that were I for a moment to
cease believing, I should at once be swallowed
up by the enemy of my soul. Were I to suffer
unbelief to slip in, to true peace of mind I must
say, "Farewell." But, I bless God, whenever
the adversary attacks me, I do feel a power to
look to Jesus; and I find his name a strong
tower and a city of refuge. I find no way to
conquer but through faith in his blood.

15th.—A few days ago, I felt such a longing
desire to save souls, that I said in my heart, to
the Lord, that if he would condescend to use me
as an instrument in his hand, to bring one soul
more to himself, I would for ever praise him for
it. When at Ponsanooth, I was informed of a
young woman who was so ill of a consumption,
that her medical attendant had given her up.
The moment I heard of her case, I felt an ardent

desire to see her. As she was known to have a strong dislike to religion and religious people, the friends told me it would be useless: But what they said no ways discouraged me; I resolved I would try to gain access to her, and, if I could, have some conversation with her about her soul. I accordingly went to the house, and informed her mother what was my business Her mother said, she was not yet come down stairs, but she would tell her of it. The answer was, that she did not wish to see me. This did not dishearten me, nor quench my desire for her salvation; but it instantly struck me, that if I would see her at all I must come upon her unawares Two hours afterwards I again called at the house, and found her sitting by the fire, exceedingly pale and deathly in her appearance. I was well assured in my mind, that if I would have access to her heart, I must attempt it in the gentlest manner, by the tenderest love and affection, and by indirect approaches; so I asked her several questions concerning her complaint, and found it such as was likely soon to bring her to the grave. I then asked her if she believed there was a God; she answered, " Yes," in a rather high and forbidding tone of voice. " And do you believe," said I, " that he knows the secret thoughts of your heart?" " Yes." " But do you think you have ever sinned against this God?" " O yes," said she My heart rejoiced to hear from her such admissions as these. " And now," said I, " are you willing to die in

your present state of mind?" She candidly
confessed she was not. I then told her Jesus
Christ came into the world to save sinners, that
he had died to purchase salvation for her; but
that he had said in his word, except we repent
of our sins we should eternally perish; and that,
after she had repented, in order to be saved,
she must believe that Jesus bore the punishment due to her sins " in his own body on the
tree." Her heart now began to soften; and
she burst into tears, while I endeavoured more
at large to show her from the Scriptures, and
from our expressive Hymns, the willingness
there was in Christ to save her. At my leaving, I proposed prayer, to which, she readily
assented. The next day I visited her again;
and no sooner did I enter the room where she
was, than I perceived her to be a very different
creature from what she was when I approached her the preceeding day. She now opened
her mind, and freely entered into the important subject; and while I conversed and prayed
with her, the Lord wrought powerfully upon
her heart, and she wept much. Four days
after this, it pleased God to set her captive soul
at liberty, by the manifestation of his pardoning
love; and soon after she died happy in the
Lord.

16th.—To-day I had a conversation with one
of the members of our society, on the subject of
the witness of the Spirit. Like too many others,
he was resting short of this privilege. Finding
he had not read Mr. Wesley's sermons on this

subject, I earnestly requested him to procure and read them as soon as possible. What a thousand pities it is, that the excellent sermons of Mr. Wesley are so little known or read among too many of the Methodists !

18th —Last night in the midst of much pain and affliction of body, the Lord wonderfully supported me by his presence. O how sweet was that union which I had with the Father, Son, and Spirit, and how harmoniously do they unite together in the great scheme of my redemption ! I bless God, all my desires are satisfied in Him ! He is my reconciled God in Christ Jesus; I feel his presence with me in sickness and in health, at home and abroad, in reading and in writing. O may my every breath be praise !

Dec. 24th.—This day I left home on a visit to Mr W. Hendy. With him and his happy family, I staid several days On the Sunday, Mr. W. Thomas came to Cury to preach ; and very earnestly pressed me to go to Mullion. I was reluctant, on account of the distance, and thought to plead myself off; but he would take no denial. Accordingly, the next day he came himself for me Religion had been rather at a low ebb in Mullion for some years ; and there seemed, at this time particularly, a dark cloud of unbelief to pervade the minds of God's people. I felt as if I was brought into an atmosphere in which my soul could not live. Oppressed with grief, on account of the state of things around me, I began to cry mightily unto the

Lord for help.   The third night, while in bed,
it pleased God to reveal himself to me in a
wonderful manner.   From this gracious visitation, my faith and hope revived; a Divine
power descended into my soul, and I felt like
one made all anew.   I knew the change was
of God, because of the power which was now
given me to speak to the people about their
souls   At Mr. T.'s I unexpectedly met with
one of Breage, in whose salvation I had taken
much interest; but, hitherto, she had stoutly resisted the striving of the Spirit of God.   I now
earnestly interceded with the Lord on her behalf, and conversed much with her, in the most
affectionate and faithful manner, on the necessity to meet her God.   I urged her to begin to
pray, and at once to give the Lord her heart.
It pleased God to bless my efforts, and seal
truth upon her conscience.   When I saw this,
I invited her to the class-meeting.   The second
time she came, while I was meeting the class
in Mullion chapel, the Lord graciously manifested to her soul a sense of his pardoning love.
The change wrought in her was so manifest,
that two young men in the family of Mr. T.
were thereby powerfully awakened to a sight
and sense of their lost estate as sinners, and
were both soon converted to God.   This quickly spread abroad, the fire began to kindle, and
there was a blessed stirring up among professors, many of whom were enabled to believe
unto full salvation.   Mr. F. insisted on my
coming to spend a Sunday with him at Newton.

Before I went, I earnestly besought God to make my visit to the family a blessing to the souls that composed the household. The eldest daughter was a sensible young woman, about nineteen years of age. As soon as I saw her, my soul was drawn out with ardent desire for her salvation; and compassionate love constrained me to invite her to come to Jesus, and give herself up to the service of Him who had redeemed her. At first, she stood aloof from every overture, and seemed to make light of it; but one evening I pressed her to go with me to the chapel to a prayer-meeting; that night, the Lord touched her heart; and she was soon brought to enjoy a very clear sense of God's pardoning mercy. I conversed much with her, and rejoiced to find her mind so well informed; her views of the plan of salvation so correct; and her heart so fully set on things above. The Lord grant that she may be faithful unto death. I went with a friend to the Lizard, and felt much of the Divine presence while I was speaking to the people. Many hearts seemed deeply affected: may the good seed take root! From this place I went to Ruan, where the Lord began a good work among the people. I gave an exhortation on the nature, fruits, and necessity of faith; and published for a meeting the following evening; when I urged on all who were living in sin, to prepare for a dying hour and a judgment-day. Many present were deeply wrought on; I told them we should have a class-meeting the next night, and should

be glad to see as many present as were willing
to forsake their sins, and flee from the wrath to
come   In compliance with the invitation, eight
new members came, and seemed greatly in
earnest to save their souls.   I lodged at Mr.
and Mrs. R.'s at Cadgewith, where I was most
kindly entertained.   In conversation with Mrs.
R., I was grieved to find her mind so much
weighed down by the sad effects of unbelief.
I told her it was her privilege to be freed from
all the deadly evils of unbelief and its fruits;
that God had commanded her to reckon herself
dead indeed unto sin ; and that it was her privilege at that moment thus to reckon with God,
because Christ had paid all her debt, having
purchased for her both pardon and holiness;
and therefore it was at once her duty and her
privilege to believe and enter it !   God enabled
her to take the advice; she did believe; and,
having plunged into the fountain which is
opened for uncleanness, she rose every whit
whole.   Jesus granted her all her desire, and in
the fulness of her grateful heart she cried out :—

" I'll praise Him for all that is past,
    And I'll trust Him for all that 's to come."

Nor was it a transient feeling, for I found by
subsequent intercourse, that she was built on the
Rock of Ages.   I cannot close this account of
my visit to Mullion and its neighbourhood, without mentioning the wonderful change that was
produced in my dear brother, J. T. : I often
lodged at his house, and took frequent opportu-

11

nities of conversing with him on the subject of perfect love. Though a man of piety, and steady deportment, yet his mind was often so weighed down and dejected through unbelief, that he was not unfrequently shut up in Doubting Castle. I laboured hard to point out to him the way of simple faith in the Son of God; and soon he was enabled to lay hold on the great salvation. From the moment he was brought to enjoy full liberty, be became like a flame of fire. Instant in season and out of season, abroad and at home, he was preaching Christ; and the Lord used him as the happy instrument of much good, especially in deepening the good work in the minds of God's children Many of his friends thought, a more manifest change was seldom wrought in any man.

In consequence of a promise to return at an appointed time to Mr. Hendy's, I left Mullion sooner than I otherwise should have done. When I was last at Cury, a respectable young female was deeply convinced of sin. Her mind continuing in a state of bondage through unbelief, she imbibed a notion, that if she had another interview with me, her soul would be set at liberty; and through the expected medium, it pleased the Lord to reveal himself unto her in his pardoning mercy. Like many others who have the means of gratifying the taste of the carnal mind, she had previously indulged in the vanity of dress and fashion; but now, God having clothed her with humility, she made a striking sacrifice of all conformity to the world. And, what is more remarkable, she had the courage to tell the young man to whom she had given her company, that he must not calculate on enjoying her company any more unless he became decidedly religious in his character. This firm and exemplary conduct on her part had the desired effect on him. It may seem hard for some to credit this; but I was an eye-witness, and can vouch for the truth of it. Some others got good while I was there: May the Lord make them steadfast and unmovable! The great kindness of Mr and Mrs H., and the rest of the dear friends, under whose roof I have been entertained and lodged, can never be erased from my mind. I believe I may say in truth, that, since the first day I knew the Lord, I never spent eight weeks more happily or usefully. But, O my God, my soul knoweth right well, that all the good that is done upon earth, thou thyself doest it; and cheerfully do I ascribe to thee all the praise: Yes, my Lord and Saviour, thou shalt have the glory in time, and to all eternity.

March 14, 1823.—Since I last wrote in my journal, O how greatly has my mind been weighed down, to see the indifference, coldness, and deadness of the people at Mylor Bridge! I can scarcely see one young person in the place who has a serious concern for his soul. O that God would speedily put a stop to this torrent of ungodliness!

25th.—Yesterday the Lord visited my soul in an extraordinary manner: I was constrained to shout aloud for joy and gratitude, to think that

He should make such a worm as I am the instrument of bringing sinners to repentance. By
a letter from Miss F , of Mullion, I have just
received a pleasing account of the happy effects
of the revival in her father's family, and among
her neighbours. " Wherever I go," she says,
" I find religion is the chief topic of conversation.   My two brothers, a sister, and two servants, have all joined the society, and are the
subjects of a gracious change." I have received
another excellent letter from one of the young
converts.   When she was made happy in God,
I advised her to seek out her former companions,
and do what she could to bring them to partake
of " like precious faith." It appears she has
followed up the advice with much zeal and
perseverance; and with some she has been
happily successful.

[Under the above date, my father writes to a
local preacher, to whom he had been useful:
The following is an extract from the letter :—]

"MY DEAR BROTHER,

" I HOPE you feel the same pleasure in
preaching a full salvation as when I saw you.
And while you offer the blessing to others, do
not fail to live in the daily, hourly, and momentary possession of it yourself; else you will
lose the sweetness and Divine satisfaction you
once enjoyed in this blessed work   You know
we have need to take care of being discouraged
in our own minds when we meet with difficulties, and do not succeed in that way and manner

we wish and expect. We must not reason
about it for a moment, but believe and go forward, leaving every thing quietly in the hands
of God; still acting with a single eye to his
glory, in all we think, or speak, or do. While
we thus live, we shall continue under the Divine influence, and be enabled to rejoice in the
kingdom fixed within. Are we "soldiers
fighting for our God?" let us take care that
our spirits never flag, but that we keep our faith
and courage up. I would say to you, my brother, as Paul said to Timothy, ' Fight the good
fight of faith, whereunto thou art called, and
hast made a good profession before many witnesses.' And remember, if we wish to be more
useful to our fellow-mortals, we must still strive
to be more holy; to get more of the image of
God stamped upon our souls. O for more of
that faith which casts out sin, purifies the heart,
and conquers and puts to flight all our enemies!"

APRIL 12th.—For several days past, the
enemy of my soul has made repeated and fierce
attacks upon me; it seems as if he had rallied
up all his forces to try what he could do to
shake my confidence in God; but, blessed be
his name,

> " Still, in spite of sin, I rise,
>   Still to call thee mine I dare.

Without much of this holy violence, I find I
cannot conquer, or drive back the armies of the

aliens. But, glory be to God, neither their magnitude nor their number discourages me; for it is not in my own strength I go against them: No, because I feel I have none; but—

"Who in the strength of Jesus trusts,
    Is more than conqueror."

Gladly do I join with one of old, and cry out with my whole heart, "Thanks be to God, who giveth me the victory, through our Lord Jesus Christ!"

MAY 1st.—This morning, in meditating on the word of God, I felt it was precious to my soul. I could exclaim, the Lord is my portion, saith my soul, therefore will I hope in him;" and when I remembered it is said, "The Lord's portion is his people," I thought within myself, "If the Lord has taken me for his 'portion,' and I have taken Him for mine, then truly I have the best of the bargain." O yes, I have greatly the advantage; "Nothing but sin I call my own;" but he has given me the riches of his grace here, and reserved for me the riches of his glory hereafter. O how delightsome the thought! He has indeed given me not only his gifts, but himself also. While I indulged in this train of meditation, my heart was sensibly affected with the Divine goodness.

3rd.—To-day, while on the road returning from Penryn, I was reflecting on the gain a Christian derives from trading with "the heavenly country." In a moment, as if a voice had spoken to me, it was inquired, what interest

I had there. My heart instantly replied," I am a son of the King of that country, and a joint heir with Jesus Christ." My conscience did not give me the lie, but all within seemed to rejoice in the truth of it.

7th.—Through the tender mercy of my God, and the kind intercession of my dear Redeemer, I am spared on earth, to see the return of another of my spiritual birth-days. I see sufficient cause to be humbled as in the dust before God, on account of my short-comings, imperfections, and little improvement of my precious time. O, it is well for me that I have an Advocate! But, on the other hand, what abundant cause have I for gratitude and thanksgiving! Yes, glory to thee, my God, I see I have! I bless thy name, I have beheld thy mighty power displayed this year in the conviction and conversion of sinners; particularly of Gunwalla, Mullion, and Ruan. It is now fifty-two years since the Lord spoke peace to my troubled mind. Then I could say, "Behold, God is my salvation, my strength and my song;" and, after the long lapse of so many intervening years, O what a heavenly sweetness do I still feel springing up in my soul! Yes, glory be to God, I still feel I am built on the rock of eternal ages!

8th.—This morning, early at the dawn of day, when I seemed entering on a new year, I renewed my covenant with God, and solemnly engaged to be his for ever; and, glory to his adorable name! my God and my Father condescended to renew his covenant with me. In a very remarkable manner this promise was applied to my mind, " I will put my laws into their mind, and in their hearts will I write them; and I will be to them a God, and they shall be to me a people." Three times God spake with power to my soul; in such a wonderful manner did he speak the third time, that had he not veiled his glory in a moment, I could not have lived under it. I cried out, " Lord, it is enough!" I was then enabled to believe from my heart, that my Maker had again renewed his marriage-covenant with me. O! what an increase of confidence in him did I feel after this; and what fresh vigour of soul to pursue my way to the realms of bliss and glory! Never, I think shall I forget this morning's covenant with my God.

JULY 3rd.—I am just now returned from a tour of six or seven weeks, in visiting the different societies at Breage, Mullion, Gunwalla, Ruan, and Helston; and trust my humble efforts to convince the sinner, and to establish and build up believers, have not been in vain in the Lord. During this time of travelling and exertion, I have often been led to adore the goodness of God, in so wonderfully strengthening my body: I have scarce felt an hour's pain since I have been absent O my Saviour, may I never forget to praise thee! I rejoice much to meet so many of those to whom God had made me the instrument of good, still standing fast in the faith. One of them, who fetched me to Ruan with a horse, informed me, as we journeyed

on together, that before he saw me, he was
for seven years in an awful state of backsliding
from God, and could not see by what means he
was to escape from his unhappy bondage.   I
well remember the conversation that passed
between us.   I would not let him go till I had
his promise that he would again give himself to
God, and commence a life of prayer, before he
lay down that night.   He now told me that he
kept his promise.   At present he seems to
have a good work of grace upon his mind :
May he be found faithful unto death !   I also
met with the young man with whom I had the
conversation about his soul, while he was smoking.   For some time I laboured hard to awaken
his conscience, but nothing affected him.   I
then requested him to lay aside the pipe ; and
no sooner had he done it, than the truth of God
touched his heart, and he became a penitent at
the feet of Jesus.   Greatly did we rejoice again
to meet each other in the flesh ; and I trust we
shall also meet above.   I spent three days with
the friends at Hellston, going from house to
house, conversing of Jesus and the things of
eternity.   In three of the houses which I visited, the awakening Spirit appeared to seal the
truth on the consciences of sinners   Some of
them wept bitterly. May these gracious impressions never be effaced.

Aug. 11th —I have recently returned from
a visit to my much-respected friends, at Saltash.
They nobly hold fast the blessing of full salvation, and are more and more established in it.—

They still meet in a select band; and, instead of four enjoying perfect love, there are now more than twice that number. I had the great pleasure of meeting in band with them, and also of seeing another brought into full liberty. In this little place, there are several of the excellent of the earth. I should have staid longer with these truly respectable friends, but was obliged to hasten home, from an attack of my old complaint, an inflammation in the leg.

SEPT 17th.—Since I last wrote, I have been confined to bed four weeks, by a malignant fever, and have been brought nigh to the gates of death. But I have great cause to be thankful for the wonderful support which the Almighty afforded me in the time of trial He applied many great and precious promises as cordials to my fainting mind. I felt that his eternal power was my refuge, and that underneath were the everlasting arms. The third morning after I was laid by, while looking up for Divine aid, Jesus appeared to the eye of my faith, and said, in his well-known voice, " Thou art all fair, my love; there is no spot in thee." My heart bounded with transport, my eyes flowed with tears, and all within me shouted aloud for joy. This blessed visitation afforded me lasting strength and comfort, and will, I trust, never be forgotten. I praise God, he has now so far restored me, that I am able to walk about a little, and attend the means of grace, to the great profit of my soul.

Nov. 30th.—A few days ago, I was requested

to visit a person who was dangerously ill; there being no hope of her recovery. I was well acquainted with her, and had often warned her of her danger as a sinner, and invited her to give her heart to God, but she did not close in with the offers of mercy. After a close conversation with her, she seemed to obtain some knowledge of her lost estate, and showed marks of repentance. I was sensibly affected by her cries and tears, and gave her all the encouragement I could. The next morning, I called again to see her: She wept much, but I told her it was a nice point to say whether her repentance was genuine or not. I, however, felt much love and pity for her; and, while endeavouring to prove and illustrate, from the word of God, the willingness of Jesus to save sinners, and earnestly interceding with God in her behalf, it pleased the Lord to answer for himself, by bursting her bands of guilt and sin asunder, and shedding abroad his love in her heart. She cried out, "Jesus is here, Jesus is here!" She now felt clearly assured that God had pardoned all her sins, by the Spirit which was given unto her. The following day, I found her standing fast in the liberty wherewith Christ had made her free; and, in a short time, she entered the world of spirits, witnessing the power of Jesus to save unto the uttermost. Is not this a brand plucked out of the burning? A short time before this occurred, I had been breathing my ardent wishes to God, that he would again permit me to see his holy arm dis-

played in the salvation of another sinner.   He
has now granted me the desire of my heart;
glory, glory, be to his holy name!   No one
knows the happiness this affords, but those who
taste it by experience.

Dec. 6th.—I received a message from my
brother, at Mousehole, informing me that if I
would see him once more in the body, I must
hasten to him without delay.   I set off with all
speed, and found him very low, but very happy
in God.—

> " Strong in the Lord of hosts,
> And in his mighty power."

I was with him five days before he took his
flight to paradise.   Such was his assurance of
salvation, and such the heavenly manifestations
on the occasion, that I sat by him with sweet
composure and Divine satisfaction of mind, and
beheld him fall asleep in Jesus.   Thus, after
fighting the good fight of faith for more than
fifty-two years, he finished his course with joy;
leaving behind him a name that will long be
precious to those who knew him   From the
time he joined the society, to the day he entered
into the joy of his Lord, he was one of the most
unblamable of men: I never knew or heard of
a stain on his character.   The cause of God
lay near his heart, and to the utmost of his
power he struggled to promote it.   For many
long years, he was one of the principal pillars
of the excellent society at Mousehole.   Many
of the preachers, who in succession have visited

this favourite place, held him in high esteem, and remember his name with pleasure. The regularity with which he attended the prayer-meetings, and every other means of grace, was proverbial. Few men more revered the Sabbath than he did. In common with other fishermen, he was often tempted to profane the Lord's day, by pursuing his ordinary calling; but, in this respect, he was an example of selfdenial and pious trust in God. So generally was he beloved and revered for his piety, that all parties, in the neighbourhood, seemed to regard him as the most fit person to instruct, comfort, and pray for them in a dying hour. He filled the office of class-leader for more than forty years, and greatly was he beloved and respected by his members; and, as a man of uprightness and general integrity, his name was known far beyond the immediate circle in which he moved. Truly it may be said of him, "He feared God above many;" but now he rests from his labours, and his works do follow him.*

* Among his excellencies unmentioned above, was his strong attachment to his Bible. As far back as I can recollect, while he was on a visit to my father, I remember he said, " When I have been detained at sea two or three days, and have not had an opportunity of reading the word of God, on entering my house, after I have come ashore, at the very sight of the Bible my heart has leaped for joy within me." Of my father's piety he thought very highly. I was present at a prayer-meeting, when my father gave a short exhortation in his usual strain. My uncle was there also, and afterwards stood up to speak a few words to the people. In the course

On my way home I visited Breage, Mullion, and Constantine; and rejoiced to find so many of those who had but recently entered on the work of God steadfast in the paths of duty. While I was at Constantine a gracious revival commenced, and I had the happiness of seeing many sinners awakened and brought to the knowledge of the truth. Hearing that God had very wonderfully visited Ponsanooth, I hastened thither, and found some of the distressed souls in the chapel, who had been there several days and nights struggling in prayer and crying for mercy At Mr. Lovey's factory the Spirit of conviction was operating so powerfully, that many who had been triflers were falling down on their kness to pray in the midst of their work. Indeed, for many days, little else was done but attending to those who were deeply agonizing with God for their soul's salvation. Multitudes were the subjects of a gracious change; the exact number I cannot say, but upwards of a hundred gave their names to meet in class But not only at Ponsanooth has this glorious work broken out: It has gone forth into all the societies and congregations round about to a great extent. Thousands of sinners are said to be awakened. How many, in conse-

of what he said, when referring to my father's remarks, he was much affected, and with a full heart and streaming eyes, he observed, I have now known my brother William, as a Christian, nearly forty years, and have always been constrained to regard him as one of the best men living."—EDIT.

quence of this general shaking among the dry
bones, will find their way to heaven, O Lord,
thou knowest! These are fair blossoms; and
in due season it shall appear who will bring
forth fruit unto perfection May God deal gently
with them, and show them mercy unto eternal
life! Amen and Amen.

[I doubt not but it will be both pleasing and
profitable to the reader to append to this chapter
a brief account of that eminently pious and ta-
lented man, the late Stephen Drew, Esq., Bar-
rister at Law, of Jamaica, from whom my father
this year received an excellent letter, in answer
to one which he had written to him.   The circumstances of this gentleman's conversion are
rather striking, and for different reasons deserve
to be recorded; particularly as they are not
known to the public. For many years he lived
in Jamaica an entire stranger to God, far apart
from religious people, without the means of
grace, and surrounded by sensuality and sin.
In 1814 his sister, Mrs. C., of Saltash, was sa-
vingly brought to God, joined the Methodist society, and soon became eminent for her faith, and
zeal in her Master's cause The following year,
being stationed in the Liskeard Circuit, my
father and I became acquainted with this accomplished and devoted woman. The case of her
unconverted brother, dwelling in the darkness
and dissipation of Jamaica, lay near her heart,
and was not unfrequently the topic of her conversation She longed for his salvation, and
studied by what means she should attempt to

effect it. Religious books she thought a likely instrument, and among these, Mr. Wesley's Sermons stood first in her esteem. Such was her conviction of the point and force contained in these volumes, that she expressed her belief, if she could only get them safely conveyed into her brother's hands, God would bless the pe rusal of them to his soul's salvation. At her request I undertook to assist her in forwarding them. The books being committed to my care, with some considerable difficulty, I at length succeeded, by the assistance of my brother, in getting them delivered into Mr. Drew's own hands. After I left the circuit, I received a letter from Mrs. C., enclosing the amount of the expenses, and conveying the highly gratifying intelligence that her brother was awakened by reading the Sermons: " I have heard from my brother," she says, " and have no doubt but the Lord has already made them a blessing to his soul. In his letter to me, he says, ' Now I have read Wesley's Sermons, I seem to see with new eyes. In these Sermons every thing is as distinctly marked as if the writer possessed a powerful optic glass, to bring things, the most distant, home, as it were, to our very selves, so as to affect us as we were never before affected. I do believe he has the key to unlock the very mysteries of Scripture doctrine.' In the same strain he has written a long letter; speaking also of his helplessness as a sinner, and his conviction of the necessity of an entire change in heart and life. May God, in his mercy, make me thank-

ful for this blessing!"* Another letter, soon
after conveyed to her an account of his conversion,
and of his having received the witness of the
Spirit.   He now saw the privilege and duty of
seeking purity of heart, and not long was it before he was enabled by simple faith to lay hold
on the blessing   From this time his life and
conduct discovered the happy effects of the pure
flame of love that filled and actuated his soul.
He quickly began to preach, and the Lord
made his testimony an abundant blessing. Many
were converted through his instrumentality, and
a church was formed in his own house   But
in his Christian life he had many trials to encounter, especially in his profession of perfect
love; and his affectionate sister, wishful to make
him, as far as possible, a sharer in every good
that she enjoyed, requested my father to write
him an encouraging letter.   He did so, and
Mr. D., in a letter to his sister, acknowledges
it in the manner noticed in the preface.   Some
time after this he wrote an answer to my father.
From this interesting and deeply spiritual letter
the following is an extract —]

* Since the above extract was transcribed I have
received another letter from Mrs. C.; and I cannot
refrain from adding a part of it in this note.   She
says, her brother wrote to her as follows: " Aug.
11th, 1816 —I hope I shall to the latest hour I live
be more and more thankful for Wesley's Sermons.
I know not how to speak the utmost I think of them;
for they are, on the whole, calculated, in their form
and manner, to be more effective in reforming the
corruptness of our nature, than any I ever met with.

"*Bellemont, St. Ann's, Jamaica, Feb.* 5, 1823.

"MY VERY DEAR SIR, AND FATHER IN ISRAEL,

"THE letter which you were so kind as to write me was a source of comfort and edification beyond any that I have ever received. I read it at our quarterly-meeting, and it confirmed the faith of many. It is a great encouragement to be so kindly noticed by one who can say, 'I have fought a good fight, I have finished my course; henceforth there is laid up for me a crown of righteousness.' When the chariot

They speak with astonishing authority as to doctrine and practice." In a letter written a few months after, he states, " The Bible seems altogether a new book to me; before I read the Sermons of Mr. Wesley, I thought erroneously, like others, that it belonged almost exclusively to the Jews; whereas he shows that it more truly belongs to us. The necessity of regeneration appears to me as clear as demonstration could make it. I mean in the spiritual sense of being actually made a new creature by the operation of the Spirit of God." I give these extracts here as a valuable additional testimony in favour of Mr. Wesley's Sermons, and also further to make known their excellent writer. I now rejoice greatly at having it in my power to announce, that Mrs. Carpenter has it in contemplation to prepare for publication a volume, containing the Christian memoirs of her late brother. Mr. S Drew. A man of such fervent, distinguished, and enlightened piety ought to be extensively known to the church of God. Most heartily do I wish that Mrs. C. may meet with every encouragement and stimulus to prosecute and accomplish her pious undertaking.—EDIT.

of Israel and the horsemen thereof come for the
Lord's aged servant, to him may an abundant
and glorious entrance be administered ! and on
some favoured witness may his mantle fall, and
a double portion of his spirit on many !   Your
own experience of the work of full salvation
on your soul has assisted me to gain a correct
view of that invaluable blessing.   I, for a little
time, entertained an erroneous notion, that,
when it is once attained. the soul has acquired
the utmost fulness of holiness and perfection that
it can attain in this world   This I see was a
snare, and satan turned it against me; for after
the Lord's Spirit witnessed this blessing to me,
and enabled me to witness the good confession
before many, I was assailed with such a storm
of temptations of various kinds as I never had
before experienced; and satan suggested my
then weakness as an argument that I had de-
ceived myself. But I was graciously supported,
and found it impossible to disbelieve   This I
now continually experience ; so that I can no
more doubt my spiritual life than my natural :
And occasionally the intrinsic knowledge and
assurance of this is very strong   However, I
found from this, that I was but a babe in sanctification . I learned that I was infirm ; yet. as I
loved the Lord with all my heart, and served Him
with all my powers, that infirmity no longer
alarmed me, there being no particle of sin mixed up with it.   I am thankful in being enabled
to say, that, my faith being increased, the work
of faith has proceeded, and the fruits of faith

become more apparent. I feel more unreservedly devoted to the Lord; more love to God, and to every child of man; more deadness to the world, and more power over whatever is evil, or from the evil one. I feel that I am growing in stature; and I have an abiding and an assured faith that the Lord will preserve me until I attain the fulness of the stature of a man in Christ. But I feel that I need all your prayers, and I know I shall have them, for we are one. My temporal and spiritual trials are very great; but the Lord's deliverances are wonderful. I will mention one, because it is right with the mouth to make confession to the Lord's glory. I was this week called to make payment of one hundred pounds without delay. The evil of procrastination would have been very great in some important chancery suits, in which I am a suitor. To raise the money instantly, I proposed to a neighbour to sell some things at a great loss: He was the son of my opponent, and a witness against me, and a great enemy to my attempts to spread the knowledge of redeeming love. My application was unsuccessful; the time arrived for my answering the demand; I was on my knees making it a matter of prayer. I felt assurance; and, while at prayer, a servant arrived bringing the money from the same person, who, in the kindest manner, desired I would on no account, in these distressed times, think of selling at a loss, as I was welcome to keep the money as long as I pleased. Does not the Lord turn the hearts of

our enemies, and make them to be at peace, if
we humbly strive to serve him? In the matter
of building a chapel here, I am wonderfully
supported. I have so far been enabled to bear
the whole expense The roof is erecting; and
I feel an indescribable, awful joy at seeing the
heavy timbers lift their heads. The building,
including the minister's apartments, is seventy-
two feet long by forty-four wide; and my wife
and I mean to give it to the society on the Con-
ference-plan, with about three hundred and
eighty feet square of fine land surrounding it.
I trust it will be sufficiently finished to admit of
preaching in it by May or June. By the
Lord's mercy there has never been an omission
of worship in this house any Sunday for these
last five or six years; the Lord, having empowered and directed my labours, has owned
and blessed them to the salvation of many; and
the work is greatly spreading. Seventy-one
meet in class under this roof every Sunday;
the whole of whom I led myself till within a
few months back, when my wife was made
class-leader, and took the females. In addressing those who attend me, I scarcely ever omit,
more or less, to show the necessity of full salvation—entire heart-holiness—as alone qualifying
us to enter into that place where only righteousness shall dwell Nothing but a free, full, and
present salvation is the doctrine of the Gospel of
Christ, and where it is preached, there will the
blessing of God be manifest. At the time I
heard from you, I was labouring under very

dangerous illness; during which I was supported by the most merciful manifestations of the
love of Christ, filling me with joy unspeakable.
He was my Friend and my Physician. My
health is now graciously restored and confirmed, and I am enabled to rise at four o'clock in
the morning and begin my studies. I drink
nothing now but milk or water, and twice a
week abstain from animal food; being desirous
of setting an example of self-denial, in a country remarkable for self-indulgence of every kind,
even among many of those who profess religion.
Having attained the limits of fifty years, and
seeing nothing I have ever done but what I
should pray the Lord would blot from the book
of his remembrance, I now, after I have been
so long borne with, though so unprofitable,
would strive with increase of years to increase
in every self-denial, and live closer and close"
to God. I have, by the blessing of the Lord,
been brought through the writing of a book to
demonstrate the truth of Christianity against
the cavils of Infidels. I have given it to the
society for the benefit of our Missions, and hope
it may be productive of good. I am occupied
in writing a Scriptural Illustration of Faith,
with a view of inciting Christians to the practice
and exercise of it, as the condition on which
we attain an assurance of present pardon, and as
a means whereby we receive grace, and work
out a free, a full, and an everlasting salvation.
This, therefore, should I ever be brought
through it, will be a practical work; and I

have presented it to the Lord, and pray for his guidance, instruction, and blessing You see I mention all my little concerns with the confidence of one who is addressing his father and friend, but my remarks are incoherent and ill-digested, as I am labouring under much anxiety, having three of my children dangerously ill. I cannot refrain from telling you, the Mission cause is greatly prospering here Friends are raised up to the cause in many a quarter among men of the first respectability, and the number of white members begins to increase considerably. The reverse has hitherto been sadly true In these parts I have walked singular and alone; having had none of my own colour and condition to converse with But the Lord has been with me, and he is Father, Brother, Friend.

    " Believe me, my dear Sir,
       " Faithfully yours in Christ,
          "STEPHEN DREW."

[LITTLE more than three years after the date of this letter, this eminent man was called to his reward above. To that holy cause, on the promotion of which his benevolent mind was so intently set; God permitted him to fall a sacrifice. A riotous assault being made on the house of Mr. Radcliffe, our Missionary stationed in St. Ann's, Mr. Drew being a magistrate promptly interposed to quell the rioters, and defend the Minister of Christ. By the exposure of his person, in this act of piety and benevo-

lence, he got a severe wetting, which threw him
into a violent fever, that terminated his valuable
life in four days. During the illness his mind
was abundantly supported by the consolations
of faith and love. When near his death, he
directed his pious negroes to be brought into
his room, when he addressed them in the most
solemn and affectionate manner. And then
gave out and sung with astonishing energy,—

> " Our souls are in his mighty hand,
>   And he shall keep them still ;
> And you and I shall surely stand
>   With him on Zion's hill.
>
> O what a joyful meeting there !
>   In robes of white array'd,
> Palms in our hands we all shall bear,
>   And crowns upon our head."

To Mrs. D., whom he was leaving behind with
nine children, he said, " Lavinia, have faith in
God." Lying at the feet of Jesus, confessing
himself the chief of sinners, full of faith and the
Holy Ghost, and exhorting and blessing those
around him, he awaited the final summons:
when his purified and happy spirit rose in
triumph to the skies. The poor negroes were
deeply affected at their loss. One of them, who
afterwards came to England, observed, that,
had they each had nine lives, they would have
given them all to have saved his. The regula-
tions of our Missionary Society not permitting the
Committee to accept the work of Mr. D., above
referred to, that, together with the treatise on

faith, has since been published in England by subscription, in two volumes octavo, under the general title of, "Principles of Self-Knowledge."]

CHAPTER V.

March 11th, 1824.—I have now finished the seventy-fourth year of my age. Taking a retrospect of my past life, I am constrained to say " Goodness and mercy have followed me all my days." And, glory be to God, my last days are my best ! I often think with gratitude, what a mercy it is, that in my old years I am enabled to live free from all the distracting cares of this world. Herein I clearly see the kind hand that has led me, as well as fed me, from my infancy, and in those days when I knew him not. My soul is humbled in the dust, to think of the goodness of God. I can truly say, I have proved him a Father to the fatherless.

> " O how shall I thy goodness tell,
> Father, which thou to me hast show'd !"

My prospect is unclouded, and, I believe, I never before felt such an establishment in grace, such an inward recollection of thought, and such a heavenly frame of mind. Truly, my Divine Shepherd makes my soul to lie down in green pastures.

May 7th.—This is a day which I have been

anticipating with pleasure and sacred delight.
Gloiy be to thee, my God, that I am permitted
to see another annual return of the memorable
day in which my soul was brought out of darkness into marvellous light! Never, I trust, shall
I forget to praise thee for what thou didst for
me, a poor sinner, this day fifty-three years ago.
Unworthy worm as I am, surely I may ask,
"What shall I render unto the Lord for all his
benefits towards me ? "

15th —Being at Ponsanooth, I was requested
to visit a sick woman ; who had for several days
been distressed about her soul.   When I entered
the room and sat down by her, she clasped her
hands, and looked earnestly at me, crying out,
"What shall I do? what shall I do?" I inquired if she felt herself a sinner. " O yes," she
replied, " a guilty sinner." I no sooner offered
her Christ as an able and willing Saviour, a
Saviour ready at that moment to receive her,
than she exclaimed, "He died for me" This
was an exercise of faith that brought the power
of God at once into her soul, when she cried
out, " Glory, glory be to God, my load is gone,
my sins are pardoned!" The change was so
evident, that happiness sparkled in her eyes, and
all her bones seemed to rejoice within her.
Several friends were present, and we all joined
to give praise and glory to her Great Deliverer.
I called on her again some days afterwards,
and found her still in the same blessed state of
mind.

JULY 5th.—I believe I never had greater

pleasure in meeting classes; in labouring to
prop the feeble knees, strengthen the hands that
hang down, and press on believers to all the
depths of humble love. Blessed are those who
live in the possession of all this glorious salvation. O my God, I bless and praise thee
that ever thou didst bring me acquainted with
that faith which is of the operation of the Holy
Spirit; that faith which works by love, and
purifies the heart! I have lately had the joy of
seeing three old backsliders return to God, and
their backslidings healed O that others of this
class would also return to the Lord before repentance be hid from their eyes! In the death
of one of these poor unhappy wanderers, I have
lately had many sorrowful reflections For some
years she was a member of my class; but her
heart departed from God, and then she left his
people. I followed her closely in her wanderings from the " fountain of living waters," and
frequently warned her, invited her, and entreated her to return ; but at length she gave
me a flat denial, saying, " I will never join the
society at ———" The Lord still strove with
her; One night she had a most terrific dream,
and, by her horrid screams in sleep, she alarmed
the house in which she lived When pressed
the following morning to tell what it was that
induced her to utter such cries in the night, she
was at first not willing it should be known ;
but, after a while, she said, " I dreamed I was
dying unprepared, and that I saw satan standing
by the bedside, waiting to carry away my depart-

ing soul." When I heard of this, I told her, it
was certainly an awful warning from God, and
that she ought not any longer to quench the
Spirit. But all was in vain; her heart continued obdurate. When she got married, feeling
I could not yet entirely give her up, I went to
her house for the purpose of once more trying
to persuade her to return to that Saviour whom
she had forsaken; but my efforts were apparently fruitless. Judge what were my feelings when,
a short time after, I heard she was dead! She
was ill only from the Friday till the Tuesday
following. The doctors who attended her saw
the disease was mortal, and told her husband
of it. She had no apprehension of danger
herself, and her husband had not the courage to
communicate the Doctor's opinion till just before she expired! I would not limit the mercies
of God, or set myself up as a judge of those who
are gone hence; but surely this is an end which
ought to be a warning to the unfaithful.
Another case of the kind, more awful than this,
came under my notice some years ago. A man
with whom I was well acquainted, being a professor of religion for a long series of years, departed wickedly from God by the sin of drunkenness. In his backsliding state I had many
opportunities of conversing with him; and
often did I earnestly entreat him to return unto
the Lord. But he waxed worse and worse.
One Saturday, attending market at a neighbouring town, he staid at a public house, with
two sons of Belial, till near midnight. On his

way home, he fell down, and died in a moment! His wife told me he was brought home, in a state of intoxication, about ten days before, by one of his companions. "Shall I not visit for these things, saith the Lord?"

AUGUST 22nd —This morning I have proved the Lord to be my rock and my strong tower against the face of my enemy. I have often, of late, been attacked by vain thoughts It is no little thing, at all times, to conquer self. O for a power continually

> " To catch the wand'ring of my will,
> And quench the kindling fire."

These are "the little foxes that spoil the vines ; for our vines have tender grapes" More than ever I see the value of the atoning blood, which speaks and pleads for me every moment.

SEPT. 3rd.—My soul has of late been much pained to see the indifference of the people in attending the means of grace May the Lord shake away from us this deadly slumber, and stir us all up to set out afresh for the kingdom.

19th —In the silent watches of the past night, the Lord wonderfully revived and cheered my soul by his presence He makes my heart his home : I am become a temple of the indwelling God At present I feel "the speechless awe,— the silent heaven of love." What is all creation compared to this? It is lighter than vanity ; yea, it is dung and dross. " Praise the Lord, O my soul !" Well might the Prophet Isaiah say, " Cry out and shout, O inhabitant of Zion,

for great is the Holy One of Israel in the midst
of thee."

> " This, this is the God I adore,
> My faithful, unchangeable Friend."

Nov. 15th.—After a tour of seven weeks
among various societies, I have returned in
health and peace ; having scarcely felt an hour's
pain or indisposition since I left home. O
what cause have I for gratitude to my heavenly
Father! In meeting classes, visiting from
house to house, singing and praying, and talking freely of the great things of God's kingdom in the heart, I have had many blessed opportunities, melting times, and precious seasons with the people of God. Several who had
lost the witness of the Spirit, or let slip the blessing of full salvation, were encouraged again to
lay hold on Christ for a supply of all their
wants. At Mullion, a much-respected friend,
who had for some time lived in the enjoyment
of perfect love, had cast away her confidence,
and fallen into a state of fear and unbelief. But
one day, while conversing with her on the unhappy effect which unbelief has on the mind
that yields to it, she was enabled, by a simple
act of faith, again to lay hold of the blessing ;
and afterwards made a good profession of it before many witnesses. Here I had the pleasure
of meeting several of my spiritual children,
whom the Lord gave me about two years ago.
As they still hold on their way well, I pray
thee, O Lord, keep them unto the end! No

one knows the love that is felt for such, but those who have begotten them in the Gospel. St. Paul knew it, when he said to his Thessalonian converts, "For what is our hope, or joy, or crown of rejoicing? Are not even ye, in the presence of our Lord Jesus Christ at his coming? For ye are our glory and joy" One rather remarkable circumstance occurred, while I was at Mullion. A friend who had been confined to her house for a long time, by a sore leg, sent a message by her son, requesting me to come and see her. She began her mournful story, by relating to me how greatly she had suffered from the wound in her leg, and that now it had spread downwards to her foot, and assumed the character of a permanent and settled affliction. I inquired how her mind was affected under the chastening rod: She told me her soul was in a very uncomfortable state. It appeared, on further conversation with her, that for many years she had known the love of God, but had afterwards cast away her confidence; and now, like the foolish Galatians, she was seeking to be made perfect by works. She said it was suggested to her, that she should never regain her peace of mind till she had gone through such and such distressing exercises, and had submitted to the performance of various painful duties She accordingly did voluntarily exercise herself in many ways grievous to one in her state of body. " Before I could lay down to rest at night, I have been on my knees," says she, " by the bed-side,

till three o'clock in the morning." I told her
God was not such a hard master as to require
impossibilities of her; and, indeed, that all she
did was nothing in his sight. I asked her if
she found herself any thing the better for all
that she had thus performed: She confessed
she did not. Indeed, it appeared to me there
was not a grain of faith in all her performances;
and her case clearly illustrated to me the
truth of that scripture, " Without faith it is impossible to please God; for he that cometh unto
Him, must believe that He is a rewarder of
them that diligently seek Him." After I had
explained to her more perfectly the way of
faith, we went to prayer; and the Lord graciously answered for himself, set her free from
her distressed bondage, and filled her soul with
peace and joy in believing. In a few days
after this happy change in her mind, the affliction by which she had been so long before confined to her house, was so far removed, that she
walked to the chapel, though the distance was
full half-a-mile; and she continued to do so
while I remained there. When I mentioned
my surprise at seeing her out, she said to me,
" In healing my soul, the Lord has healed my
body too."

Whilst at this place, I met with Lady Maxwell's Life, and read some parts of it with much
pleasure and profit; especially the following remarks;—" From day to day, I am made to taste
of that perfect love which casts out fear; and
often I experience a plenitude of Divine pre

sence. But I most sensibly find it is only by a
momentary faith in the blood of Jesus, that I am
kept from sin ; and that my soul is more or less
vigorous as I live by faith.' I have never
known so much of the nature of simple faith,
and of its unspeakable value, as since I have
tasted of the pure love of God ;—by it how has
my soul been upheld in the midst of temptation !
The Lord has taught me that it is by faith, and
not joy, that I must live. He has, in a measure, often enabled me strongly to act faith on
Jesus for sanctification, even in the absence of
all comfort : This has diffused a heaven of
sweetness through my soul, and brought with it
the powerful witness of purity. I would say
to every penitent, ' Believe, and justification is
yours ;' and to every one who is justified, and
sees his want of sanctification, ' Believe, and
that blessing is yours also.' I seem to derive
the greatest advantage from a lively faith in
constant exercise ; this secures what I now already possess, and increases my little stock. At
times, my evidence for sanctification is as strong
as a cable fixed to an immovable rock, and as
clear as the sun shining at noon-day." I have
recorded these remarks, because they so perfectly agree with my own views and experience.

Dec. 3rd —This morning while meditating
on the riches of Divine grace, how was my
soul filled with the fulness of God, and lost in
wonder, love, and praise ! Heaven appeared
so attracting, I was constrained to check the
desire of departing to be with Christ, lest there

13

should be too much of my own will in it.   I
bless God, "to me to live is Christ, and to die
is gain."   Never had one, every way so un-
deserving, so much reason to praise the God of
love.   Day by day; nay, every hour that I
breath, He loadeth me with his multiplied
mercies.   If I did not love him with all my
redeemed and consecrated powers, I should of
all mortals be the most inexcusable.   O, his
love to me is boundless!   I prove it an ocean
without bottom or shore.   O, that all the world
knew the riches of Divine love; especially the
rest from all sin,—that rest of perfect love which
is received by simple faith alone.

5th.—By the urgent request of the friends at
Stithians, I attended a love-feast there.   The
preacher having disappointed the congregation,
I was pressed by many to give a word of exhortation.   In doing it, I found great liberty,
while faithfully addressing those who were
living without God in the world.   At the love-
feast, I was delighted to hear the people speak
so freely, scripturally, and experimentally, and
so much to the point   The chapel, at times,
seemed filled with the glory of God.   I lodged
at brother J. Hearle's.   He has three daughters,
all bidding fair for the kingdom; and I think I
never saw three sisters more united in love.
The youngest, who had been brought to God
in the last revival, was longing to love the Lord
with all her heart.   This I told her was her
privilege, and that God's time was the present
moment; but I found she could not venture on

the atonement. The next day, conversing with her again, I asked her, " Can you now believe ?" She replied, " No : I still feel a bar that prevents my laying hold." I saw what she wanted, and requested her to fetch me Mrs. Rogers's Memoirs. I opened to the part applicable to her experience, and bid her read for herself; where Mr. Fletcher invites all who felt their need of full salvation, to believe now for it. He observed, "As when you reckon with your creditor, or with your host; and, as when you have paid all, you reckon yourself free : So now reckon with God. Jesus hath paid all; and hath paid all for thee ! Hath purchased thy pardon and holiness. Therefore, it is now God's command ; reckon thyself dead indeed unto sin ; and thou art alive unto God from this hour ! O begin—begin to reckon now ! Fear not ! Believe, believe, believe ! And continue to believe every moment ; so shalt thou continue free " This had the blessed effect which I longed to see. The words, "Fear not," &c., touched her heart ; and she wept, believed, and entered in. And so powerful was the change wrought in her soul, that her whole frame was thereby greatly affected.

22nd —At the kind and pressing request of Mr. Carter, I went to Breage, and remained with him a fortnight. Accompanied by Mr. C., I visited every house belonging to several of the villages round about, endeavouring in every family to scatter the seeds of eternal life. What may be the result, will be known in the

great day of account   The people received us
kindly, and several of them have since attended
class-meeting.   I then went to Mr Glasson's,
and adopted the same plan in his neighbourhood.   One day, while conversing with a poor
backslider, who was just beginning to turn
again to the Lord, a young woman, who was
living without God, came into the house, and
listened very attentively to the conversation.   I
felt my mind impressed to say something to
her before I left.   I had talked to her but a
very short time, before the word reached her
heart; and the silent tear stole over her cheeks.
While praying with her she wept bitterly.
The next night she came to the prayer-meeting,
and the Lord set her soul at liberty.   Another,
an old man, was deeply convinced that night,
and soon after found pardon.   Four that week
were brought to enjoy the peace of God.   In
going from house to house, I met with one
woman who appeared to know nothing of
prayer. · I earnestly desired her to try to pray
in her heart that God would bless her at that
moment.   I was some time before I could prevail upon her to do it; but no sooner did she
lift up the desire of her heart unto the Lord,
than I perceived that he answered.   Her hard
heart was quickly melted, and the waters of
contrition gushed out   She now promised she
would give herself to God.   On the Sunday
following, with her soul deeply burdened with
the guilt of sin, she came to the class-meeting:
my heart rejoiced to meet her there, and soon

the Lord turned her sorrow into joy. Another mourner, who came with her, was also made a partaker of the joys of salvation.

FEB. 3rd, 1825.—In the past week I have visited Ponsanooth : I rejoiced to find so many of the young converts steadfast in faith and practice. I met the Sunday, Monday, Tuesday, and Wednesday's classes; and we had most blessed seasons together The following Sunday I was at their monthly meeting, and surely the power of God was with us. Three entered into the enjoyment of entire sanctification, and bore a lively testimony to the power of Christ to save to the uttermost. In meeting the class the following evening, another young man entered into the rest of perfect-love ; and " with a loud voice gave glory to God." These were seasons never to be forgotten.

MARCH 2nd.—In the Methodist Magazine for last month, I this day read the memoir of Mr. Robert Spence, of York. · I know not when I have met with any man's experience to come so near to mine as his does. A conversation with Mrs. Mather was made an unspeakable blessing to his soul. It was by her he learned his privilege to claim the promise of full salvation, and expect the evidence in believing. Afraid of mistake, he artlessly interrogated, " Is this Methodism ?" It was replied, " It is old Methodism—proved Methodism." Yes, and I bless God, that I have the pleasure of putting my hand to the truth of this: I can say, " It is old and proved Method-

ism*" for, on the thirteenth day of this month,
it will be fifty-three years since I obtained the
evidence in believing, that "the blood of Jesus
Christ, the Son of God, cleanseth from all sin."

4th —The following observations are delightful, and deserving of particular notice :—" A
calm and recollected mind generally produces
a heartfelt union with a Holy God. God is
love! sweet truth; and love is the Christian's
all! Love in us is the Divine nature impart-
ed; it is the fulfilling of the law, the perfect
law of liberty. Whosoever loveth his brother
hath fulfilled the law to his neighbour; and he
that loveth the Lord his God with all his heart,
and soul, and mind, and strength, hath fulfilled
the law to Him also. To such His commandments are not grievous; not a task, or a burden,
but a delight; they are ways of pleasantness,
they are paths of peace. His wisdom to guide
and teach; his power to protect, help and
strengthen; and his faithfulness, his truth, his
mercy, &c, are all sealed over, and secured to
us by covenant privilege, and covenant blood."
This is strong language, but, glory be to God,
it is all true.

6th.—Yesterday, while I was in my closet
pouring out my soul in prayer, the Lord the
Spirit applied these words to my mind, with
great power and energy: "I have loved thee
with an everlasting love." At this time my
soul is encompassed with mercy, and full of the
hope of immortality. To the praise and honour of his grace, who is the glorious Giver of

all good, I can say with good Lady Maxwell,
" My evidence for sanctification is as strong as a
cable fixed to an immovable rock, and as bright
as the sun at noon-day."

> " To know thou tak'st me for thine own,
> O, what a happiness is this !"

7th.—The more I meditate on Divine things,
the more my soul is lost in the immensity of redeeming love. This has an influence so wonderfully attractive, that it draws all the powers
of my heart and mind into it. Well might the
poet say,—

> " Who that loves, can love enough ?"

> " Jehovah himself doth invite
> To drink of his pleasures unknown;
> The streams of immortal delight,
> That flow from his heavenly throne."

Methinks I hear him saying, " Ho, every one
that thirsteth, come ye to the waters, and he
that hath no money, come ye, buy and eat ; yea,
come, buy wine and milk, without money and
without price." O what a glorious invitation is
here! Might not rebel man cry out with astonishment, and ask, " Can it be possible that
this is the voice of God to me ?" Yes, poor
sinner, it is God's voice to thee; if thou art
athirst for salvation, salvation by grace. " Sing,
O heavens, for the Lord hath done it : shout, ye
lower parts of the earth: break forth into singing, ye mountains, O forest, and every green
tree therein; for the Lord hath redeemed Jacob, and glorified himself in Israel."

26th.—Since I wrote last, I have had to mourn over my short-comings and imperfections. I long for every thought and desire to be continually swallowed up in God. O what depths of humble love, and lengths of Gospel truth, do I sometimes see! I want to sink into the former, and rise into the latter. I see I must cast myself upon Christ from moment to moment, in order to make any progress in the Divine life. One act of faith will help me to a lift; but one act of faith will not do; faith must be my life,—I mean, in connexion with its grand object. The Lord has lately very sensibly taught me this lesson, that, as I cannot live by one inspiration or breath, but must breathe on, and draw the electric, vital fire into my lungs, together with the air; so I must believe on, and thereby draw into my soul the Divine power and the fire of Jesus's love, together with the truth of the Gospel, which is the blessed element in which believers live.

APRIL 14th.—I have lately been reading Mr. Fletcher's Letters, and they have been made a great blessing to my soul. He exhorts believers to hold fast their confidence, but not to trust or rest in it; but to trust in Christ, and remember that he says, " I am the way," not for you to stop, but to run on in him. This is a wise and important observation, which has much included in it. Happy would it be for believers did they all comprehend and practically observe it!

20th.—A few days ago I was called to visit

a sick man. I had been with him before, and
found him very dark and ignorant. I asked
him if he prayed; he told me he did I inquired what he played for. That God would
take him to heaven, he said And what would
you do, said I, in heaven in your sins? Heaven
is no place for an unregenerate soul. God's
word is gone forth, " Without holiness no man
shall see the Lord;" and, therefore, I said, except you repent you must perish I now found
him much distressed in mind; he said he had
not rested since my conversation with him.—
When I beheld him in this state on the brink
of eternity, it is impossible to describe the love
and pity I felt for him. He knew but little,
having never been able to read the word of
God. I gave him all the help I could; and
though a kind of despairing gloom pervaded
his mind, yet a ray of hope would occasionally
animate his feelings. In speaking to him of
the consolations of Divine mercy, I was wonderfully assisted; but in the course of a few
hours he died. The strong compassion I felt
for him, connected with those marks of penitence which he manifested, forbid me to entertain the thought that he is eternally lost; but
this matter must be left to the decision of the
great day.

24th.—This morning I read that blessed portion of the word of God contained in the first
three chapters of the Epistle to the Ephesians.
O what did I discover in the great truths contained herein! I can truly say, I feel them to

be a reviving cordial to my mind! But with
all his spiritual possessions—his wisdom, piety,
and usefulness—St. Paul considered himself,
"less than the least of all saints." How deeply
humbling were his views of himself! Methinks I hear something within me, saying,

> " For ever here my soul would be,
>   In such a frame as this."

26th.—My heart, I feel, would soon stand
still in the ways of God, did I not receive those
regular supplies from above, by which I am
enabled, daily, to make a fresh start for the
kingdom. I often compare my heart to a
watch or a clock, which must be regularly
wound up, or it will be found quite useless.

> " Still stir me up to strive
>   With thee, in strength Divine ;
> And every moment, Lord, revive
>   This fainting soul of mine."

29th —In all my life I never felt a greater
need of praying to my heavenly Father, that he
would continually cleanse the thoughts of my
heart. I see I must take great care, or vain
thoughts will lodge within me. I must confess that I have sustained a loss from this quarter If not repelled in a moment, they are of
such a pernicious nature that a sting will be left
behind; and, were it not for a fresh application
of the " blood that speaketh better things than
the blood of Abel," it would prove fatal. But,
O what a mercy it is, the Christian has a shield

which, when well exercised, repels every fiery
dart of the adversary; but if, for a moment, the
shield should slip, and a wound be received,
there is no room for a moment's despair, for,

' He has an Advocate above,
   A Friend before the throne of love."

O how great my privilege! even above that of
Adam, for now it is written, " If any man sin,
we have an Advocate with the Father, Jesus
Christ the righteous." And of his advocacy I
never saw so much the need as I do at present.
Not that I am now more unfaithful than formerly, but I now more clearly see that I depend on the intercession of Christ for every
thing.

MAY 7th—It is fifty-four years, this day,
since God, in his rich mercy, first visited my
soul with his pardoning love; and blotted out
my sins as a cloud, and mine iniquities as a
thick cloud, for his own name's sake. Yes,
glory be to God, it was that night that my
chains fell off, and I partook of the freedom of
a follower of Jesus Christ. Nor am I yet weary
in well-doing, or cut down as a cumberer of the
ground. O the boundless mercies of my God
to me!

" I would praise thee—I would praise thee ;—
  - Where shall I thy praise begin ?"

26th.—I have lately been greatly blessed
under the ministry of the word; and in reading
the blessed book of God. O what beauty do I

discover in it! It is sweeter to my taste than I ever before felt it.

> " I love thy name, I love thy word,
>   Join all my powers to praise the Lord."

I have just received a letter from a dear child in the Gospel, M. B. It affords me much gratitude and joy to think, that the Lord has now kept her six years in the slippery paths of youth. O, my heavenly Father, keep her unto the end!

30th.—" Conviction is not condemnation ; as children of God, we may be convinced, yet not condemned ; convinced of useless thoughts and words, and yet not condemned for them. We are condemned for nothing while we love God, and give him all our heart!" These remarks are, I think, just and important; for the want of heavenly wisdom to discern between conviction and condemnation many sincere souls have been foiled by the grand adversary : They have yielded to unbelief, entered into temptation, and cast away their confidence. Again do I bless God for my present privileges; having so much time and opportunity to retire from the bustle of the concerns of this life ; to read, meditate, pray, and to write to so many of my much-respected friends on the deep things of God. What a heaven have I felt this day in reflecting on these mercies! Christ was truly precious, and I felt a holy longing to depart and be with him for ever.

SEPT. 12th.—I have of late been much confined at home by reason of lameness and the infirmities of age. Except a few times to Ponsanooth, I have only been abroad once for the last three months, and that was on a visit to Constantine, when the Lord condescended to use me as an humble instrument of pointing another poor sinner to the out-stretched arms of mercy. While meeting brother Harvey's class I saw a respectably dressed young man, a stranger to me, sitting rather apart from those present, who did not belong to the class. I afterwards inquired who he was, and found it to be Mr. James Box, who was in an afflicted state of body, but did not enjoy religion. I then felt regret I had not spoken to him; but the next day I received a message requesting me to visit him On entering the room where he was, I found him on a sofa, in a very feeble state of body, and his soul heavy laden, dark, and comfortless. He expressed strong desires for salvation from guilt, and sin, and hell, but knew not the way to attain it. Finding that he was already of a broken and a contrite spirit, I immediately pointed him to the Lamb of God. Nor had I long been talking to him of Jesus, before the blessed light of truth shone upon his mind. and while he was repeating with his lips, and endeavouring to apply to himself, that precious passage of Isaiah, " He was wounded for our transgressions, and with his stripes we are healed," he was enabled to believe to the saving of his soul. The overwhelming power of the Spirit so descended upon him, that his feeble

frame shook under it; while, in the fulness of
his heart, he cried out, " Now I can love God."
After this I saw him several times, and found
him still holding fast his confidence, and rejoicing in the God of his salvation.

15th — During several of the days last past,
and I may add, of nights too, for I have slept
but little, my soul has been in the "land of
Beulah," where the sun and moon shine together, and never go down. This is a delightsome country.   It is

> " A land of corn, and wine, and oil,
>   Favour'd with God's peculiar smile,
>   With every blessing blest;
>   There dwells the Lord our righteousness,—
>   And keeps his own in perfect peace,
>   And everlasting rest."

18th —I never in my life so fully understood,
and so felt the blessed effects of, these words as
I do at present : " He that abideth in me, and I
in him, the same bringeth forth much fruit."
By abiding in Christ we get rooted, and
grounded, and built up in our most holy faith
O the inexpressible blessedness arising from a
heart-felt union with a holy God !

19th —I have just received a letter from my
dear son in New South Wales, in which he
mentions the conversations which took place
between him and me fourteen years back, that
led to his conversion.   As far as my recollection goes, I think he is correct   He says,
" You may be assured I have not forgotten the
conversation about the salvation of my soul

which took place while we were standing together near the entrance of the stable-door.
But the remarks which you made to me, on
the following Sunday, I think, while I was
occupied in my old way, about your declining
health, and the disquietude which it would give
you in a dying hour to leave me behind in an
unconverted state; enforced as they were by
the eloquence of falling tears, and the sighs of
a full heart, produced on my obdurate mind a
deeper impression than any previous effort of
your faithfulness and love. But the most effectual and best-remembered of all your paternally
kind attempts to effect the great change in my
soul, was the invitation to attend the class-meeting, which you gave me on the succeeding
Tuesday evening. Though at this distance of
time, and very much greater distance with regard to place, every thing that occurred that
evening is as vivid in my recollection as if it
had taken place but yesterday, and in the house
in which I now sit. I was then sitting in my
usual position, with the books open before me
which had so long kept my heart from God.
Half-past six o'clock was the time;—I knew it
was the meeting-night, and, from what had
taken place between us on the Sunday, I anticipated another attempt that evening. At length
the fastening of the door moved; it produced a
thrill within me; you entered, prepared for the
meeting, and I was affectionately urged to go
with you, and cast in my lot with the people of
God. I could hold out no longer: the conquest.

was won; and I yielded to the reasonable request to accompany you to the hallowed and hallowing assembly of those that feared God. In so doing I found my soul stimulated to seek that grace by which I was enabled to turn my feet to the testimonies of the Lord; and, having obtained help of God, I continued to this day. To Jesus, my Saviour, be ascribed all the honour and the praise!"

I have often thought, if parents were to plead more importunately with God in behalf of their own offspring, He would surely hear their cry; and we should not see so many professors' children living in a state of ungodliness and sin. I remember my wife told me, that, after she had once been fervently pouring out her soul to God in behalf of our children, on rising from her knees,—the Bible being on the table before her,—she opened it on these words, which she regarded at the time as given her in answer to prayer: "One shall say, I am the Lord's; and another shall call himself by the name of Jacob; and another shall subscribe with his hand unto the Lord, and surname himself by the name of Israel." The Lord granted her the desire of her heart, for she lived to see her three children converted to God. Now I consider, that, as God has promised to pour out his Spirit on our seed, and his blessing on our offspring, He has graciously bound himself to hear prayer; and we have an unquestionable right to pray for the fulfilment of the covenant; nay, He himself has gone so far in encouraging us to ask the fulfilment of his promises, that He has condescended to say, " Put me in remembrance ;" as if he had said, " When you pray, be sure to bring the promises with you." Hence I conclude, if I have faith to give full credit to God's word, that promise which I lay hold of is mine, and all it contains, so far as my wants are concerned.   On the other hand, if I entertain a doubt, or stagger at the truth of God, I consider I have no claim, and my prayers will not find access.   Such is the dreadful effect of unbelief, that, speaking after the manner of men, it binds the hands of God.   It is said of Jesus on one occasion.   " He could do no mighty work, because of the people's unbelief."   I see a great deal included in that verse of our Hymn, which says, " Faith looks at the promise," and sees that *alone*, and cries, in spite of all impossibilities, " It shall be done." But we must not forget, that, however great may be our faith, it may be tried to the uttermost.   This is very evident from the cases of Abraham, and the woman who came to our Lord for her daughter.   Both these had mighty faith, yet were they severely tried before either of them obtained their suit.   The great object is to persevere in the prayer of faith.   While all things are possible to him that believeth, we must endeavour so to believe as never to faint in crying to God.   This is the conduct that honours him : and the Lord saith, " Them that honour me, I will honour."

25th.—The word of God never appeared so

valuable in my eyes, as at the present moment. Truly it is a lamp to my path, and a light to my feet. All language fails to express the regard which I feel for it. "How sweet are thy words unto my taste; yea, sweeter than honey to my mouth. Thy testimonies have I taken as an heritage for ever; for they are the rejoicing of my heart." Blessed be God, this is not only David's experience, but through grace it is mine also. I feel an ardent desire and holy longing within me to outvie, if I could, all the heavenly host in loving and praising the God of my salvation :—

"Vying with the heavenly choir,
Who chant thy praise above;
We on angels wings aspire,
The wings of faith and love."

28th.—Yesterday Mr. J. Box, of Constantine, sent for me. I found him confined to his bed, still holding fast his confidence in God. O how did we rejoice to see each other! He has had severe conflicts with the adversary of his soul, particularly on this point,—that God will at some future period leave him; (a com mon temptation;) but against which, God has provided an express remedy by saying, "I will never leave thee, nor forsake thee;" and again, "They shall never perish, neither shall any pluck them out of my hand." Precious promises! and happy is that man who is blessed with precious faith to claim them for his own. The following remarks, which I have just met

with in a favourite author, contain spiritual
directions which appear to me particularly
worthy of observation :—" Fly from the cooling
influences of unbelief, and get under the rays,
the melting rays, of the Sun of righteousness.
If any idol has got possession of our hearts,
there is no other way of casting it out, but by
getting them filled with a nobler object, even
Jesus ; and then all the charms of our idols
will sink into nothing ; and we shall hate the
intruders which so long possessed the place of
Christ."

· Oct. 10th.—Mr. J. Box again sent to fetch
me, requesting that I would come and remain
with him some days. I found him full of faith
and love. He rejoiced greatly to see me, and
said, " You are my spiritual Father : I never
knew what faith was, till I saw you." I told
him he must give all the glory to God. At
this time no one expected death was near ; but
the next day he was taken violently ill. In
this conflict, which was the struggle of death,
he suffered greatly for fourteen hours ; but
throughout he held fast an unshaken confidence
in his Redeemer ; and at last came off more
than conqueror. As he drew nearer and nearer
the closing scene, his faith and hope grew
stronger and stronger. At last he cried out,
" The angels are coming !" and soon after, with a
heavenly smile on his countenance, he breathed
his last. One thing is rather remarkable, and
seems to show as if angels themselves are not
sufficient to help in a dying hour ; when he

exclaimed, "The angels are coming!" he
turned to me as I sat by his dying pillow, and
asked, "Will Jesus come too?" I replied,
"Jesus is already here." Thus died this excellent young man in the 25th year of his age.
He died in the house of his elder brother, Mr.
M. B., a man of much respectability in the
world. For some time his kindness would
not suffer me to quit the family; and, being
thus detained, I took every opportunity of conversing with him on the subject of preparing to
meet his God. The circumstances were favourable to such conversations, and I soon found
his heart was open to conviction. The day
after his brother's interment, while reasoning
with him on the great truths of religion, and
the importance of enjoying God, the Spirit of
God rested upon us, his heart became deeply
contrite, and he expressed his readiness to covenant immediately to be the Lord's. When I
saw this I felt no hesitation in preaching to
him Jesus and the atonement. I urged him at
once to rest his guilty soul on the merits of
that blood which Christ had freely shed for the
remission of his sins. From the testimony of
the word of God, I assured him that his ransom
was already paid, and that the duty which re
mained for him was to believe with all his
heart. Soon he was enabled to believe with
his heart unto righteousness, and with his
mouth he made confession unto salvation. He
received the inward witness, and testified that
God, for Christ's sake, had pardoned all his

sins; and we rejoiced together with "joy unspeakable and full of glory" Knowing the
difficulties and dangers he would have to encounter, in holding fast his faith in Christ, I recommended him to take the first opportunity of
uniting with the people of God; to this he
readily assented, saying, "And you must remain with us till next Sunday, when I will go
to the class-meeting with you." Being then
about to leave home on some public business
in which he was engaged, he requested that I
would intercede with God in his behalf before
he went. "Pray," said he, "that my faith fail
not." So we kneeled down together before
God, and, under a blessed sense of his presence
we rendered to him the praise and glory due to
his name; and entreated him henceforth to
afford help to his servant in "time of need."
According to his promise the following Sabbath
he accompanied me to the class-meeting; and
great was the rejoicing which he occasioned,
while, with melting simplicity, he declared
what God had done for his soul. O Lord, do
thou grant that he may prove faithful to the
grace given; and may I meet him, as well as
his happy brother, with the sheep at thy right
hand! Amen, and amen.

Dec. 19th.—About two months back my soul
was drawn out to pray for a certain person. I
entered into a solemn covenant with God, that,
if he would bring her to the knowledge of the
truth, I would eternally praise him for it.
From that time to the present, I have pleaded

hard, and "travailed in birth," for her. Several times while at a throne of grace interceding for her, I felt a degree of assurance that the Lord would answer my prayers; but something like a doubt or fear following the impression, I still pleaded on for a clearer and stronger evidence of it. Last night, while praying for her, I felt more than usual on her behalf; and, not willing to give up, after praying nearly two hours, I said, "Lord, methinks I could stay all night praying for her, could I gain my suit." In a moment these words were applied, as if spoken, to my mind—"Thy prayer is heard, it shall be so." At the same moment, the circumstance of Cornelius was brought before me, that his prayers had come up as a memorial before God. Assured hereby that God would grant me the desire of my heart, I was constrained to shout, "Glory! glory!" and for two hours I was drawn out in such a heavenly strain, that I could say nothing else but, "Glory, glory, glory!" Now Isaac was not born immediately on God's making the promise, nor on Abraham's believing it; yet, according to his faith, it was at length done unto him. Lord, may not I stagger through unbelief! Speak the word only, and it shall be done. for thou art the same yesterday, to-day, and forever! I remember, a similar circumstance occurred in my experience about thirty years back, which is now as vivid and fresh in my mind as it was when it took place. My wife's sister lived with us. She had a cancer in her breast. It was cut out, but, being left

too long before the operation took place, it proved fatal. She was a moral young woman, but
had all her days lived a stranger to the new
birth. I frequently conversed with her about
the necessity of her experiencing this Divine
change, without any visible effect. One day,
while reflecting on the awful consequences of
her dying in an unconverted state, I thought
with myself, "How shall I ever be able to bear
the idea of a soul being lost out of my house!"
The reflection was too painful for me to endure!
In the barn where I was, I bowed down before
the Most High God; and, I believe if ever I
prayed in my life, I prayed then. Before I rose
from my knees, God gave me a Divine assurance
that he would save her. I said nothing to her
of this, but still exhorted her to be in earnest
with God for the salvation of her soul. Soon
after this occurrence, being on a distant part of
my farm, I received a message desiring me to
come to her immediately. I hastened with all
speed, and found the Spirit of God had graciously awakened her conscience, and that she
was now distressed with the burden of guilt
and sin. Before I left her bed-side it pleased
God to reveal his mercy to her broken heart;
and she could feelingly say, with the poet,

> "See there my Lord upon the tree!
> I hear, I feel he died for me."

Methinks I now see her, with her lifted hands,
and streaming eyes, steadfastly looking up like
dying Stephen. Shortly after this happy change,
it pleased the Lord to take her to himself.

CHAPTER VI.

FEB. 17th, 1826.—I SEE I have need to be truly humbled before God on account of my not always keeping faith in lively exercise. Though cleansed from sin this moment, through the efficacy of the all-purifying blood, this purity cannot be retained but by a momentary dependence on Christ.

> " Every moment, Lord, I want
> The merit of thy death."

Of the necessity of dependence on a Saviour's blood, none are so deeply conscious as those who feel its utmost efficacy.

MARCH 3rd.—My lameness and the infirmities of old age have generally confined me at home of late. In this state I have often thought of the words of Kempis. " Leave desire, and thou shalt find rest." I bless the Lord I feel no murmuring or complaining, but I have a longing desire to have my heart more enlarged and filled with God.

10th.—[Under this date he writes to his old correspondent, the local preacher, as follows :—] " I wish to know how your faith stands, and how you are getting on in the ministry; whether in fishing for souls you have of late been as successful as in former days. I trust the Lord is still with you, and does not leave you to go a warfare at your own charge. How does your little class thrive? Are all the members

alive to God? all healthy and strong? all fruitful branches in the heavenly vine? I am afraid
that both preachers and leaders too often lose
sight of the importance of full salvation. It
clearly appears to me, did I lose sight of this,
my faith would soon lose its edge. I hope you
have not lost your zeal or your love for precious souls; whenever this occurs, our usefulness is all over Never, I trust, will it be the
case with my dear brother T I can assure you,
that, since my first acquaintance with you, I
have not ceased day and night to remember
you at a throne of grace. May a double portion
of Elijah's spirit rest upon you!"

MAY 7th.—Thank God, I am preserved to
see another return of the day on which I was
born from above. Fifty-five years have now
expired since I was plucked as a brand from
the burning, and brought to taste the riches of
my Saviour's grace Giving glory to him, I find
he is still precious to my soul. Upon serious reflection, I think I do love him more than ever.
O what a blessed day has this been to me! In
meeting the class this morning, I could say,

> " My hope is full (O glorious hope!)
>   Of immortality!"

Not being able of late to visit my friends at a
distance, my time has chiefly been taken up in
writing to many inquiring souls on the deep
things of God; and, blessed be his holy name,
not altogether in vain. I have heard of five
who have entered into the glorious liberty of

the children of God. O my heavenly Father, I pray thee that thou wouldst keep them steadfast, till we all meet at the marriage-feast of the Lamb!

13th.—[The following is an extract from a letter under this date, addressed to the correspondent mentioned in the preceding page.—] "Should it please my Heavenly Father to remove my pain, and enable me to walk, I should rejoice once more to visit you; but I find my happiness consists in living in the will of God. I am thankful, if I cannot visit my friends, that I can write to them, and in this way the Lord has been pleased to make me successful in my attempts to do good. Never, I believe, did I feel a greater pleasure in the work of the Lord. Not that I have any thing to boast of; I am a poor hell-deserving sinner; but Christ is my Saviour, and he is my all in all. In reading over one of Mr. W. P. Burgess's sermons, I lately met with some remarks on a present and full salvation, which are much to the point. I think they set the subject in the clearest light I ever saw it; and because I know you are fond of 'strong meat,' I will give these to you.— He says, 'The great salvation of the Gospel is communicated moment by moment from above, and is apprehended by simple faith It is our duty every moment to expect, and our duty every moment to receive, a full salvation The act of faith must be repeated, to be ripened into a habit; and when faith in Christ is become the habitual and uniform disposition of the heart,

it will secure a constant participation in all the
blessings of the covenant. Our privilege is to
enter now into the enjoyment of the salvation
we need; and, having once apprehended, never
to lose it, but hold it fast unto the end.' O that
every preacher, and leader, and private member,
were living in the happy possession of this faith
and this salvation! How would it rejoice my
heart! Thank God, the heavenly flame is
spreading; but luke-warm and half-hearted professors are the greatest enemies God has in
stopping the progress of this glorious work.
Satan knows it is vain for him to put the ungodly and the wicked to do this; for they would
rather add oil to the flame, and make it spread
the faster; but they are those within the pale of
the church, whom the grand adversary employs
to arrest the progress of the work of holiness.
It appears, St. Paul had to do with some such
characters in his day: ' And I, brethren, could
not speak unto you as unto spiritual, but as
unto carnal, even as unto babes in Christ. I
have fed you with milk, and not with meat;
for hitherto ye were not able to bear it, neither
are ye now able.' I hope you are still the
same humble, loving, and zealous follower of
the bleeding Lamb, that you were in days and
months that are past; and no ways discouraged
in your work, if you do not immediately see all
the fruit you expected. We must always act
from a consciousness of duty, and then leave
the event to God."

15th.—I think it is the duty of those who

take the lead at the public means of grace, to
have their eye on such as appear to be under
the particular strivings of the Spirit; but in this
respect our people are not always on the look-
out as I could wish. I was at a prayer-meeting
a short time ago, when there was a young
man, in the back part of the chapel, who appeared somewhat affected. When the meeting
was over he went out, but our people did not seem
to regard it. I asked who he was, and where he
lived; and found him to be a young man with
whom I had some time before a conversation
about his soul. Two of the friends accompanied
me to his house; and I had not spoken many
words to him before he began to weep. When
I saw he was wounded, I told him there was a
Physician at hand, waiting to heal his soul,
We then knelt down; and while I was at prayer
with him, the Lord filled his soul with peace
and joy in believing. The next morning I rejoiced to find him at the class-meeting; and now
he bids fair for the kingdom.

28th.—I am just now returned from visiting
my dear friends at Ponsanooth, and many are
the blessed seasons which I have had with them.
Here I had the pleasure of meeting with one
who happened to be there on a visit, with
whom I once had some profitable intercourse.
She had now been a Methodist for some years,
but was still complaining of an evil heart of
unbelief. From the carnal mind, which is enmi-
ty against God, she manifested great anxiety to
be delivered, but was unacquainted with the way

of simple faith. While conversing with her on
the subject, God was pleased to enable her to
trust her all in his blessed hands, and he filled
her soul with unspeakable joy. " Never," said
she, "did I feel the like before." I advised her
to commit it to writing, which she promised
me she would do ; for want of this, many, I believe, let slip and lose the blessings of God.
May God have this handmaid in his holy keeping!

Sept. 6th.—[To his old correspondent he
wrote as follows.—[" I rejoice that you are still
so successful in seeking the good of souls. This
is the most important work in the world, as the
day that is swiftly approaching will fully make
manifest. ' They that be wise shall shine as the
brightness of the firmament; and they that turn
many to righteousness as the stars, for ever
and ever. It is not said that this great work
must be effected by any one particular means;
whether by preaching, exhorting, conversing,
or praying: No; but if they are God's in-
struments, they shall surely have their reward,
—if they ' turn many to righteousness.' May
the God of heaven make you, my dear son, one
of the happy number! And the hope of being
by your side in that day causes the silent tear
to flow down my cheeks while I write. God
has opened my faith's interior eye, and at this
moment so displays his Divine glory, that I
am overwhelmed, and lost in astonishment and
love. And shall we, from the rivers of his
grace, drink in endless pleasure? Glory, glory,

glory be to God, for such joys and prospects! At this time I may say, with Mr. Fletcher, 'God has laid an embargo on my body.' But I now leave desire; and find His will sweet. Great part of my time is taken up in writing to various friends, on the subject of inward holiness; and I cannot express a thousandth part of the pleasure I feel in being thus employed for God. I bless the Lord, I hear, many have lately found their way into that Fountain which cleanseth from all sin."

26th.—Not able for some months past to go abroad, as usual, to visit the friends of different societies, many, who reside at a distance, have visited me for the purpose of conversing on the subject of full salvation; and I trust some of them have been profited. I have a letter from one of them now before me; the writer says, " I believe I shall have cause to bless God eternally for directing me to you. Before that time I was like a ship without a rudder, beaten about by the pitiless storms of pride, self-will, and other temptations; but now, I feel I am redeemed from sin through the blood of Jesus Christ. Glory be to God for this fiee, this full salvation! I no longer contend with temptation: but, on the appearance of the tempter I instantly fly to the foot of the cross: where I immediately find redress, and obtain fresh strength for combat. I have had the pleasure of seeing several others enter into this happy liberty, while conversing with them on the subject."

FEB. 8, 1827.—I am now returned, after an
absence of sixteen weeks: which I have spent
chiefly among the societies in the St. Austell
circuit. The first three weeks I spent at Sticker;
where I saw the power of God displayed in
cleansing many sinful lepers. I lodged at the
house of Mr. and Mrs. Carthew: whose kindness, while I remained with them, I shall never
forget. Many came to converse with me on
the subject of perfect love: among other, W. B.,
who was a class-leader. After some conversation with him, he said, " I have long been
convinced of my want of purity of heart, and
have long sought the blessing in vain." I said
to him, " My brother, the cause of this is in
yourself: you have most probably been seeking
it by works and not by faith. By this you
will know whether you have been seeking it
by works or by faith: If by works, you have
always something to do; if by faith, why not
now ?" He saw at once where his error lay:
and in a short time was enabled to believe with
all his heart, and was so filled and overwhelmed
by the Spirit of God, that he could scarcely
support his body under it. His strength was
so affected by the joy of the Lord within him,
that he could not walk home without the assistance of a friend. From this place I went to
St. Austell, and met with a very kind reception
from Mr. Lawry, at whose kind and urgent
request I had come to visit the friends in the Circuit. Here I remained ten days, and beheld the
work of the Lord wonderfully prospering. My

next place was Charlestown, where I was glad·
ly received by Mr. Banks and family.   One
night, while meeting Mr. B.'s class, I was holding out the privileges of God's people; when
one young man present felt the refining fire go
through his heart, and bore a clear testimony
that God had cleansed him from all sin.   Two
others, while I was there, were also made partakers of the great salvation.   I have often observed that where God revives his blessed work
there is a power in operation which cleanses
believers, as well as convinces and converts sinners.   This I have more particularly remarked
in the revivals which I have witnessed of late.

   After I had remained at Charlestown eight
or ten days, a conveyance being kindly sent to
fetch me, I proceeded to Mevagissey, where I
was affectionately welcomed, and lodged, at the
house of Mr. James Dunn.   For about a week
I went from house to house in my usual way,
but nothing particular transpired in the way of
movement among the people ; at last I heard
that a young woman was convinced of sin, and
wished to see me.   While I was conversing
with her she wept much: and, at the prayer-
meeting in the chapel that night, she cried aloud
for mercy.   This was the beginning of the
revival at Mevagissey.   Afterwards we had
prayer-meetings every night for seven weeks:
and I witnessed some of the most remarkable
conversions I ever saw in my life, especially
among a number of old people.   One day
while musing on the wonderful works of the

Lord, these words came with much light and power, " Whoever shall call upon the name of the Lord, shall be saved." They had such an effect upon my mind, that for a moment I cannot tell how I felt; but something within suggested, " This day is come." In the course of that day, I had seen the truth of it exemplified in three different houses which I had been requested to visit. None of them who were the subjects of the change had been at the chapel. I asked one of them, " In what way did the Lord work on your mind?" She replied, " I was reading a Hymn; and when I came to these words.

' I the chief of sinners am,
    But Jesus died for me ;'

I turned over these words in my mind again and again, 'Jesus died for me! Jesus died for me!' I then felt a desire to pray: but, while on my knees, my husband came in, and I was ashamed; when he went out I fell on my knees again, and told the Lord, I never would rise more till my soul was set at liberty." Soon the Lord gave her the desire of her heart.

" No matter how dull the scholar whom He
Takes into his school and gives him to see;
A wonderful fashion of teaching he hath,
And wise to salvation he makes us through faith."

There were several converted who had been in the habit of attending the Calvinist chapel: this made no small stir among them. One of

these sent for me to come and converse with her.
I knew not what place of worship she attended, and therefore at once came to the point
with her, and asked what she wanted: she immediately began to exclaim, "What a sinner I
have been!"   Seeing she was wounded by the
Spirit, I endeavoured to lead her to the Physician without delay; and as soon as I had explained the way of faith to her, the Lord set her
soul at liberty.   Tears of joy streamed from
her eyes, and gratitude overflowed her heart,
We then knelt down together, and gave God
the glory.   This was soon spread through the
town: and the Calvinist minister, having heard
that I had robbed his church, came to the
woman to inquire what I had said to her.   She
replied, " Sir, I am not a member of your church
nor ever was: so that you have not suffered any
great loss: and as to the man you allude to, he
never inquired what place of worship I attended,
but showed the way to come to Christ, in order
to be happy, and now I know I am a new creature."   This surprised him: and he wondered
how the work could be done so soon.   The
woman replied, "I was made happy in five
minutes after he explained to me the plan of
salvation by faith.   Though I sat under your
ministry for some time, you have never shown
me the way to happiness by believing in Christ."
    I was sent for by another; when I came, she
was in a despairing state, writing bitter things
against herself, and fearing she was one of the
reprobates.   I said, " Is there no balm in Gilead,

no Physician there, no Saviour now to save sinners?" I then exhorted her to look to Jesus, who had verily shed his blood for her, and exercise faith in the atonement. In a few minutes her load of guilt was removed, and she was filled with peace and joy in believing. Soon after this she gave up her seat in the Calvinist chapel, and regularly attended ours; as did several others.

One day I called to see an aged woman who had met in class for thirty years: and while I was telling her of the danger of resting satisfied without the evidence of her acceptance in the Belóved, and the impossibility of getting to heaven without being born again, she was pricked to the heart, and fell on her knees, and began to cry for mercy. Her prayer was, "Lord, save me from dropping into hell!" In her loud and vehement cries for mercy, my voice was soon lost. It was affecting to see and hear her. daughter: who, though not possessed of religion herself, said, "O my dear mother, hold out, hold out!" The Lord dealt very graciously with her, and soon granted her the " knowledge of salvation by the remission of her sins." Her face shone as it had been the face of an angel. and she went round the room, clapping her hands, and shouting the praises of God; apparently with all the activity of a girl of fifteen, although she was then fourscore.

The blessed influence so generally rested upon the minds of the people, that cries for mercy were frequently heard in the houses as we

walked the streets.   It was thought by the
elders, that such a revival had never before been
witnessed at Mevagissey.   Upwards of one
hundred and fifty were brought to the Lord, besides a great number of children.   While I was
there, I was often led to think whether the Lord
did ever more strikingly bless my feeble endeavours.   The eight weeks I was with them,
I could seldom get to bed before one in the
morning; and sometimes I was called again before breakfast to visit persons in distress.   But
the Lord gave me strength according to my day.

Among the aged who were converted, there
were two brothers, who were brought in about
the same time; one was sixty-three, and the
other in his sixty-seventh year.   The wife of
the elder brother had long been a pious member of the society; he was her persecutor, and
seldom or never attended the house of God.
The Lord found him out in his dwelling; and,
hearing that he had begun to pray, I was requested to visit him   I had not long conversed
with him, before he was more deeply awakened,
and began to cry aloud for mercy   After praying with him I left him.   In the evening I
called on him again; and while I was pointing
him to the Lamb of God that taketh away the
sin of the world, God revealed his mercy to his
soul, and he cried out, " My burden is gone,
the Lord has pardoned all my sins: Glory, glory,
be to his name!" I saw him several times afterwards, and found his confidence unshaken; and
what is rather remarkable, he told me he could

never sing before, but now he was singing, and praising God all day long.

May 7th.—Another year of my spiritual life is rolled away. Blessed be God, my face is still Zionward, and I am happy in a Saviour's love! O what return shall I make to my God for all his benefits towards me? I would for ever

> " Fall at his feet, and the story repeat,
> And the Lover of sinners adore."

10th.—I would not undervalue the grace which I have already received, because nothing is more likely to hinder the soul's progress in holiness; but O, how clearly do I see I could not stand acquitted before God, one moment, without the atonement! After fifty-six years spent in the service of God, I find I have nothing to keep my soul in motion, but faith in the blood of Christ. Without this, I should at once be as a ship becalmed. Glory be to God for precious blood, and precious faith! I am much delighted with Mr. W. P. Burgess's views of the atonement. In one of his excellent sermons, he observes: "The merit and atonement of the Saviour are the price by which all the blessings of the new covenant may be purchased,—they constitute a full equivalent; for their value is inestimable and infinite. Whoever, therefore, approaches the footstool of Jehovah, trusting solely in the merit and atonement of Christ, pays down the full price for every blessing that he claims, and may expect it on the ground of justice. If, in our dealing

with our fellow-creatures, we bring a full equivalent in our hands, and pay down a fair price
for any commodity which we need, it would be
injustice to withhold it: Even so when we ask
in the name of Jesus, for full redemption and
entire purity; justice requires that our prayers
should be heard, and our petitions granted.
So that if God be just, he will not only pardon
our sin, but cleanse us from all unrighteousness. Thus, then, we see the justice of God,
in furnishing us with strong encouragement,
and emboldening us to ask and receive every
blessing purchased for us by the adorable Saviour." There is much included in these remarks, and they deserve to be well pondered
in the heart of every believer. On the necessity of having constant recourse to the blood
of sprinkling, he remarks, (in perfect accordance with my views and experience,) " Even
when we are cleansed from all the pollution of
sin, we shall be sensible of numberless frailties
and deficiencies, which will render it necessary for us continually to have recourse to the
atoning blood of Jesus ; and our best services
are so imperfect and unworthy, that. were they
not offered in the name of Christ, and on the
ground of his all-availing sacrifice, they could
by no means be acceptable to God. But, while
we live in the constant exercise of faith, em-
bracing the whole record that God has given
concerning his Son, we shall have constant experience of the efficacy of the Redeemer's
blood, and shall from moment to moment enjoy

a complete salvation from sin. Nothing short of this comes up to the standard of apostolical experience; and nothing short of this should ever satisfy us." May these glorious truths be more and more known and felt, among all the members of Christ's church!

14th.—Much of my time has of late been taken up in answering letters: Since my first attempt at writing, I was never so busily employed in this way. In three weeks, I have written twenty-five letters. My visit to the St. Austell circuit, especially to Mevagissey, has greatly added to the list of my correspondents. I feel the employment delightful; it is rendered a very great blessing to my own soul.

JUNE 16th.—For many years, the church of God in this parish had remained in a barren and winter state; but, blessed be the Lord, he has lately been pouring out his Holy Spirit upon us, both at Flushing and at Mylor Bridge! Many have been awakened and converted from the error of their ways; and what adds to the joy is, that some of the branches of my own family are among the happy number. My daughter's son, William Rundle, is one of them: For many long years had I prayed for him: He is truly converted, and has a zeal about him, which promises to make him useful. May God preserve him, and keep him steadfast unto the end!

JULY 25th.—Since I wrote in my journal, under the above date, a solemn and most unexpected change has taken place in the family.

My dear grandson, William Rundle, so recently
brought to God, and so hopeful in the church,
has been snatched away from us by the hand of
death. He was ill only a very short time; but,
glory be to God, he died in sure and certain
hope of a glorious resurrection to eternal life!
How merciful are the dispensations of God!
His conversion took place about six weeks
before his removal from hence. He did not
long groan under the burden of guilt, and his
evidence of pardon and adoption was very clear.
At a prayer-meeting, two or three weeks before
his death, he received an overwhelming manifestation of the Spirit, in which every doubt and
fear were utterly put to flight. He attended his
class, a few days before his death, and seemed
to be filled with unspeakable joy: "My soul,"
says he, "is like a ship in full sail on the bound
less ocean of redeeming love." His death was
occasioned by the rupture of a blood vessel. In
all the conflict, he was perfectly tranquil and
serene; fear was not permitted to come near
him. This was the more striking, because, in
every little indisposition before, he was much
alarmed and distressed at the thought of death.
But now he seemed at once ready-winged for
the flight. To his father, who had fondly hoped
that he would be the help and comfort of his
advancing years, he said, "Father, you can do
very well without me; and I would rather die
than live." The Lord, whom he had so heartily
chosen for his portion in the vigour of health,
was now his abundant support in the struggle

of pain and death. Just before be expired, he said to me, " I used to be struck with terror at the thought of dying, but now I can meet death with a smile." He died in his nineteenth year. When at a neighbouring place of worship the Sunday preceding his death, it was remarked by some who knew him, what a fine, healthy, blooming youth he appeared. What a lesson is this to all who seek their happiness in this world! Mr. Hayman, this evening, applied the solemn event, by preaching to a crowded congregation, from 1 Samuel xx 3, " There is but a step between me and death."

Nov. 27th.—I have just received an affectionate letter from Mr. Lawry, in which he urges me to pay another visit to the friends in the St Austell circuit. He says my warm friends at Mevagissey propose to man a large boat, and send it to Flushing for me, that my lameness may be no obstacle to my visiting them. In the dealings of the Lord with me, with respect to my bodily health, there is something remarkable. Last year, about this time, I was at Sticker, St. Austell, &c., in the midst of various revivals, and felt but very little fatigue, or pain, or feebleness, from all the labours I engaged in. For ten months after this, I was chiefly confined at home, by weakness, lameness, and the various accumulating infirmities of age: I could not walk without much pain and difficulty; but now, within the last three or four weeks, the Lord has in a great measure removed all my bodily ailments. Bless the Lord,

O my soul, and forget not all his benefits!
Last night, I had a wonderful display of the
Divine goodness and mercy; such a plunge,
indeed, in the ocean of God's love, as I thought
exceeded all I ever before experienced.   It was
such a weight of glory—such an overwhelming sense of the Divine presence, that I seemed
lost in wonder, love, and praise!   My happy spirit
appeared to mingle with the glorified throng,
around the throne of God.   It seemed to me
there was but a very thin partition between me
and the world of glorified spirits.   I thought I
could sweetly join with them in singing, "Unto
Him who hath loved us, and washed us from
our sins in His own blood, and made us kings
and priests,—to Him be glory for ever and
ever!   Amen."

JAN. 11th, 1828.—I am just now returned,
after a tour of eight weeks among the different
societies at Sticker, St. Austell, Charlestown,
Mevagissey, &c.   I rejoiced to find that the
numerous young converts stand exceedingly
well.   At the quarterly-meeting, held at St.
Austell, we had one of the best love-feasts I
ever attended.   The testimonies borne to the
reality and blessedness of the doctrine and experience of purity of heart, exceeded every
thing of the kind I had before witnessed.
While at Mevagissey, a young woman came to
me at Capt. Dunn's, and said her mother wished to speak with me.   I went to the house, and
found she had been a regular hearer at the Independent chapel.   On my inquiring what had

induced her to send for me, she said, "Her
mind was so greatly oppressed by the burden of
grief and sin, that she knew not what to do."
I requested that a Bible might be given to me;
and while I was pointing her to those portions
which were suitable to her state, and explaining to her the privilege which the Gospel holds
out to penitents, God was pleased to reveal himself to her, and she found liberty through the
blood of the Lamb.   With tears of joy running
down her cheeks, she cried out, "I will now
go to a class-meeting."   Before I left the place,
I had the pleasure of meeting her there twice;
May I also meet her in "the general assembly
and church of the first-born!"   Mrs. R., of St.
Austell, mentioned to me a person who was
then lying very ill, and in a despairing state of
mind.   I said I should wish to see her.   When
I was conducted to her bedside, I inquired the
state of her mind: She, said, "I am afraid I
shall be a lost soul."   I reproved her for enter-
taining such hard thoughts of God; and told her
she ought not to do it.   "God," said I, "is a
God of love, and Jesus hath died to save you."
I then showed her how she was to receive
Christ, by believing the precious promises God
had made to penitents; and, while I was in
structing and encouraging her to trust in the
atoning Saviour, God revealed his mercy to her
sorrowful mind, and set her soul at liberty from
the grievous bondage under which she groaned.
Feeling the blessed deliverance the Lord had
wrought out for her, she lifted up her eyes and
hands to heaven, and joyfully exclaimed,—

" Now I can tell to all around,
    What a dear Saviour I have found."

The load of guilt being removed, filial confidence filled her heart; and therefore, in the true
spirit of Christian resignation, she said, " I can
now give up my children and all into the hands
of the Lord."　After this I visited her several
times, and always found her in the same com-
fortable state of mind.

Oct. 11th —Through the great goodness
and mercy of God I am now returned from a
tour of nearly six months.　The first three
weeks after I left home, I spent with my various friends at Camborne.　Thence I went
once more to see my old friends at Mousehole;
whom I had not visited for nearly five years.
When I arrived, the life and power of religion
seemed to be, comparatively, at rather a low
ebb among them : And what increased the
gloomy appearance was, some little unpleasant
things had just before occurred in the church,
which contributed to estrange some of their
hearts one from another.　I used my humble
endeavours to remove stumbling-blocks, and
unite them all together in Christian love, and
to stir them up to pray for a revival of God's
blessed work.　During the first week we
saw no particular displays of the quickening
power of the Spirit in any of the means of grace.
On the following Tuesday we changed the
house at which the usual prayer-meeting was
held · We had it at a friends Wallis's, instead of
friend Jeffry's; and here we first felt the en-

couraging tokens that God was about to afford
gracious answers to our prayers. It was published, that the following night the meeting
would be held in the chapel. There was an
increased attendance, and I exhorted the friends
to plead hard with God, and expect an outpour-
ing of the Spirit After this meeting, a general
concern took place in the minds of the people.
The prayer-meetings were crowded by hundreds of attendants, and all the inquiry was,
" What must I do to be saved ?" Some of the
most hardened sinners were cut to the heart,
and cried aloud for mercy; and the work of
God went forward with mighty power. This
extraordinary visitation from above continued
four months; and the " revival at Mousehole,"
resounded far and near Vast numbers, moved
by different motives, came from a distance of
many miles, to see the wonderful works of God;
and not a few of the strangers who came from
curiosity, were converted in the chapel at
Mousehole; and, like the eunuch, were found
on their road home going on their way rejoic
ing. Thus the heavenly fire was carried to
different villages and societies in the Circuit;
and the thanksgiving of many redounded to the
glory of God. This revival was carried on in
the best order I ever saw one in my life From
the best information I could get, I think about
two hundred have joined the society; and I
have good reason to hope, that by far the greater part of them have not only been awakened,
but have been also brought to experience a clear

sense of God's pardoning mercy. Some of
them, probably, will prove unstable; but that I
shall meet many of them in the great day, with
the sheep at God's right hand, I have no doubt.
Mousehole now appears like a new town; instead of scores of men of different ages standing
in groups on the cliff, talking about worldly
things, and idling away the Sabbath, as they
used to do; there are now scarcely any but
such as seem to " remember the Lord's day to
keep it holy." It has been a custom at this
place, from time immemorial, for men, women,
and children, to go out to the island on Mid-
summer-day; but this year a subject of greater
importance so occupied their attention, that not
a single individual was seen there on the occasion. Even the children were also so impressed
with seriousness, that not one of them would
kindle a bonfire on Midsummer-eve. These
little facts serve to show what a universal seriousness pervaded all ages and classes. When
the revival took place, and for some time afterwards, there was very little fish taken, and consequently much poverty prevailing; but I heard
no complaining among them. The wonders of
the Lord, daily displayed in the conviction and
conversion of sinners, seemed to engross nearly
the whole conversation of the place. During
the four months that I was with them, there
were very few houses in Mousehole but I visited them from religious motives; and very few
men, women, or children but I conversed
with them on the necessity of preparing to

meet God The effect of this on their minds
will be known only in that day, when God
shall assemble all nations, and "the judgment shall be set, and the books shall be
opened." So happily did my time pass away
while actively employed in this good work,
that four months appeared only as four days.
It was astonishing to all the friends, as well as
to myself, how the Lord supported my strength.
Day and night I was employed in visiting, in-
structing, and exhorting; and in praying with
the distressed, both in their own houses and in
the chapel. Truly I found verified, in my experience, the truth of that promise, "As thy
days thy strength shall be." That I should, at
the advanced age of seventy-nine, be enabled to
endure such a continuance of extraordinary toil
and labour, is surely by the Lord's special
help and goodness. I believe God never more
visibly owned my poor efforts than he has in
this blessed revival in my native place and
society O the boundless mercy of my heavenly Father to unworthy me! He has saved me
and kept me in his ways these fifty-seven years;
he has given me favour in the eyes of the people in every place, and he has also given me
spiritual children, some of whom are landed
safe on the eternal shore, and others are on their
way to glory "Bless the Lord, O my soul,
and forget not all his benefits!" O my Saviour,
cheerfully do I ascribe to thy name all the honour and the praise!

20th.—Yesterday two persons came from

Falmouth to converse on the subject of full salvation. A few days before God had very graciously visited them, and revealed to their
souls much heavenly light on the subject, but
they said they wanted to be more established
in the truth. They appeared full of simplicity and holy resolution, longing to be Christians according to the measure of God's word.
Our interview was profitable: They declared
that all their scruples were removed; and they
returned home rejoicing, giving glory to Him
to whom alone it is due. "When Jesus is our
peace, strength, righteousness, food, salvation,
and our all, we are penetrated with the consciousness of it; Without this feeling we should
never rest; nor ever think we have it strong
enough. This it is to 'keep the faith.' "

27th.—Of late I have felt the truth of the
following remarks :—" Pain and sickness follow ease and health in quick succession. But
amidst all the possible changes of this life,
Christ is a rock. To see him by faith, to lay
hold of him, to rely upon him, to live upon
him,—this is a refuge from the storm, a shadow
from the heat. Jesus Christ! What a gift;
a gift of free grace! And for whom? For
me, a sinner; and, as such, I believe in his
name." I always feel my heart refreshed when
talking, or writing, or thinking of Jesus. To
meditate on the glories that compose his adorable name, is food to my soul. O Jesus,
teach me to know more of thy infinite and unsearchable riches, thou incarnate Deity, that I

may love thee with a never-ceasing love, and serve thee with increasing zeal till thou bring-est me to thy glory! Amen.

30th.—I have just now received a long and well-written letter from one of my children in the Gospel. The dealings of the Lord towards his creatures are often very singular. We have an instance of this, exemplified in the case of the writer of this letter. I have already mentioned my visiting from house to house, during the revival at Mousehole; In my calling on different families, I happened to enter a friend's house where she was. Desirous of shunning an interview with me, she fled by the back-door. On seeing this, I expressed my regret, and my inclination to follow her. I was told it would be useless, as I could not over-take her; but, on stepping to the front-door I saw her running into a neighbour's house. Unwilling that satan should triumph in obtain-ing a victory that way, I went to the house after her. When she saw me approaching, she ran up stairs. I did not think it proper to pur-sue her any farther; but knowing she was within the hearing of my voice, though I could not see her, I delivered to her my message from below stairs. And having done so, I closed my remarks, by saying, "Remember, God says, 'Except you repent, you must perish.' I have now faithfully warned you of your dan ger, and you must meet me at the bar of God, to give account of the use you make of it." As she did not make her appearance, I with-

16

drew, and left her to her own reflections. Before the close of the day, it was reported that E. T. was under the awakening influence of the Spirit of God. The next morning, I went to her own house to inquire after her. No longer now disposed to shun me, she came down stairs bitterly weeping, because she had so long and grievously sinned against God. "Every word," said she, "that you addressed to me yesterday went to my heart, though I could not see you; and such an impression was thereby made upon my mind, as I could not shake off." Finding that she was now of a broken and a contrite spirit, I offered her Christ as a present Saviour; and she was soon enabled to believe with her heart unto righteousness, and rejoice in the God of her salvation She now says in her letter,— " I feel I am a sinner saved by grace; and my prayer is, that I may be kept faithful, till my heavenly Father shall gather me home. While memory lasts, I hope never to forget the first interview I had with you. O how sweet the recollection of that happy morning when I first felt the Saviour's pardoning blood applied!"

Nov. 14th.—For several weeks past, I have been confined at home by rheumatism, and have been chiefly employed in writing letters. Though labouring under much pain and weakness, I have lately written eleven letters tc different friends, and have found it a sweet occupation of my time from d y to day. At times I am so feeble, that I seem ready to sink into the dust; but just now while I was thinking on the poor condition of my shattered frame, suddenly the thought occurred, " Yet Jesus deigns to dwell in it." I was struck with wonder and amazement at such infinite condescension, to think that the God of heaven should dwell in such a mean house of clay. While I was thus indulging a moment's reflection, these words were applied : " Ye are the temples of the living God." O what a lift did this give my faith, and what a heavenly intercourse did it open between God and my soul !

24th.—I have just sent off a packet of letters to Mousehole : May the blessing of God accompany them, and render them useful ! One day while I was contemplating the riches of Divine grace, and the greatness of that salvation which Christ has purchased for sinners, this passage was brought to my mind with uncommon life and power : " Wherefore he is able to save unto the uttermost them that come unto God by him, seeing he ever liveth to make intercession for them." I cannot describe what I felt when I attempted to fathom the meaning of the word "uttermost." Surely, thought I, it must at least include salvation from all sin. And when I thought on these words, "ever liveth to make intercession for them," I saw enough in them to make my very heart leap for joy. O how did this endear the priesthood of Christ to my soul ! Nor did I ever feel I needed the intercession of Christ more than at the present moment. Such is the sight and sense which I have of my manifold weaknesses and little returns of gratitude to the Author of all my mercies, that I feel I have no footing but in the cross of Christ. But this is the mystery of faith, that while I have on one hand a painful consciousness of my deserts as a sinner, I have on the other, at the same moment, "boldness to enter into the holiest by the blood of Jesus." "Blessed is the man to whom the Lord imputeth not sin." I thank God through Jesus Christ He is "the way, the truth, and the life:" We must ever bear in mind, that we can only be saved unto the uttermost while we "come unto God by him."

Dec. 10th.—[Under this date he wrote to a class-leader at Mousehole: The following is an extract of the letter:—] "When I removed from you and my other dear friends at happy, happy Mousehole, I was like one brought into a different atmosphere. I then heard but little of Jesus Christ, and his wondrous doings for poor sinners O that our people felt more of the power of religion, and were better acquainted with the nature of living Gospel faith! Many of those who are most sincere do not understand the appropriating act of faith. There are some remarks in Mr. Fletcher's letter to Mr. Vaughan, which have been rendered a great blessing to me and to many others. He says,—'Fight the good fight of faith; break through all temptations, dejections, wanderings, worldly thoughts, through all unprofitable companions, and the backwardness of an unbelieving heart and carnal mind: Struggle, I say, till

you touch Jesus, and feel healing, comforting
virtue proceeding from him ; and when you
know clearly the way to him, repeat the touch
till you find he lives in you by the powerful
operation of his loving Spirit. Then you will
say with St. Paul, ' I live the life of God, yet
not I, but Christ who liveth in me.' I rejoice
that you inquire where Christ maketh his flock
to rest at noon; the rest from the guilt and
power of sin you will find only in inward holiness . And this I apprehend to consist in what
St. Paul calls, 'the kingdom of God ' Righteousness, which excludes all guilt; peace, which
banishes all fear that hath torment; and joy,
which can no more subsist with doubts, anxiety,
and unstableness of mind, than light can subsist
with darkness. That there is a state, wherein
this kingdom is set up, firmly set up in the heart,
you may see from our Lord's sermon on the
mount; by his priestly prayer in St. John; by
the epistles of that apostle, and by various parts
of the epistles of St. Paul and St. James. To
aim aright at this liberty of children of God,
requires a continual acting of faith ; of a naked
faith, independent of all feelings, in a naked
promise; such as: 'The Son of God was manifested to destroy the works of the devil;' ' The
law of the Spirit of life in Christ Jesus hath made
me free from the law of sin and death;' 'I can do
all things through Christ, who strengtheneth me,'
By a naked faith in a naked promise, I do not mean
a bare assent that God is faithful, and that such
a promise in the book of God may be fulfilled to
me; but a bold, hearty, steady venturing of my

soul, body, and spirit upon the truth of the promise, with an appropriating act : 'It is mine,
because I am a sinner, and am determined to
believe, come what will.' Here you must shut
the eye of carnal reason, and stop the ear of the
mind, to the reasonings of the serpent, which,
were you to listen to him, would be endless,
and would soon draw you out of the simple
way of faith, by which we are both justified
and sanctified You must also remember, that
it is your privilege to go to Christ by such a
faith now, and every succeeding moment; and
that you are to bring nothing but a careless, distracted, tossed, hardened heart ; just such a one
as you have now. Here lies the grand mistake of many poor, miserable, but precious,
souls : 'They are afraid to believe, lest it should
be presumption; because they have not yet comfort, joy, love,' &c ; not considering that this is
to look for the fruit before the tree is planted.
Beware, then, of looking for any grace previous
to believing —Now, my brother, you have here
my thoughts upon this subject; this self-despe-
rate, appropriating act of faith, which Mr.
Fletcher and Mr. Wesley wrote so largely
upon For my part, I think I shall never sufficiently praise God for putting their Works
into my hands. That Mr. Wesley's views
were exactly the same as Mr Fletcher's, is
plain from this verse of one of his hymns :—

'In hope against all human hope,
  Self-desp'rate, I believe;
Thy quick'ning word shall raise me up,
  Thou shalt the Spirit give.'

It must be acknowledged, this language is strong; and I know it has frightened many, perhaps, sincere penitents; but it is no more than what is included in the word 'believing;' and is the direct and simple way to pardon and purity."

22nd.—[Under this date my father wrote, in answer to a letter which he had received from a highly respected friend and brother at Mousehole; in which, after giving him a pleasing account of the further advancement of the work of God in the society, mention is made of the remarkable circumstance of a pious and aged member having very confidently asserted that one evening, while worshipping in the chapel, he heard supernatural music of the most melodious kind, proceeding, as he thought, from that part of the leaders' pew, which was so long and so regularly occupied by those two extraordinary men of God, Benedict Carvosso and Richard Trewavas, sen. This was a fact which highly accorded with my father's strong views of invisible realities; as it will be perceived by the use he makes of it in the following extract from his letter —] " I had a blessed time last night while pleading with the Lord for those who yet remain unconverted among you at Mousehole. I felt such love for them, that I could not give up till my heart dissolved with compassion, and my eyes overflowed with tears. Such a love to them I never felt before, nor can language describe it; but I thought of Jesus weeping over Jerusalem. I seemed to be carried away till I was found among you, with Jesus in the midst of us. O what a glorious visitation has Mousehole lately had! I do not wonder at what you mention about friend R. having heard heavenly music; for our Lord tells us, 'There is joy in the presence of the angels of God over one sinner that repenteth.' Now I have thought, if there be joy among the angels on account of one sinner's repentance, what must be their joy over the two hundred whose conversion you have witnessed during the last few months. St. Paul, speaking on this head, says, 'Are they not all ministering spirits, sent forth to minister unto those who shall be heirs of salvation?' And, at the birth of Christ, these heavenly messengers were employed: 'And the angel said, Fear not, for behold I bring you glad tidings of great joy, which shall be unto all people. And suddenly there was with the angel a multitude of the heavenly host, praising God,' &c. In further confirmation of this doctrine, I may add what is said of the death of Lazarus: 'And it came to pass that the beggar died, and was carried by the angels to Abraham's bosom.' I remember, about fifty years back, I heard something myself of the same nature as what friend R. mentions. I allude to Jane Hosking, who died at Trungle. She expired in my brother's arms, saying to him, as her last words, 'They are come, they are come!' and died in a moment. I was in the adjoining field at the time, and just at that instant I heard the most delightful singing in the air I ever heard in my life. O what a wonderful sight does your society now present; and what an overthrow has satan's kingdom had in the last eight or nine months! A great many of these precious souls, who have now joined God's people, spent last Christmas in ' rioting and drunkeness, chambering and wantonness, strife and envying;' but now they can say, with the poet, from happy, heart-felt experience,—

' Suffice that, for the season past,
    Hell's horrid language fill'd our tongues:
We all thy words behind us cast,
    And lewdly sang the drunkards' songs.

' But, O the power of grace divine !
    In hymns we now our voices raise ;
Loudly in strange hosannahs join,
    And blasphemies are turned to praise.' "

CHAPTER VII.

JAN. 6th, 1829.—THE following is an extract from a letter just received from one of the young converts at Mousehole. He is a young man in whom there is pleasing promise of future use-fulness: " Shortly after I obtained mercy by faith in Christ Jesus," he observes, " I discover ed the need of a still deeper work of grace in my soul. I felt the carnal mind was not des-troyed: my heart seemed full of evil; ' a cage of every unclean bird ;' and often it betrayed me into bondage. But, with David, I earnestly cried, ' Create in me a clean heart, O God !' I

longed to have all my inward enemies destroyed, and to be fully renewed in the image of
my Saviour. And, glory, glory be to God! on
Sunday morning, the 7th of September last,
while engaged with the Lord in secret, pleading the promises of sanctification, I felt faith
suddenly spring up in my heart; my soul was
abundantly blessed, and I was enabled to believe
the work was done; yet was my faith not so
strong as I could wish:—I want a more powerful witness. I rose from my knees, and went
to my class-meeting fully resolved to tell what
God had done for my soul; and, glory be to
His holy name, I was not long there before I
was so completely overwhelmed by the Divine
presence and joy, that, for a while, I was deprived of the power of speech or motion. Truly
it was the

> ' Speechless awe that dares not move,
> And all the silent heaven of love.'

Since that period, blessed be God, the enemy
has not been able to prevail, for one moment, to
shake my confidence in that blood which
cleanseth from all sin "

MARCH 21st.—After being confined at home
by feebleness and pain for some months, I paid
a visit to my dear friends at Ponsanooth; and
was happy to find the work of God in such a
prosperous state amongst them. By Mr.
Lawry's kind and pressing request I went to
Gwennap, where the good work is also advancing. I lodged at Mr. J. Mitchell's, and was

most kindly received by him and his excellent
family; among whom, I trust, my humble
efforts were not wholly in vain Some appeared
to receive the seed into good ground, may
it be manifest in the last day, that the good impressions were ripened unto perfection !

22nd —I have now entered my eightieth
year. O the mercies of God still richly displayed towards me all flowing through the
kind intercession of my Advocate at God's
right hand !

> " My dying Saviour and my God !
>   Fountain for guilt and sin !
> Sprinkle me ever with thy blood,
>   And cleanse and keep me clean."

I am conscious I can form no language of
my own adequate to this, to express my views,
and thoughts, and feelings respecting the atonement.   This is a favourite hymn of mine, and
has often proved a blessing to my soul. I have
many times thought, that did I possess the
talents of Mr. Wesley, I should preach and
write just as he did My views of the salvation of the Gospel, and of the atonement, correspond exactly with his May I live this year,
which I have entered in so heavenly a frame
of mind, more to the glory of God than any
former year of my life !

June 28th —I am now returned from a tour
of eleven weeks, during which I have visited
the societies at Mousehole, Penzance, Helston,
Mullion, &c. It rejoiced my heart to find the

young converts standing so well at Mousehole.
Many had been added in my absence, and several more souls were gathering in all the time I
was with them. On the day I left, I had the
pleasure of seeing three converted to God. One
of the conversions, which I witnessed while I
was there, was such an instance of the mercy
and power of God, to save unto the uttermost,
as I have scarcely ever met with. On the preceding day, which was the Sabbath, he was in
a state of continued intoxication. When his
wife returned from the chapel in the evening,
where she had received her quarterly ticket
from the preacher, not finding him in his own
house, she sought him elsewhere, and found
him drunk at a public-house. Seeing him in
such a place, and in such a state, on the Lord's
day, she could not forbear talking faithfully to
him on the great impropriety and sinfulness of
his conduct. However ill-timed this might
appear to some, it was a word in season to him;
for it pleased God to fasten the reproof on his
conscience. And so powerfully did the Spirit
of God arrest him, that, to the astonishment of
all who beheld him, the fumes of the intoxi-
cating liquor, which he had drank so plentifully, left him entirely, in a few minutes. His
mind was now awake to the evil of drunkenness,
and he said to the person who kept the inn, that,
so long as he lived, he would taste no more
strong liquor. He returned home in an agony
of mind; and his wife told me he never slept a
moment during the night. Early in the morning,

I received a message, requesting me to visit him. I found him in deep anguish of soul, bewailing his manifold and great sins against his God. After conversing with him for some time, I advised him to go into his chamber, and again pour out his soul to the God of mercy in secret prayer. After a short time I went to his house again, and desired his wife to call him out of his room, as I wished to pray with him. The load of his guilt was overwhelming; but I was conscious, if I could only get him to look to the atonement, his sins would be no barrier to his justification. When I had directed him to look to that suffering Saviour who had borne his sins in his own body on the tree, we fell on our knees; and while I was engaged in fervent and mighty prayer in his behalf, the Lord turned his darkness into light, and his hell to heaven. He now stretched out his hands heavenward, and cried out,

"I'll praise my Maker while I've breath!"

He has since held on his way steadily and joyfully, and is a wonder unto many. May God grant that I may at last meet him and his dear wife,—to whom the Lord was pleased also to make me useful,—safe lodged among the jewels of the kingdom above!

Another interesting and rather remarkable conversion occurred, in which, I think, the short-sightedness of Satan is very clear. One of the members of the society being forbidden by her husband, in a very peremptory manner, from

attending class-meeting that day; she meekly
submitted, and retired to her chamber to spend
the time in prayer. Without being aware that
her unkind and ungodly husband was within
hearing, she was drawn to pour out her soul to
God very earnestly in his behalf. This was
more than even his hard heart could bear; it
touched a tender string, and the Lord fastened it
as a nail in a sure place. He became thoroughly
and deeply awakened to his lost estate; and so
overwhelmed was he with a sense of his misery,
that his son came to me with great speed, requesting that I would go with him, because—
" Father was so distressed about his soul, he was
not able to go to sea" I went to him, and
talked to him, and prayed with him for about
two hours, till my bodily strength was quite
spent out; and I was obliged to retire to a
friend's house and lie down to take a little rest.
When I awoke from a short sleep, these words
came with light and power; " The blood of Jesus
Christ, his Son, cleanseth us from all sin " Knowing for what purpose they were given, I replied
in a moment, " This will do ;" and instantly putting on the part of my dress which I had laid
aside, I hastened to the house of the penitent.
He was still on his knees. I told him I
had a proper discharge for him from the King
himself; and put him to read the words with his
own eyes God applied to his broken heart the
healing balm contained in this precious portion
of his word; and the contrite sinner, believing
whit all his heart, and lifting up his hands and

eyes to heaven, cried out, " Glory be to God,
Jesus hath died for me!" He afterwards said to
me, " I have never entered the chapel doors
these twelve years : and forty-four years have I
lived in the world, and knew nothing of my God
till this day." Now I think satan would not have
shown much of the serpent, in hindering the
woman from going to class-meeting, if he could
have foreseen that that circumstance would have
occasioned the loss of one of his most faithful
servants

July 17th.—In the following remark, there
is much that is worthy of observation by those
who wish to walk with God :—" Without recollection God's voice cannot be heard in the soul.
It is the altar on which we must offer up our
own will. It is instrumentally a ladder to ascend
unto God.   By it the soul gets to its centre, out
of which it cannot rest. Man's soul is the temple
of God ; recollection, the holy of holies. As the
wicked, by recollection, find hell within their
hearts, so faithful souls find heaven.   Without
recollection all means of grace are useless, or
make but a light and transient impression."

Aug. 15th —I bless God, all is calm again :
I feel a heavenly sweetness—peace, joy, and
love—springing up within my soul. But I have
lately had some sharp conflicts with myself and
with the adversary of my peace. O what a necessity do I still find of using self-denial! More
and more I see self must be mortified. But I
have again proved by experience, that it is faith,
and faith alone, which brings certain victory

over self and sin. What a blessed union with Jesus do I sometimes feel in the night-season, while all are sleeping around me! The night-watches are favourable to meditation; no earthly object to draw away the attention.

[THE following is an extract from a letter without date, but was evidently written about this time. It was addressed to a respectable young female, for whose salvation it is manifest he felt a deep solicitude: and shows the manner in which he was accustomed to follow up the impressions that he had made, when he had reason to fear they were too slight, or not duly attended to. I introduce it also in the hope that it will be read to profit, by some of the many who felt the force of his thrilling appeals and reproofs in personal conversation, but are yet making no adequate preparation for the awful day which he, in this letter, brings before us so impressively.]

" MY DEAR MISS ⸺,
" I CANNOT account for it, how I should feel such a concern for your immortal, never-dying soul, but so it is: and by it I am now constrained to write to you. I thank you for your very kind remembrance of me: it is a proof that you have not forgotten me: nor, I trust, the conversation I had with you in the parlour the last time I saw you, when the Spirit of the Lord strove with you in a most powerful manner. I sometimes think I hear your sobbings, and see your

tears; They will never be forgotten by me, nor
by you either, I hope: for I am sure they cannot be forgotten before God.   You know that
you then promised me you would give him
your heart: Whether you have done it or not, is
best known to himself, and to your own soul.
I was just thinking, my dear Miss——, what
are all the pleasures, riches, and honours of this
world, compared to the soul? Or, as our Lord
says, 'What shall it profit a man, if he gain the
whole world and lose his own soul?' If we had
had no Bible, and had never heard the Gospel,
we might make some excuse.   But born and
brought up, as you have been, in the midst of
Gospel-day, you can make none.   Then, 'how
shall we escape if we neglect so great salvation?'
I wish you to bear in mind, that that same Jesus,
who poured out his blood on the cross to make
an atonement for your sins, will come again, ' in
flaming fire, to take vengeance on them that
know not God, and obey not the Gospel of our
Lord Jesus Christ: Who shall be punished with
an everlasting destruction from the presence of
the Lord and from the glory of his power.'
(2 Thess. i. 7–9,) O my dear Nanny, how awful,
how striking; and yet how true!   This is the
word of God, and not the word of man.   And
if you read your Bible, you will find that the
prophets, as well as the apostles, speak of this
awful day.   Daniel speaks of it in a very striking manner: ' I beheld till the thrones were
cast down and the Ancient of Days did sit,
whose garment was white as snow, and the

17

hair of his head like pure wool; his throne was
like the fiery flame, and his wheels like burning
fire: a fiery stream issued and came forth from
before him; Thousands, thousands, ministered
unto him, and ten thousand times ten thousand
stood before him, the judgment was set, and the
books were opened.' (Dan. ix. 9, 10.) Compare
these portions of God's word with the twentieth
chapter of Revelation, from the eleventh to the
fifteenth verses.   There you will see what are
St. John's views also of this awful subject; I
saw a great white throne, and him that sat on
it: from whose face the earth and the heaven
fled away, and there was no place found for
them.' Mark what follows!—'And I saw the
dead small and great stand before God;' (and
you and I must be there;) 'and the books were
opened; and another book was opened which
was the book of life : And the dead were judged
out of those things which were written in the
books according to their works.'   This, you
know, will be an awful scene; but what is more
awful is yet to come: 'And the sea gave up the
dead which were in it; and death and hell delivered up the dead which were in them; and
whosoever was not found written in the book of
life was cast into the lake of fire." O my dear
Miss ——, I wish to speak plainly to you,—this
must be the portion of every soul that does not
repent; every one who lives and dies in his sins.
God declares, 'The wicked shall be turned into
hell with all the nations that forget God.'
(Psalm ix. 17.)   Read also the last chapter of

he second epistle of St. Peter. I hope you will
not think I am wanting in respect to you because I have laid before you these awful truths.
If you know the love which I have to your
soul, you could not entertain a thought of the
kind. At any rate, you know you have been
twice unexpectedly, but I have no doubt providentially, thrown in my way; and on both
occasions, while I was talking with you, but
especially the last, you were deeply affected,
and promised me, in the presence of God, that
you would be his: and now the love of Christ
constrains me to write, to remind you of your
vows and promises, otherwise I could not be
clear in my own mind. It is my fervent prayer
that God would make this letter a lasting blessing to your soul; read it in your closet, and
pray earnestly over it and then send me a few
lines in answer. If you felt so much love for
your own soul, as I do for it, you would at once
cheerfully give up all for Christ, and quickly
be happy in him. I now commend you to God,
praying that the Holy Spirit may seal the truth
upon your heart!"

Oct. 17th.—For some time past I have been
very busy in writing letters to friends in various
places. I received a packet containing nine,
from various persons at Mevagissey, every one
requiring an answer. These various requests I
have fulfilled; and I have sent twelve more to
Mousehole and other places. O that all the
precious souls whom I have addressed, may
find their way to heaven !

28th.—[An extract from a letter addressed to a class-leader :—]

"My DEAR BROTHER,

"I WISH to know how you and your little flock are getting on; and whether any have strayed from the fold or not 'in a dark cloudy day.' I trust none of them are lost by your fault or negligence. My prayer is, that all your members may be more and more united in love to one another, and that they may grow up in Christ, their living Head, in all things. O that the Lord would make them fruitful branches in the heavenly vine! In reading God's most holy word, I have been struck with the tender love and compassion St Paul manifested towards those who had sustained a loss in their souls : ' Brethren, if any of you be overtaken in a fault, ye which are spiritual restore such a one in the spirit of meekness, considering thyself, lest thou also be tempted' Again, addressing himself to those who had been unfaithful, he says, ' My little children, of whom I travail in birth again, until Christ be formed in you.' To the same effect he elsewhere says, ' Bear ye one another's burdens, and so fulfil the law of Christ.' On another occasion, we read, that when he had called the elders of a certain church together, he gave them a particular charge, saying, ' Feed the church of God which he hath purchased with his own blood.' A dear rate this ! And I am certain we ought to take very great care of that which is bought at so high a price. Before Jesus, the Chief Shepherd, left this lower world, he gave to Peter a strict charge respecting the flock, saying, 'Feed my lambs.' You will observe my brother, he calls them, 'my lambs;' his own blood-bought property. I have often observed, he first mentions the lambs, because he well knew they would require much care and nursing. But he gave him also a particular charge respecting the sheep, twice saying to him, 'Feed my sheep.' May the Lord endue you, my respected friend, with all that heavenly wisdom, grace, and understanding, necessary for you, to conduct your little flock in safety to the care of the great Shepherd and Bishop of souls above. In due time you shall reap, if you faint not. And now, my brother, I would ask, How does your faith stand? Are you like Abraham, strong in faith, giving glory to God? Without this you will do but little when surrounded by the powers of darkness. It is the shield of faith alone which shall quench all the fiery darts of the wicked. But we must remember, too, to take the sword of the Spirit with us, which is the word of God; otherwise our faith will soon fail us. It is the promise of God which whets the edge of our faith; and all the promises are yea and amen to them that believe. '.Fear thou not, for I am with thee; be not dismayed, for I am thy God: I will strengthen thee, yea, I will help thee: Yea, I will uphold thee by the right hand of my righteousness.' Now, my dear brother, I would .

ask you whether a few such promises as this will not set a good edge to your faith.

> 'Faith, mighty faith, the promise sees,
> 'And looks to that alone.'"

Nov. 9th.—For several days past my soul has been earnestly longing for a more clear inward testimony of the Spirit I pleaded hard with the Lord for it; and, glory be to his holy name, he granted me the desire of my heart, by applying these words, "I have loved thee with an everlasting love." This was a word in season.

Dec. 21st.—I am now again mercifully restored, after being confined to bed for several weeks by reason of a wound in my leg. Blessed be God! this affliction has been sanctified to the good of my soul One day, reflecting upon my state as the prisoner of the Lord, it was suddenly suggested, "Jesus is in the prison with thee." My heart leaped for joy, and my eyes overflowed with tears of gratitude, at the thought of such infinite condescension I thought of the three Hebrew children: How the Son of God was with them in the midst of the flames, and preserved them unhurt "Who is a God like unto our God?" "When thou passest through the fire," says he, "thou shalt not be burned, neither shall the flames kindle upon thee." I have since had many plunges into the glorious fulness of Deity, which have greatly encouraged and strengthened my faith. Just before this took place, every grace was tried from a particular quarter, on which the enemy had not been accustomed to attack me. But, blessed be the Holy One of Israel, I can now triumph in victory over all my enemies.

JAN. 11th, 1830.—I HAVE begun this year with a fixed determination to live for God alone; Nothing besides is worth a thought. As I have been much confined at home this winter, my time has been chiefly occupied in writing to my different Christian friends, from Saltash to nearly the Land's End.

14th.—This morning, while turning my thoughts and attention to myself and my circumstances,—being generally much confined from the public means of grace by indisposition and the infirmities of age,—it was instantly applied .o my mind, as if one had spoken to me, " Thou must now learn to feed upon Christ in thy heart by faith." In a moment I saw more clearly than ever before, that every believer's heart is the temple of God, and that he has promised to dwell and walk therein. O the blessedness arising from such a reflection! Christ in me the hope of glory! That he should dwell in my worthless heart! O how this endears to me the name of Jesus! How it lifts up my faith, and yet humbles my soul into the dust before him!

MARCH 5th.—Within the last few weeks I have written nearly twenty letters, chiefly on the subject of entire sanctification. Deprived as I am of the pleasure of visiting my dear friends, I have found it very good to write to them.

The Lord knows my motives in this employ
ment ;—I aim at the good of their souls ; and
to me it is just the same as if I had been praying and conversing with them.   In all my pilgrimage I have never known so many clear
testimonies of the power of God to save from all
sin, as I have of late.   Surely it may be said
that knowledge is increasing ;—the knowledge
of believing with the heart unto righteousness.
Three letters that I have just now received bear
testimony to the truth of this.

11th.—My birth-day. This is a day to which
I have long looked forward; and often felt an
earnest desire to see it.   As I was born in the
year 1750, I am now beyond four-score.   I
thank God for giving me to behold this day ; and
I earnestly pray that the blessed end may be
answered, for which I am spared to see old
age.   Blessed be God, I can say at present, I
am happy.   Christ is more precious to my soul
than all the world besides   O for ten thousand
thousand tongues to praise my God, my Saviour, and the blessed Spirit !

> " To Father, Son, and Holy Ghost,
>   Who sweetly all agree
> To save a world of sinners lost,
>   Eternal glory be."

In singing over this verse in past years, which
is now nearly lost sight of, I have often, with
pleasure and profit to my mind, contemplated
the mystery of redemption, in which Father,
Son, and Spirit sweetly agree to save a ruined

world. At present, gratitude is the language
of my heart as well as my tongue; and it is
easy for me to sing and rejoice. It is, however, not always so with me; not long since it
was quite otherwise. I had head-winds and
rough seas to beat through, in order to gain the
port; but now, glory, glory be to God! I
have fair wind and smooth water. My harp is
in tune; and,

> " Of Him, who did salvation bring,
> I could for ever think and sing."

July 3rd.—Still confined at home on account
of lameness and pain. But this day I have received a very powerful manifestation of the
Spirit of God, for which I cannot sufficiently
praise him. The blessed effects of this gracious visit I sensibly feel at this moment while I
write. It puts to flight all the armies of the
aliens, and greatly brightens my prospects of
future glory. O how infinitely do I fall short
in gratitude to the Author of my mercies!

August 3rd.—Glory be to thy holy name, O
thou most high God! Thou hast now accomplished and fulfilled the promise concerning my
son Benjamin, given me more than ten years
ago, when I felt reluctant to give him up to go
out as a foreign Missionary; thou then re-
provedst me, and said, " I gave my Son to die
for thee, and canst thou not give up thy son to
go an errand for me? I will bring him again
to thee." And, glory, glory be to thy adorable
name! thou has brought him back again, and

his dear wife and children also, in safety, in health, and in peace. For these mercies, eternal praises be ascribed to thee, my God! And now, as thy presence was with him to give him favour and to prosper him in distant lands, so do thou grant, O Lord, that thy presence and blessing may still accompany him and his ministry, wherever thy kind Providence shall, in future, direct his steps! Amen and Amen.

10th.—[The following letter, containing some important remarks on a subject too much neglected in the church of Christ, was addressed to an excellent young man, a class-leader, for whom, and for the souls committed to his care, the writer felt a strong regard ·—]

"MY DEAR JOSEPH,

"SOUL-work is important work. You have now three classes committed to your care. To attend properly to these and your prayer-meetings you have enough to do; too much, I, fear, for your constitution. As to prayer-meetings, I always considered it a duty incumbent on me as a leader, regularly to attend upon them It was there I had an opportunity of discovering who in my classes were in earnest. and who were not; and to inquire of those absent, what was the reason they did not attend this means of grace. You know, if the outward means are neglected, our souls cannot prosper With respect to visiting from house to house when you were first fixed as a leader, I know it was your meat and drink to do it; for the

alvation of their souls lay near your heart. If
hey discover less diligence and love manifested
owards them in this respect, it is apt to dis-
ourage them, and lessen their esteem for their
eader. You will bear, I hope, with my plain
lealing. It is because I love you that I speak
hus. I wish you to look well to those pre-
ious souls under your care; that, in the great
lay, when you will be called to give an account
if your stewardship, you may be enabled to
ay, 'Here am I, Lord, and those committed
o my care; not one of them is wanting.'

"I am glad to hear the young men stand so
vell; and I pray that the Lord may make
hem abundantly more useful than ever! But
. sorrow to find so many of the young females
riving their company to young men who are
arnal and without religion. This, you know,
ny dear Joseph, is quite opposed to the word of
God. He commands us to 'be not unequally
roked together with unbelievers. For what
ellowship hath righteousness with unrighteous-
iess? and what communion hath light with
larkness? and what concord hath Christ with
Belial? or what part hath he that believeth
vith an infidel? and what agreement hath the
emple of God with idols? As God hath said,
I will dwell in them, and walk in them. and
I will be their God, and they shall be my peo-
ile. Wherefore, come out from among them,
ind be ye separate, saith the Lord' (2 Cor.
vi 15-18.) 'SAITH THE LORD,' not man.
Awful, indeed, to reflect upon it,—whoever

breaks this command! But who lays this to
heart? Not those who marry out of the Lord,
or with unbelievers; because God himself has
forbidden it. Have you, my dear brother, explained to the young people who meet in your
classes, the awful consequences of breaking
this command of God? You see it is as much
forbidden by him as any other sin. To plead
the commonness of it will no ways do away the
evil of it. For instance, suppose we see men roll-
ing in the streets in drunkenness from day to day;
shall we say, ' Drunkenness is no sin?' God
forbid.—It is forbidden by God; that is enough
to satisfy me. If I were to relate to you, my
brother, the many awful circumstances which I
have seen to attend these unhappy marriages, it
would make you tremble. Some time back a
young man, a Methodist, came to me to ask my
advice on this head. He was at that time very
promising for usefulness in the church of God.
I earnestly entreated him, if he had any love
for his own soul, or the cause of God, to have
nothing to do with the young woman he mentioned, because she was not a professor of religion. I told him he would be ruined if he
did; and that his conduct would be such a stab
to the cause of God in that place as he would
never be able to make satisfaction for. All
this did not avail;—he soon got married. He
invited me to call to see him. I did so; and
his wife said to him in my presence, looking him
stark in his face and calling him by name 'James.
I will never be a Methodist.' It was like as if a

sword pierced my heart. He thought, like many others, that when he got married he was going to do great things; but he found he was quite mistaken. He soon gave up his profession, and became a drunkard, a swearer, and a Sabbath-breaker; and a most wretched kind of living they have had ever since. I hope you will for ever set your face against this sin, and do all you can to prevent it. At least I wish you to clear your own soul of their blood, that you may meet them all with boldness in the day of judgment, if their souls should be lost by this dreadful evil which is got amongst us. My dear brother, methinks I could on this account say with Jeremiah, 'O that my head were waters, and mine eyes fountains of tears, that I might weep day and night for the slain of the daughter of my people!' It will require a great deal of that wisdom which is from above, to train up souls for heaven. The Great Shepherd of the sheep himself gave Peter a strict charge to feed his lambs; and St. Paul likewise exhorted the 'overseers,' perhaps such as leaders are now, to 'feed the church of God which he hath purchased with his own blood,' I have suffered a great deal of pain while I have been writing this letter to you. I can now rest but little at night from a violent pain in my left thigh. I often think I am in the hands of a very skilful Physician, who is to wise to err and too good to be unkind."

JAN. 1831.—SEVERAL months have now

elapsed since I set down any thing in my journal. During this time I have received many blessings at the hand of God, and have passed through many inward conflicts. Day and night I have felt the need of crying for help unto God. It is well for me that there is an open fountain, and that I have an Advocate above.

MARCH 13th.—I have been spending some weeks at Ponsanooth. While there, I had the pleasure of seeing the wonderful works of the Lord displayed in the conviction and conversion of many sinners. The subjects of this gracious work are persons of all ages. Upwards of fifty have received notes of admission. From what I have seen of them I have reason to think the greater part of them have been brought to enjoy justifying grace. I hope my labour among them was not in vain. This will be best known when God makes up his jewels.

MAY 7th —Bless the Lord, O my soul! He has spared me to commemorate another return of the day of my conversion. It is now sixty years since the blessed change took place within my heart. From the first day to the present moment I could never doubt of the reality of the work. What shall I render unto the Lord for all his mercies to such an unworthy worm ? "O to grace how great a debtor!"

> " Sweet is the memory of thy grace,
> My God, my heavenly King!
> Let age to age thy righteousness
> In sounds of glory sing."

27th.—I think I never felt my feeble frame so crushed with the infirmities of age as in the past week. But it is very pleasing to know, that while this earthly house of my tabernacle is dissolving, " I have a building of God, a house not made with hands, eternal in the heavens " Glory be to God for such a knowledge as this! Amen and Amen.

Aug. 29th.—At present I am led to admire the mysterious ways of providence and grace. For some considerable time I had been praying to the Lord that he would work a saving change upon a certain person, but could not obtain a convenient opportunity of conversing with her, till about five weeks ago. The result will be best described in her own language, from a letter which now lies before me· She says, " I lived for many years in a state of indifference about the salvation of my soul, till it pleased the Lord to lay his afflicting hand upon me. I then saw in part my danger as a sinner, and promised, if the Lord would raise me up, I would give my heart to him. He did raise me up, and I began to pray and to attend the public means of grace; but no one taking me by the hand to lead me further, I rested in the form without the power. Having a knowledge of your character, I often felt a longing desire to converse with you, but never had an opportunity of opening my mind to you till the 25th of July, when I met with you quite unexpectedly. You then told me the desire you had long felt to converse with me, and asked me if I was happy. I said I was not. You then inquired if I prayed: and when I told you I did, you showed me I wanted faith to receive the blessings of the Gospel, and invited me to attend the class-meeting. I went accordingly, and was much affected, especially by the first hymn you gave out:—

> ' Come, Saviour Jesus, from above,
>   Assist me with thy heavenly grace;
> Empty my heart of earthly love,
>   And for thyself prepare the place.'

This was the prayer of my heart; and the meeting proved to me the most profitable I ever attended. But still I knew nothing of the nature of living faith, till I came to Downstall, and had another conversation with you; for which I think I shall have cause to bless God to all eternity. Blessed be his name, my guilty fears are now all removed, and I feel my faith daily strengthened; I can love God above every thing, and trust I shall henceforth, through grace strengthening me, be ever numbered with the humble followers of the Lord Jesus."

[About this time the following letter was written, which serves farther to exemplify his style of letter-writing, and the affectionate earnestness and striking fidelity with which he pursued those who professed to get good from his personal instructions and admonitions:—]

" MY DEAR S——,

"I HOPE you will, for my sake, take care of the letters which I write you, and read them over often when I am sleeping in the dust. Remember you are to meet me at the bar of God, to give an account to him of all the kind admonitions you have received from unworthy me. You know it has pleased God to make use of me as an instrument in his hand for your soul's good; as you have often confessed amidst many tears. Since you came to P——, God hath opened the eyes of your understanding, and given you to see the dangerous state your soul was in by sinning against him. And although you have not that clear witness of the Spirit which it is your privilege to enjoy, yet I should not have a doubt of your salvation if I were called to follow you to the grave. I believe whatever is lacking in you God will accomplish. I have seen the tears of penitence running down your cheeks; and, more than once, your very limbs trembling under you. While I write these lines methinks I see you before me, as I have described: You know the truth of this. I believe you are a sincere follower of Jesus, so far as you have heavenly light. O continue to watch and pray, and walk humbly with God! O may the eternal Jehovah destroy all unbelief in your heart, and enable you more fully to understand what is meant in these words, 'Jesus hath loved me, and given himself for me!' I was never so fully convinced in my life as I am at this moment, that you ought to be as fully persuaded in your mind that Jesus bore your sins in his own body on the tree, as if there was no other sinner in all

18

the world. When you read the following
lines, be sure you hold fast what is included in
them :—

> ' Thou hast my full ransom paid,
> And in thy wounds I rest.'

When I first conversed with you, you little
thought you could ever consent to go to class-
meeting. But the prejudice you then felt
against the Methodists God has taken away;
and I trust, if you are spared to return to E——,
you will not be ashamed to acknowledge what
the Lord has done for your soul, to such as
fear God. My dear S——, there is a great
danger here, and I wish to admonish you of it
in Jesus's own words : 'Whosoever shall confess me before men, him will I confess before my
Father which is in heaven:' Mind what follows. 'But whosoever shall deny me before men,
him will I also deny before my Father which is
in heaven.' (Matt. x. 32, 33.) Be sure you read
for yourself, for 'we must all appear before the
judgment-seat of Christ' Another caution I wish
to give you, which I consider is of the greatest
importance; because it is God's command:
'Be not unequally yoked together,' &c. (2 Cor.
vi. 14–18) Take your Bible and read the
whole passage. Now I would just ask you,
my dear S——, what can those professors of
religion expect from God, who break such a
command as this? I hope you, my dear child
in the Gospel, will never be guilty of it. I
trust you will lay this seriously to heart; and

mind, it is God speaking; not such a worm as man! No! It is the Lord Almighty. It is because of the love I feel for your soul, my dear child, that I write so faithfully to you. I almost despair of seeing you in heaven if you get married to a man who has no religion. One good man observes, ' Their very breath is infectious.' What then must be their conversation, and how much more so to be married to such a one? As you are clear from this deadly evil at present, I hope and trust you will ever keep clear. That the God of all grace may sanctify these instructions, and make them a blessing in time and eternity, is the sincere prayer of your ever-loving and affectionate father in the Gospel!"

Nov. 3rd —For several days past satan and unbelief, the two grand enemies of my soul, have laboured hard to wrest my shield from me and weaken my confidence in God. I have had to hang on Christ by a naked faith, without any sensible enjoyment. But in the past night, while all lay sleeping around me, and my soul was deeply and solemnly engaged with God, he appeared to me in a gracious manner, and lifted my head above all my enemies; not one was seen in all the coast. I was greatly blessed while thinking upon that remark of Lady Maxwell:—" I have often been enabled strongly to act faith on Jesus for sanctification even in the absence of all comfort; and this has diffused a heaven of sweetness through my soul, and brought with it the powerful witness for purity."

21st.—I can truly say, with one of old, " Giv-

ing glory to God, I feel no guilt; all is clear.
I feel no sin; God hath destroyed it.   I cannot
sleep by night; but I now think of God as naturally as I used to forget him.   He is hardly
ever out of my thoughts.   Christ is all in all!"
This morning He spoke with power to my
heart, in these words, "Thou shalt never perish,
neither shall any pluck thee out of my hand."
Before this the enemy had made his appearance; but he now fled in a moment; he could
not withstand the sword of the Spirit.

JULY 4th, 1832.—After a tour of nineteen
weeks the Lord has once more brought me in
safety to my own home; for which I praise his
holy name.   I spent seven weeks at Mousehole,
where I had again the pleasure of seeing many
sinners brought to God.   Several penitents received the Spirit of adoption while I was explaining to them the way of believing in order to be
justified; six of them indeed before I had
bowed my knees with them in prayer   This, I
think, is more than I could ever say before.
One day as I was walking in the street, a person came after me in haste, and requested me to
visit a woman who was in great distress of soul.
When I came to her she instantly exclaimed,
"If I die in this state, I am lost! I am lost!"
and continued repeating those words for some
time.   I asked for a Bible; and while I was
explaining to her the precious promises of the
Gospel, she was enabled to believe and rejoice
in the God of her salvation.   This woman had
never attended the chapel for several years.   I

spent four weeks at Penzance, there also I saw much good done; indeed, there is an extraordinary work of God in almost every society throughout that extensive Circuit. I visited Breage and Mullion, and was most kindly received by my old and dear friends. One was awakened, and two professed to receive the blessing of perfect love. I was glad to see those of my children who are still walking in wisdom's ways; and sweet was the intercourse which we had with each other, while talking over the things of God together. In riding from Mullion to Mr. Hendy's at Polgrean, the horse on which I rode fell with me while going down a hill, and threw me over his head; but, by the particular providence of God, I was preserved unhurt. Here I rejoiced to meet with my dear J. F., a child in the Gospel whom the Lord was pleased to give me about ten years ago. She is still steadfast in the ways of God. After I had visited my good friends at Helston, I returned; but had been home but six days before a conveyance from a distance of seven miles was sent to take me to visit a young man in great distress of mind, who had so far reasoned with the enemy of his soul as to believe he had committed the sin against the Holy Ghost. I staid with him four days. He got better, and was much relieved and comforted. Thence I was brought to Mr. M. Box's, of Constantine; to whom, about six years ago, the Lord was pleased to show his pardoning mercy, while I was conversing with him. He is now a much-respected class-leader. I staid with him three days, met his class, and have some reason to hope that my conversation in the family was made a blessing to some who knew not God.

Aug. 4th.—I bless the Lord, that my last visit to Ponsanooth was rendered useful. A young man, the son of a pious mother, for whose salvation I had long felt an anxious concern, was awakened while I was conversing with him about righteousness, temperance, and a judgment to come. Trembling under the arrest of the Spirit of conviction, he took hold of my hand, and said with much emotion, "Now I will go to class-meeting with you." The following Tuesday evening he came accordingly, and boldly declared what God had done for his soul.

Sept. 6th.—My kind and much-respected friends, Mr. and Mrs. Harvey, of Mawnan, having often requested me to pay them a visit once more, I accordingly went over and spent a week with them. I felt, on entering the house, as if the Lord was about to do some good in the family, and told them of it; and it soon appeared who was likely to be the subject of it. Miss E. F., their neice, who had been living with them for some years, I found in a state of darkness and despair about her soul; but she had not made known her grief and burden to any one. God was pleased to bless my conversation to her; and before I left I had the unspeakable pleasure of seeing her made exceedingly happy, and also united to the people of God. To his name be all the praise and the glory!

OCT. 1st.—I have lately been shut out from the public ordinances by a cold, a cough, and shortness of breath. But my time has passed away very comfortably in answering various letters which I have received from friends at Mousehole, Mevagissey, &c. Seeing that nature's ties are all dissolving, it affords me no small consolation to look forwards to the building of God in the heavens, which I know is mine by the inward testimony of the Spirit. Yes, for thee, my soul, for thee! Glory be to God!

13th.—I feel my bodily weakness increasing more and more; but I bless God, he gives me fresh tokens of his love and approbation, to assure me that I am his. This morning, feeling much of the helpless worm, I wanted a stronger inward testimony of my sonship; and looking up to my Advocate with God, these words sweetly flowed into my mind:—

> " Before the throne my Surety stands,
>   My name is written on his hands."

This was enough; tears of joy overflowed my eyes, and my heart dissolved in love.

> " Much love I ought to know,
>   For I have much forgiven."

24th.—[He wrote to one who made some anxious inquiries in reference to the subject of full salvation. The following is an extract from

the letter :—] " I have read your letter, my
sister, with the greatest attention, and cleaily
discover your holy and ardent desire after purity
of heart.   As I have passed through the same
feeling which you describe in your letter, I
know where you are, and what you want.
Suffer me to speak plain to you, in order to set
you right.   You err, not knowing the Scriptures, nor the power of God, I would ask, my
sister, Can you find no promise in the Bible
which can satisfy the earnest desires of your
mind ? And remember we have need of courage,
that, when we read the promises, we may believe, and make them our own.   Now there
are two of God's promises to which I wish to
lead your mind, because it pleased God to make
use of them in order to bring my soul into that
happy state which St. John calls, ' perfect love.'
Methinks I hear you say, ' O tell me, tell me
where I shall find them !' If you will promise
me to do as I did, I will tell you.   No doubt,
you say, ' I will try.'   Then when you read
them, O may the Lord increase your faith ! In
order to put your faith in lively exercise, I wish
to remind you that that God who caused them
to be written for your sake, will be present
with you when you read them to require an
act of faith in you.   And you are to believe,
not only that the blood which Jesus shed on the
cross for you was sufficient to make atonement
for the guilt of your sins, but also to cleanse you
from all unrighteousness.   Suppose I were to
ask you, Do you believe Christ will die any

more? you would say, 'No, I do not believe any such thing.' Then why not say in your heart, and from your heart, and with all your heart, looking steadfastly to Jesus by faith?—

> 'Surety, who all my debt has paid,
> For all my sins atonement made,
> The Lord my righteousness.'

"My dear sister, we must continue to believe every moment in order to feel. I wish you were so anxious in your mind about believing, as you are about feeling. Then I am sure God would soon send the witness of the Spirit into your heart, and enable you to say,

> ''Tis done; thou dost this moment save;
> With full salvation bless'd,
> Redemption through thy blood I have,
> And spotless love and peace.'

"By this you may know whether you are seeking the blessing by faith or by works: If by works, you have always something to do first; that is, you think you must be more in earnest; you must pray a little more; or, it may be, satan will suggest to your mind, 'You cannot believe now, your heart is too hard.' If you listen to any of these things, it proves that you are seeking it in a way you never can find it. It is 'not by works, lest any man should boast:' But, if by faith, why not now? Now is the accepted time with God. He commands you to believe that Christ has paid all for you; this is all he requires. I hope you have no

objéction to he saved in God's own way. You
want the wisdom which shows the difference
between the witness of the Spirit, and the simple
act of faith. For want of this heavenly light,
you are foiled by satan and unbelief. The witness of the Spirit is God's gift, not our act; but
it is given to all who act faith on Jesus, and the
promise made through him. God at this moment requires an act of faith in you, while he
holds out the promises, and saith, ' A new heart
will I give you, and a new spirit will I put
within you; and I will take away the stony
heart out of your flesh, and I will give you an
heart of flesh.' (Ezekiel xxxvi. 26.) Now
here are the two precious promises which I referred you to above. I saw in them every thing
I wanted; deliverance from inbred sin, and the
bestowing of a new nature; though I had no
man to teach or instruct me. From the time
God showed me what was included in these
words, I can truly say I never lost sight of
them. I could desire nothing else; I could
pray for nothing else; but that God would
cleanse my heart from all sin, and fill me with
his love. But all this would not do, till I believed that Christ had paid all for me; then I
felt the refining fire go through my heart, and
all within me became wholly sanctified to God."

[THE following extract is from a letter
written about the same time as the above:—]

"I AM rather jealous in my own mind, that

you have not a clear and proper view of Christ and his atonement. I believe there are thousands of sincere souls greatly distressed on this account. Till I met with Dr. Clarke's Commentary on Rev. v. 6, I am not ashamed to say, my own views of this subject were not so clear as they are now. As his remarks have proved such a great blessing to my own soul, I will give them to you in this letter : He says, 'Jesus Christ appears in heaven as if now in the act of being offered. This is very remarkable ; so important is the sacrificial offering in the sight of God, that he is still represented as being in the very act of pouring out his blood for the offences of man. This gives great advantage to faith ; when any soul comes to the throne of grace, he finds a sacrifice there provided for him to offer to God. Thus all succeeding generations find they have the continual sacrifice ready, and the newly-shed blood to offer.' None but God knows what a blessed effect these remarks have had on my mind ; and have to the present moment. I pray the Lord to give you heavenly wisdom to comprehend what is implied in them concerning the atonement of Christ. I can assure you I never read them but they give my faith a good lift ; or, if you will allow me the expression, they set a new edge to my faith. Whenever I come to a throne of grace, I now finds a sacrifice provided, and newly-shed blood to offer; this fills my soul with fresh vigour and courage to start in the Christian race. If you wish your soul to prosper, and to be a real

Christian, as you say in your letter, I would
advise you to think much of this subject, and
read the word of God on your knees in faith;
for you are an heir to all the exceeding great
and precious promises contained therein."

26th —THE language of my heart at this
time is,—

> " O Love, thou bottomless abyss,
>   My sins are swallow'd up in thee,
> Cover'd is my unrighteousness,
>   Nor spot of guilt remains on me;
> While Jesus' blood, through earth and skies,
>   Mercy, free, boundless mercy, cries."

" I will greatly rejoice in the Lord; my soul
shall be joyful in my God: For he hath clothed
me with a garment, he hath covered me with
the robe of righteousness; as a bridegroom
decketh himself with ornaments, and as a bride
adorneth herself with jewels "

Nov. 3rd —In the last two or three days I
have felt my soul particularly engaged with
the Lord, in order to keep my evidence bright
for glory, and to have a closer walk with God.
Last night, while lying on my pillow, this portion of God's most holy word flowed sweetly
into my mind· " Jesus answered and said unto
him, If a man love me, he will keep my words;
and my Father will love him, and we will come
unto him, and make our abode with him."
Such a Divine and heavenly influence accompanied the application of the words, that I felt
I was enabled to believe that the glorious truth

contained in them was fulfilled in me; and I rejoiced in it, and gave glory to God. Indeed I had such a confirmation of the truth and reality contained in these words. " We will come unto him, and make our abode with him," as I never felt before.

APRIL 9th, 1833.—I have spent three or four weeks at Tregew, and visited Flushing friends pretty much as I was able. I had the pleasure of seeing several made happy in God while I was with them. One afternoon, while taking tea at a friend's house, two young women came there in great distress of mind: Before we parted, the Lord was pleased to set them both at liberty. O may He keep them steadfast in the faith!

27th.—Yesterday I went to chapel, but was so poorly it was with difficulty I could return. At present I seem stripped of nearly all my bodily strength; but, I bless the Lord, I feel my mind perfectly resigned. Christ is all in all. I want no other portion in earth or heaven. His presence makes my paradise. Unto me, who am less than the least of all saints, is this grace given. Glory be to God!

MAY 7th.—Through the tender mercies of a kind indulgent God, and the speaking blood which pleads for me in the courts of heaven, I am spared to see sixty-two years expire since the Lord was pleased to bless me with the Spirit of adoption; whereby I was enabled to cry, " Abba, Father! my Lord and my God!"

' The gladness of that happy day,
O may it ever, ever stay !
Nor let my faith e'er lose its hold,
Nor hope decline, nor love grow cold."

Whether I shall survive another year, I know
not ; but whether I live long, or die soon, O my
God, let me be found

"Ready prepared and fitted here,
By perfect holiness t' appear
Before thy glorious face."

I bless his holy name for the prospect I now
have ; and I praise him for the Fountain which
he has opened for poor sinners, to wash their
spotted souls from crimes of deepest dye.

"Thy side an open fountain is,
Where all may freely go :
And drink the living streams of bliss,
And wash them white as snow."

Glory be to God, the atonement never loses its
virtue ! How often do I reflect with pleasure
and delight on that precious declaration of St.
John. "The blood of Jesus Christ, his Son,
cleanses us from all sin." All the powers of
the prince of darkness cannot withstand this !

JUNE 25th.—A man who was genteelly dressed
called on me to-day, and spoke very freely and
familiarly. On my saying to him I could not
recollect his person, he said, "I am your own
child in the faith, my name is F. J., formerly of
Ponsanooth." I then recollected him. He
joined the society during the great revival, nineteen years back. He was then but a child ; yet

very clearly and soundly converted to God. He soon after went to London, and, what was rather remarkable for one converted so early in life, he now told me he had never cast off the fear of God, nor had his name erased from the class-book.

CHAPTER VIII.

THE last entry in my father's narrative is that which concludes the foregoing chapter, the date of which precedes the finishing of his earthly course about fifteen months. A few days after he set off on his last visit to his beloved friends at Mousehole and Penzance. He stopped some weeks at my house. It was now too manifest that his natural force was much abated; his strength being borne down by "the rush of numerous years." But, so far as his remaining strength permitted, he was constantly employed in striving to do good to all classes that he had intercourse with. At times, he was apparently so feeble as to have little power to converse on any subject; but no sooner was a humble, enquiring soul presented before him than all his former energy and vivacity returned; and he would maintain for hours an animated conversation on his beloved topics, "pardon, and holiness, and heaven." It was on this occasion that some persons, in very respectable life, not immediately connected with us as a religious body, manifested great anxiety to converse with him. They had different interviews, professed to receive the greatest benefit from his advice and instruction, and begged to be permitted to number themselves with his favoured correspondents. As it was now with difficulty he could write at all, he did not promise to correspond. But before he left the neighbourhood one of them wrote to him, and earnestly begged that she might have, in writing, the substance of what he had said to her in his conversation. With considerable effort he wrote to her a short letter, a part of which is as follows :—

"I AM happy to find what I said to you proved such a blessing to your soul; but I hope you will give all the glory to God, who alone is worthy to be praised. Sorry I am to find that you have in any degree lost the blessed enjoyment you were put in possession of. Instead of reasoning with satan, you should have kept your eye steadfastly fixed on Jesus, ever living to make intercession for you, as if you were the only sinner in the world. This is Gospel faith :—

' The faith that conquers all
      And doth the mountain move;
   That saves whoe'er on Jesus call,
      And perfects them in love.'

If at any time you should let this faith slip, the moment you recollect yourself you have the same privilege to believe again as you had at first, because you have an Advocate with the Father. Sometimes the witness of perfect love is not so clear as at first; then you must learn to walk by faith, saying, with the prophet, ' I will trust and not be afraid;' yea, ' What time I am afraid I will trust in the Lord.' Believe and go forward; and O may the Lord enable you to hold fast your confidence and the rejoicing of your hope unto the end! I cannot promise to correspond with you; but, in reference to your request that I should pray for you, be assured I shall do it with all my heart while I have breath to utter desires before God."

Soon after Conference he paid us a visit at Redruth: where he strove, in his usual way, to make himself useful, and had much pleasure in seeing some of his old friends. From hence he went to pay a final visit to his numerous and much-respected friends at Camborne; which was made a great blessing to many souls. A local preacher, who was much interested and blessed by his company and conversation while there, observed to me, that, " as it was his last, so, in some respects, it seemed to crown all his former visits amongst them." In seeking to help the sincere inquirer he toiled to the utmost of his strength. It is said that, in one instance, he laboured for five successive hours in conversation with a person who had long been suffering under the power of unbelief; and that at last his pious and mighty efforts were happily crowned with wonderful success To a respectable young man in business, who was intently poring over his accounts, my father addressed a
19

pointed remark or two, on the necessity of having his accounts fairly made out and balanced
against the day when the eternal Judge should
come to reckon with him. This led the intelligent youth to serious reflection on the great
day of account, and the importance of being
prepared for it: the happy result soon appeared
in his conversion to God. More than one or
two of this respected family received special
good by the same instrumentality.

While at Camborne he wrote to one of his
highly-esteemed correspondents as follows ;—

"MY DEAR SISTER,

"I HAVE received your very kind and welcome letter, and am glad to find it so well with
you as it is. My daily prayer is, that you may
be preserved blameless until the day of His
coming. You know he hath said, 'I will
never leave thee: nor shall any pluck thee out
of my hand' I shall never forget the conversation which I had with you at my son's at
Penzance, the first time I saw you : I saw the
earnest longing desire that was in you to be
wholly swallowed up in God. You then told
me you wanted always to be so ; and I recollect
I said to you, that to be so always, you must
always believe ; and say, in the language of one
of our hymns,—

'All he hath for mine I claim ;
I dare believe in Jesus' name.'

Be sure, my sister, you keep your faith in
lively exercise. Live momently ; do not bur-

den yourself with to-morrow's trials: This is
the way to get on I cannot describe to you
what I now suffer from giddiness in the head:
and, of late, I have been much in this way.
But I bless His holy name, it does not shake
my confidence in God. Giving glory to Him,
I think I can say,

> 'Fix'd on this ground will I remain,
> Though my heart fail and flesh decay.'

I have no objection for you to engage in your
drawing. I think it right for you to do so. I
trust the Lord will guide you aright in all
things; and, while your eye is single, He will.
There is a good work going on here at Camborne. Since I have been here I have seen
many get into perfect liberty, while I have been
talking to them, and endeavouring to point out
to them the way to the blessing. I have been
here three weeks When I came I did not intend to stay so long; but the kind friends have
constrained me."

He returned home exceedingly feeble and
poorly, and was no more able to visit distant
societies. In this respect his great work was
done; and with much truth might it be said,
he had done what he could. But he did not
yet wholly lay aside his pen. With great
effort to himself he continued now and then to
write a letter to an anxious and favoured correspondent. I have one before me without date,
which appears to have been written in the
month of December. It is addressed to one of

his youngest born, for whose spiritual welfare he felt a deep solicitude.

" MY DEAR CHILD IN THE GOSPEL,

" I RECEIVED your letter of November 30; and thank you a thousand times for it. I am happy to find you have not got weary in well-doing; but, according to the contents of your letter, far otherwise. I rejoice to hear you mention your faith in God; and that you have now been kept in possession of it fifteen months. I often think I see you on the Sunday morning coming into the parlour rejoicing: with heaven beaming in your countenance, exclaiming, 'I am happy; the Lord has pardoned all my sins.' Methinks I hear my dear Elizabeth say,

' The gladness of that happy day,' &c.

I hope you do not let one day pass without praising God for what he hath done for you. I see it is of the greatest importance always to retain ' a sense of sins forgiven.' You used to mention in your letters how excellent you found Mr. Wesley's Sermons and Mrs. Roger's Memoirs; I entreat you, my dear child, do not neglect to read them often; and be sure and search the word of God, and treasure up the precious promises in your heart. May the Lord make you and me Bible Christians! Amen. I thank you for the information you give me of your sister, my dear Anna, that she still meets in class. I corresponded with her for some years, and have now several of her letters in my possession. I hope I shall have the pleasure to meet you both in heaven. I suppose you have heard how the Lord is pouring out his Spirit at Mylor Bridge. Such a sight, at this place, I have never seen before. Many are brought to God, and I rejoice to inform you that two of the family are of the happy number;—my grandaughter and a servant maid. We have prayer-meetings every night: but my weakness is such I can seldom attend; but I hear three souls were made happy last night.

' All honour and praise to Jesus alone.'

I hope you will excuse all blunders. All the pins of my tabernacle seem unloosed. My head is giddy, and my sight so fails me that I cannot see to make or mend a pen as I ought. My memory also fails me, as you may easily discover by my writing. My kind love to you, my dear child in the faith of the Gospel, and I hope you will not forget to write to, and pray for, your loving, though unworthy, father in Christ. I can truly say, I cease not to pray for you night and day. My heart seems knit to you more than ever. Farewell, till I meet you in heaven."

FEB. 21st, 1834.—To an accomplished correspondent, who has styled his letters " invaluable," and who earnestly solicited his correspondence so long as he could hold a pen, he wrote as follows :—

"My dear Miss J——,

"I thank you for your kind letter, and for all the good news which you have sent me. I am glad to hear the work of the Lord is so prospering with you. But whatever good is done the Lord doeth it, and he must have all the glory. You say you want a more lively faith, and desire me to tell you how to get it: You must take God at his word, my sister. He tells you, 'All is yours.' I see where you miss the simple way of faith, 'and fall into the stinking dungeon of self.' St. Paul, I conceive, had no reference to rapturous joys, when he said, 'The life I now live in the flesh I live by the faith of the Son of God, who loved me and gave himself for me.' Jesus was 'wounded for your transgressions,' and 'with his stripes,' that is, through the virtue of that blood which he poured out on the cross for you, 'you are healed.' 'Without shedding of blood there is no remission. You say the reperusing of my letters has warmed your heart with Divine love and gratitude, and that your joys 'have never been so great for any length of time as when I was blessed with your advice.' O may the Lord bless you with heavenly wisdom to understand the faith which Mr. Wesley speaks of in these words:—

'Though waves and storms go o'er my head,—
Though strength, and health, and friends be gone;
Though joys be wither'd all and dead,
And every comfort be withdrawn;
On this my steadfast soul relies,
Father, thy mercy never dies.'

I wish you to meditate upon the whole of this hymn, and pray that the Lord may reveal clearly to your mind all that is contained in it; then, I am sure, you will not be perplexed about frames and feelings, but say, with one of old, 'Though he slay me, yet will I trust in him.' May the Lord bless you with the mighty ' faith that conquers all !' No state of grace will exempt us from temptation : Christ himself was tempted. When we are tempted, we must make use of the precious promises. You know what the answer to St Paul was in the time of temptation : ' My grace is sufficient for thee.' I believe the Lord never permits any trial to befal us, while we look to him, but he will give us strength to bear it. O let us take fresh courage, and may we conquer through his blood ! Amen."

FEB 28th.—He wrote as follows, to one of his own beloved children in the faith, with whom he had corresponded for several years :—

You say you are tossed with tempests, and not comforted. Methinks I hear the Lord saying to you, 'O thou of little faith, wherefore didst thou doubt ?' ' Cast not away thy confidence, which hath great recompence of reward.' ' A bruised reed will I not break, and smoking flax will I not quench.' ' Fear thou not, I am with thee.' I wish you to lay hold on these promises ; they are bought for you with the precious blood of Christ. Do not grieve the Spirit by saying, ' They are not for me.' Yes, my dear child,

they are for you. O may the Lord increase
your faith. I think you have more faith than
you are willing to own. You say you are at
times 'encouraged to hope that even the barren
tree, such as myself, may yet again blossom,
and bear fruit to the praise of the Lamb.' Now,
I would ask you, Is this the language of faith,
or of unbelief? O I want you to take courage,
and say, with the poet,—

> ' Hence my doubts, away my fears !
> Jesus my salvation is.'

This is the way to conquer and overcome all
our enemies, and at last to shout victory through
the blood of the Lamb. My strength is nearly
gone, and I am getting weaker and weaker
every day. I feel daily that I am losing my
memory, my sight, and my hearing. I assure
you, that it is with very great difficulty I can
form one letter of the alphabet. I do not know
how many days I have been trying to write these
few lines to you, and my dear Miss J——. And
now I am ashamed to send them to you after
all. But you must excuse blunders, and the
shortness of the letter ; and take it as it is, because
I can do no better. My kind love to Miss W.,
and to all who inquire after me. I am glad to
hear Miss H. is happy. Please to give my
best respects to her. I pray she may be ever
steadfast and unmovable, always abounding in
the work of the Lord. Farewell, till I meet
you all in heaven."

HERE, I believe, terminated the pious labours of his diligent hand; this was his last letter. His *active* life, protracted to a period of unusual length, was now fairly closed: Nothing remained but to retire, to suffer, and to die. But before we attend him in his last sickness and death, a few remarks on his public character in the church, may not be deemed amiss.

To the high office of a preacher, according to the sense in which that term is generally taken, he never made any pretensions. In the absence of a regular preacher, he would consent occasionally to take the pulpit; when he would give a plain useful address to the different characters in a mixed congregation. He would often remark to his friends, when the subject was introduced, " I am a teacher, but not a preacher; that is a work to which God has not called me." In reference to this observation of his, it is remarked, in a letter before me by a judicious friend, who knew him long and intimately, and had profited much by intercourse with him: "A teacher he was of the first order, in the science of saving souls—For usefulness perhaps, Cornwall has not produced his fellow; especially in helping the sincere seeker into Gospel liberty."

It has been remarked of Methodism, that "it has a place for every man;" and doubtless this is one of its peculiar glories, that it finds office and employment for all the various talents of its members. We have travelling preachers, local preachers, exhorters, class-leaders, prayer-leaders circuit-stewards, and society-stewards; all these, and various other office-bearers amongst us, perform an important part in the great work of " perfecting the saints, and edifying the body of Christ." The subject of these memoirs was not fitted for the first or second of these offices; but others were open to him for which he was peculiarly fitted; and hereby he was furnished with the opportunity of rivalling those who shall " shine as the stars for ever and ever ;" and the church became possessed of one of the most active and serviceable agents ever employed in building her walls or beautifying her palaces.

To take a brief and connected view of the principal features of his active and useful character in the church of God :—He often gave a word of exhortation.   This was a door of usefulness which was open to him, and into which he entered, from a strong sense of duty to God, and with a longing desire to be a blessing to souls   Here he was at home ; often was a remarkable door of utterance given to him ; and he spoke as one having authority.   He would frequently take his stand on a verse of one of our hymns, and thence bring forth treasures from the hidden things of God   The effect produced was often surprising   His words of fire seemed to fasten like cloven tongues on every heart. The spirit and language of our best hymns were peculiarly his own ; and in his hand they pierced like a two-edged sword   In streaming tears, and with an emphasis not to be described, he would sometimes exclaim, "Glory be to God

that ever these hymns were written!"   "With
faith divinely bold," he would seize on the
helpless seeker of salvation, and at once assist
him to step into the water, already troubled His
exhortations were, I believe, always sponta-
neous.

As a prayer-leader, he excelled in soundness
of speech which could not be condemned; in
variety of expression, in filial confidence, in fervour, and in love and compassion for the souls
of his fellow-worshippers This was to him a
field of great usefulness; and not a few will bless
God eternally, that ever he opened his mouth at
a prayer-meeting It was a means of grace
which he held in very high estimation: He
deemed it a branch in the system of Methodism
to which too much importance could not be
easily attached, by those who wished either to
get good, or to do good. He considered that
every member of society ought to attend this
means of grace from a principle of duty. Stable
piety, growth in grace, and the extension of the
work of God in the conversion of sinners, were
viewed by him as closely connected with a regular and conscientious attendance on prayer-
meetings. What sacrifices and efforts he
would make to attend them, throughout every
period of his long pilgrimage, is known to many
O that the numerous hosts of prayer-leaders, to
whom he was well known, may increasingly
partake of the Spirit of devotion which breathed
so eminently in him !

As a society-steward he was also exemplary.

He was prompt, and diligent, and peaceful.
The pecuniary affairs of the society must not
be permitted to fall behind while the matter
was in his hands. He was neither backward
to contribute, nor bore an unreasonable part of
the burden himself: but urged on every one to
do his part; and produced those motives which
never fail to operate where there is love to God
and his cause on the earth: and to him Methodism was emphatically the cause of God. It
united in itself every thing that was dear to him.
He loved the doctrines, the discipline, the ministers, the economy of Methodism in all its
bearings and relations. Disputes, and changes
and divisions he had often witnessed; but
such things never in the least degree moved
him: With his whole heart, in life and death
he adhered to the doctrines, discipline, and ministry which formed the instrument that God had
rendered so effectual in rescuing his soul from
sin, and misery, and hell, and constituting him
an heir of glory, and a possessor of "righteousness, peace, and joy in the Holy Ghost." In
attending quarterly-meetings he occasionally
lamented the great want of a peaceable disposition of mind so apparent in some. His own
spiritual remarks and exhortations on these occasions were sometimes attended with a blessed
unction from above. It was at a quarterly-meeting held in this town about twenty years ago,
after witnessing the gracious effect of some observations which he made on the deep things of
God, that the Rev. W. Martin advised him

to make himself, and the great things of which he spoke, more generally known among the societies. This eminently devoted and useful minister did not live to see how fully, from that time, my father acted in accordance with his pious suggestion

As a chapel-trustee he also rendered himself useful in promoting the interests of the church of Christ. Trustees are a class of men not so prominent as some others in our economy; but they fill an office of infinite importance to the stability and extension of the body, being legally constituted the guardians of the purity of the ministry, the privileges of the congregation, and the property of the Connexion. They often have much toil and much pecuniary responsibility; for the reward of which they can only look to the resurrection of the just, and to the consciousness which they have within their breasts that they are personally contributing to the happiness of their neighbours, and to the upholding of the cause of Christ and his ministry in the earth. In his own narrative we have seen what part my father took in this good work. In addition to the ordinary features in this work of benevolence, he had the honour and happiness of taking the special lead in the erection of the first chapel for the benefit of that society and congregation of which he was the nursing-father so many years.

As a class-leader he was deservedly held in the highest estimation. It was an office exactly to his taste, and for the discharge of its duties he had qualifications of no common order. He is an instance of the wisdom exemplified by the founder of Methodism in employing such a class of men in gathering and building up the church of God. Few men, however great might be their attainments in theology and divinity, could excel or even equal him here. Within the sphere of the class-meeting he was a wise master-builder; and how eager, inquiring souls were to profit by him in this means of grace, is well known to thousands. In many places when it was known that he was to meet a class and the room admitted of it, crowds from other classes would come to listen to his deep, experimental instructions, and to catch the fire of his spirit. His visit to a society was often regarded as a sort of era; for the expectation of the people, and the fervour of his soul, when they met "together in one place with one accord," often conspired to bring more than ordinary influences from above. He was never harsh in meeting a class, but he would blend great fidelity with fervent, melting compassion; so that however close he came, he would rarely give offence. In an early part of my Christian life, I remember he once remarked to me, in reference to a member of his class whose unsatisfactory conduct and experience had given him much pain, "I can speak to him without much difficulty when I come to him with my own soul melting under the influence of heavenly love." He considered the class-meeting a spiritual fold, into which every soul who had a

lesire to flee from the wrath to come, and be saved
rom sin, should at once be conducted; because
ie knew from facts almost innumerable, that,
within the boundary of this infinitely important means of salvation, holy desires and resolu-
ions were more happily nourished, defended,
ind strengthened than they could be elsewhere.
A class-meeting was used by him as a grand
nstrument to promote decision of religious
)rinciple; and the good which he did in this
vay is beyond calculation.   Here I can speak
vith confidence, for I speak from experience.
The kind pressure, and the constraining love
vhich he used, to get me to the class-meeting
vas little short of compulsion.   I could not get
)ut of his hands   It is right, perhaps, I should
;ay I was not at this time what is termed immoral in my conduct; but of the immediate
;triving of the Spirit's influences upon my own
nind I was then as unconscious as I had been
'or many years before.   Yet such was the effect
)f my being brought within the hallowing
)ounds of the assembly of the saints, that, be-
'ore the lapse of twenty-four hours, I was quite
lecided in pursuit of the religion of the heart.
[make this reference to my own case, to show
he importance of parents and class-leaders, and
ill members of the church of God, using their
itmost personal influence to bring every hope-
'ul subject within the range of the sanctifying
.nfluence of the Spirit and the discipline of
Christian communion.   From this mode of
iugmenting the number of our classes there is

no danger of lowering the tone of experimental or practical piety, while leaders discharge their duty to all such as place themselves under their care; and earnestly do I pray that this trait in my father's character may tell on the hearts and consciences of many who shall read this little volume.

Visiting the sick was another department of usefulness in which God was pleased greatly to honour him. To the truth of this, the foregoing pages have borne ample testimony. He approached the sick bed with such clear perceptions of the covenant of mercy, such a strong apprehension of the efficacy of the blood of atonement, such a confidence in God, and such a compassion for the souls of the afflicted, that they almost instantly felt that they were brought into the presence of a son of consolation and a helper of their joy. By a few minutes' conversation and prayer the whole scenery of the sick man's apartment was often changed; it was, in fact, turned from darkness to light. Many who have accompanied him on these occasions have beheld, and wondered, and adored. I have before me a letter just now received from Mr. T., a local-preacher, at Saltash, a highly-respected friend of my father, with whom he maintained a close and profitable correspondence for many years. Mr. T. details several very striking cases of his usefulness: Among others, the conversion of two persons whom he visited in a state of deep affliction. As the letter is very interesting, and serves both to illustrate his character and confirm many of his own narrations, being the testimony of a bystander, I think the reader will not be displeased at my giving a pretty long extract:—

"ONE day while our dear friend was with us," says Mr. T., "we took him up the river to Beer-Alston mines. There is a pretty long row of houses, occupied by miners and their families; and as we were seven or eight in company, it arrested the attention of the people, and several of them came to their doors. This gave full employment to our dear friend, for he passed but few without talking to them about their souls. At length we arrived at the door of a person who knew something of me, and pressed us to come in. Your dear father, who seemed always to have one thing in view presently began to address himself to a young girl, the daughter of the woman of the house; and he talked so kindly and closely on the affairs of her soul, that before long her bosom began to heave with unusual emotion, and her face appeared the index of a mind strongly exercised; but the mother wanting her to go for some fruit for us, she left. His attention was now directed to the mother, who, he found, had once loved God, but had lost the evidence of the Divine favour. He begged her to come near and sit down beside him, that he might converse with her on the subject; and this he did to good purpose. I made signs to the friends present to lift up their hearts in silent prayer to God; and

20

presently there seemed such a blessed influence
in the place, that I was constrained to praise
God aloud. Shortly the woman was so much
affected, that your father said, ' Let us pray;' and
in a very little time the woman found peace in
believing. But a more striking case is yet before us. At this place we heard of a blacksmith
being very ill, and were desired to call to see
him. Although pressed for time, on our way
back to the boat, we inquired out this poor man;
and found him stretched on a sort of crib in a
little hut, in the last stage of consumption. His
wife having gone out, he was left quite alone,
and seemed surprised to see so many strangers
enter his mean habitation. But our dear father
soon engrossed all his attention. Walking up
to his bed-side, he said to him, ' Well, my friend,
we are come into inquire how you are.' ' I am
very bad, Sir,' said the poor man. ' How long
have you been ill ?' 'I have been lying here
these ten weeks.' 'Indeed ; but we are come
more particularly to inquire how your mind is ?
' Very bad, Sir.' ' Indeed : What is the matter
then ?' ' O Sir, I am such a great sinner !' ' A
great sinner are you ?' ' O yes, Sir.' ' Well;
what did Jesus Christ die for ?' ' For sinners,
Sir ; but I am——' ' Stop, now; answer my
questions. You say, Jesus Christ died to save
sinners: Did he not die to save you ?' ' Yes,
Sir.' ' Well, now, if he died to save you, should
you not praise him ?' 'Yes, Sir ; but——' 'Now
stay, my friend ; just answer my question. You
admit that Christ died for you ; then, I ask.

should you not praise him?' 'Yes, Sir.' 'Come
then, my brother, lift up your voice and praise
him Glory be to God! glory be to God! Come,
my dear brother, join with me to praise the Lord.'
The poor heavy-laden sinner seemed astonished
at the request; but being repeatedly urged, he
at length consented to attempt to open his lips
to use words of praise.   Our dear friend encouraged him.   And though, at first, he seemed to
utter words of praise, not from the lively sense
of gratitude, but rather in conformity to the
wishes of his kind and venerable instructer;
yet, being hereby insensibly brought off from
himself to look to his crucified Redeemer, the
power quickly descended into his soul in such
a manner, that he shouted with all the energy
of a strong man, 'Glory! glory! glory! praise
the Lord!' till being exhausted, he fell back
on his pillow, and for the moment I feared
what would be the consequence of his extraordinary exertions.   But I was presently relieved by his again raising himself in his bed,
and shouting as he had done before; when our
dear father called on me to pray I prayed; and
as you may suppose, with no common feeling.
Our friend and the blacksmith kept shouting
aloud for joy of heart, and the rest of the company were on their knees praising God Mean-
while the wife returned, and several other per
sons had come in, attracted by the noise.   So
that, altogether, such an extraordinary scene
was exhibited as I never before witnessed I
took him another day to see a woman ill in

bed, and fast verging to the grave. He conver
sed with her, and being satisfied with the sense
she had of her state as a sinner, and the sincerity
of her repentance, he offered her Christ as a
present Saviour; and soon did the Saviour take
the happy possession of her heart. At a moment when neither of us were speaking, she suddenly broke out into holy rapture, and continued to shout the praises of God aloud, till, like
the poor blacksmith, she sunk on her pillow
exhausted; and, like him, she quickly revived;
and we left her rejoicing in the arms of her
Saviour. I attended on her to her death, when
she sweetly fell asleep in Jesus."

THERE is another prominent feature in the
active and useful department of my father's character; it is his preaching Christ from house to
house. This was his forte; and herein it pleased God to make him a blessing, distinguished,
extensive, and never to be forgotten. His much
esteemed and judicious friend, Mr. John Boase,
of Penzance, observes in a letter before me:—
"I conceive his great sphere of usefulness lay
among private families, in his religious visits
from house to house. Here in his colloquy with
the members of the family, he would deeply
search the heart, both of the serious and the
thoughtless; applying with great power such
portions of God's holy word, as were appro-
priate to their cases, and often with great success;
the results of which I doubt not many will
'arise to call him blessed.'" It is not easy to

give those who knew him not any adequate
idea of his mode of conversing about spiritual
things. It was so simple, so affectionate, so
interesting, so faithful, and so forcible, that it
seldom failed to arrest the attention, and move
the best feelings of the heart. His tears, his
emphasis, his appeals to the conscience, his
full and manifest confidence in the reality and
worth of the things he spoke of, and his devout
aspirations for a Divine blessing on what he
said, all conspired to produce such impressions,
as it was not easy for any one to efface, however
little love he had for religion. When he had once
gained the ear of a person, and had apparently
exhausted all his artillery to little or no purpose,
he would often, in the most striking manner,
refer him to the final judgment, where he must
meet him, and give an account for the use he
made of that conversation. Of this, some cases
are mentioned already; but a very remarkable
instance of his success in this way lies before me
in his own hand-writing, which may be appropriately inserted here. It is without date, but
appears to have occurred about 1820. My father
observes, " One time when at Camborne, W. J.
requested me to go to his house, for the purpose
of having some conversation with his wife about
the salvation of her soul. When I had finished what I had to say to her, I did not know
how to leave without speaking a word to the
tenant who occupied the other part of the house.
I found him a man quite unconcerned about his
soul; so after I had reasoned with him about an

hour on righteousness, temperance, and a judgment to come, perceiving that I made no impression on his hard, impenitent heart, I wished
him well, and left him; but as I was shutting
the door, something struck me very powerfully
that I ought to return to him and give him another warning. So I went back, and said to him,
'If you do not reduce to practice what I have
delivered to you, I shall appear in the judgment
of the great day to condemn you.' I said no
more, but left him to his own reflections. The
next morning I heard that William Mean was
distressed about his soul: I called to see him,
and found it was true 'All that you said to me,'
says he, 'made no impression on my mind till
you returned and uttered the last words; it then
very forcibly struck me that God had sent you
to warn me to flee from the wrath to come' He
was now deeply humbled before God on account
of his sins, and willing to give up all, that he
might obtain an interest in the Saviour's blood.
I endeavoured to show him the willingness
there was in Jesus to receive him at once; and
he was soon enabled to rejoice in a sin-pardoning God. He was a miner; and after he had
maintained a very consistent profession for three
years, he was summoned into eternity in a mo
ment, being suddenly swallowed up in the
bowels of the earth, while at his work in the
mine. After three days his body was found, and
a funeral sermon was preached for him by the
Rev. J. Ackerman. How mysterious are the
ways of Providence!"

In seeking the salvation of souls, he was emphatically in season and out of season. Wherever he found the sinner, in this world of mercy, his case was never deemed hopeless by him : With confidence in God he seized on the smoking brand, and strove to pull him out of the fire. This was often strikingly manifest in his reproving sin Constant success in his attempts to do good in this way could not be expected; yet his pious reproofs were often not in vain, even when administered under circumstances most unfavourable. An instance or two may be mentioned. While waiting one day for the ferry-boat, on the Green Bank Quay, at Falmouth, a sailor who was also standing there, was heard using profane language. ·My father reproved him; and in his own earnest and impressive manner, spoke to him at some length on the awful consequences of sin, and the necessity of preparing to meet his God. What effect this had on the sailor's mind is not known; but a respectable woman, who stood at some distance, seeing my father talking to him with great earnestness, was induced, from a motive of curiosity, to draw near enough to hear what was said. It was a word in season to her; for the arrow of Divine truth penetrated her heart; and after the lapse of some considerable time, my father had the happiness of accidently hearing that it proved the means of her conversion and salvation.

But a case much more singular and remarkble remains to be told; it is that of a drunk·

ard's being awakened to a sense of sin, by a
striking and thrilling reproof administered to
him while in a state of actual intoxication. The
person is now a very steady, active, useful leader in this circuit. The fact was first brought
under my notice at a love-feast about twelve
months ago, and was unknown to my father till
I informed him of it I will give the narrative in J. D.'s own language, as he related it to
me.· "I was," says he, "a hard-working man;
and, by extraordinary exertions in weighing
ore at the mine, I got a great deal of money.
But just as fast as I got it, I spent it in strong
drink. I used often to be absent from home
for several days and nights together in a state
of continued drunkenness. On one occasion,
after I had been out three days and nights on
a drinking bout, at Falmouth, my wife came
on a Sunday morning to seek for me, to take
me home. Returning with her and another
person, while passing through Ponsanooth in a
state of intoxication, there were some persons
coming out of a meeting; your father (whose
name I got to know some years afterward)
was among the number. Seeing my state, he
came up to me, and, laying his hand upon my
shoulder, said, 'Young man, do you know
where you are going ?' As well as I was able
to answer him, I told him I was trying to make
the best of my way home. 'This is not what I
mean,' says he : 'do you know that you are
now in the road to hell, and if you do not stop
you will soon be there ? Such was the effect of

his reproof upon my mind, that in less than
two minutes after he left me, I was as entirely
freed from the effects of liquor as I had ever
been in my life; and, before I had walked a
mile, my soul became so filled and burdened
with a sense of my guilt and sin, I was constrained to see an opportunity to turn aside into
a solitary place in a field, and there fall down
upon my knees, and cry to God for mercy.
Nor could I leave the spot for some hours I
got home with my burden in the evening, and
after a severe struggle of some months' continuance, I found peace with God "

To these traits in his public and useful cha-
acter, may be added another, in which he was
eminent and mighty: that is, in his intercessory
cries and struggles in his closet. The ardour
of desire, and strength of faith, which he threw
into these holy pleadings and wrestlings before
God in secret, were very great, and truly cha-
acteristic of his other efforts to do good. He
firmly believed that God heard and answered
'the prayer of faith" in behalf of others, and
he proceeded with all his soul to act upon this
conviction of the truth. The preceding pages
bear ample testimony to this. In the conversion of his children, he tells us, he took hold of
the promise, and retired to make known his
wishes and his confidence to the Searcher of
hearts. Here, " in audience with the Deity,"
he had " power with God and with men," and
often did he "prevail." There was one thing
remarkable, which he often mentioned, it was

the communion of spirit and familiar intercourse which he held with those for whom he prayed much, if they were persons enjoying spirituality of mind. He sometimes spoke as though he hereby got a kind of knowledge of the state of the absent, whether depressed or joyous. Once, while I was very far distant from him, he gave me some reason to think there was more reality in this matter than I was at first ready to admit. Be this as it may, he laboured much, and delighted much in the duty of intercessory prayer: and if the "fervent effectual prayer of a righteous man availeth much," it is not unlikely that it will at last appear, many have been more indebted to his benevolent interposition on their behalf than they were aware of. Above twenty years ago, a little before the Lord poured out his Spirit in an extraordinary manner on the people, and multitudes were converted from the error of their ways, I remember hearing him speak of the agony he felt in secret, while engaged with God for sinners. " The weight of their awful state," he observed, " is so laid on my soul that even my body seems crushed with the load, and I can scarcely stand upright."

One other department of useful and benevolent exertion, in which the subject of these memoirs laboured with uncommon assiduity, was his pious epistolary correspondence. Whether he was herein more useful, or less useful, than in any other department, I have no doubt many who did not personally know him will

regard this as the most extraordinary trait in
his character; when they are informed that, at
he age of sixty-five, his utmost performance
vith a pen was barely to subscribe his name.
Up to this period, I cannot discover that he had
ever attempted to put to paper a single thought;
ind, according to what he told me in his last
sickness, he then deemed himself quite ignorant
of the art of writing.   But he was naturally a
nan of an active mind, and was aimed with
much patient resolution in pursuing any object
ie took in hand; and the circumstances in
which he was now providentially placed made
writing a most desirable acquisition   I was re
moved from him at the distance of fifty miles.
our sweet intercourse was dissolved, and he
longed for the ability to tell me his thoughts
ind feelings by letter. He took a sheet of paper
ind sat down, for the first time, to speak by such
i medium; and though the performance was
humble, yet, I doubt not, he succeeded far better
han he expected   It answered a valuable purpose to him, and was the occasion of much
gratitude to God.   After this, when he became
he father of many spiritual children in different parts of the county, he was moved to ex-
hort, and to counsel and comfort them by letters.
Thus in the course of a few years, he had a
circle of correspondents more numerous than
that of most men: And if he never attained the
character of a complete scribe, he learned to
communicate his thoughts, with ease and comparative perspicuity, to any part of the globe, in a

hand little short of elegant for an aged person.
He put to paper matter enough to fill many
volumes; lived to see his epistles alike esteemed and desired by the humble labourer and
the learned counsel, the illiterate servant-girl
and the accomplished lady; and, what was far
better to him than all this, he had the great
happiness of knowing that his letters did good to
souls redeemed by the blood of Jesus. But
for this unparalleled effort of his pious, benevolent, and ardent mind, the present volume had
not existed; which, if rendered the means of
gratifying his numerous friends, and doing
good to others as far as may be reasonably
hoped for, will, in addition to what was done
in his life time, fully justify his uncommon
effort, and be of more real benefit to the world
than many noisy undertakings which promised
far more at the outset.

CHAPTER IX.

On entering 1834, my dear and honoured
father expressed a presentiment which occupied
his mind, that he had then commenced the
year which was to terminate his earthly pilgrimage. He stated that on one occasion, when
from home, amidst the displays of the power of
God among the churches, he was taken ill;
and not knowing how it might go with him,
while looking up to Him who " giveth to all

life and breath and all things," a voice spoke
to him and said, " I will add to thy days fifteen
years." That period was just now expired,
and the same authoritative voice seemed to say,
" This year thou shalt die."

The affliction by which it pleased God to remove him to his heavenly reward commenced
about the beginning of August. It was painful
and protracted, and to some it appeared rather
mysterious, that one who had so long and so
eminently walked with God, and who had in
such an extraordinary manner gone about doing
good, should, at the close of his life, be called
to pass through affliction's furnace, heated even
hotter than it is wont to be heated. Many had
fancied that he would enter into the joy of his
Lord, by a sort of translation When, therefore, they heard of his severe suffering for many,
many weeks, their faith in the Divine bene-
ficence was almost staggered. But where do we
learn this doctrine, that saints must be exempt
from suffering, or the goodness of God impeach-
ed? Had this state been the final reward of
the saints, instead of the arena of their probation
and trial, there would, perhaps, be some ground
to question the love of God. But seeing their
stay here is but for a moment, that they are on
their way to "another and a better world," that
they are to be rewarded there according to their
works, and that the "faith tried with fire, shall
be found to praise, and honour, and glory, at
the appearing of Jesus;" pain, with grace to
bear it, must now be ranked among the most

precious gifts of heaven. Hence the God of our mercies has so laid down the path to glory, as to lead his people through much tribulation to enter the kingdom. In the order of things, and to render them the more desirable and blissful, ease, and rest, and glory, are to succeed pain, and toil, and dishonour. Thus it was with Jesus, the Captain of our salvation, and thus it was with that " cloud of witnesses" who " obtained a good report through faith." We know who has said, " As many as I love, I rebuke and chasten." And, again : " Every branch that beareth fruit, he purgeth it that it may bring forth more fruit."

AUG. 13th.—I yesterday visited my dear father in his deep affliction. He has now been ill about a fortnight. His disease is an inflammation in the bladder ; a complaint often incident to old age. Alas! " his strength is now labour and sorrow." I was never before so struck with the truth contained in these words The pain is at times excruciating. It was a very afflicting scene. This is a dispensation which calls loudly for faith in God, both in him, and in those who from sympathy suffer with him. Soon after I entered the room he turned to me, and said with much emotion, " My present experience is contained in this verse of our hymn :—

> ' He has engross'd my warmest love
> No earthly charm my soul can move ;
> I have a mansion in his heart,
> Nor death nor hell can make us part.' "

He afterwards told me, that, in the beginning
of his affliction, the adversary had been permitted to thrust sore at him.   Extreme pain had
bereft him of his joy, and it was then powerfully
suggested, that, so long as he continued in the
body, it would no more return to him.   And to
enter the valley and shadow of death, without
one ray of heavenly joy, appeared to him
gloomy indeed.   But whilst he was striving to
look up for help, and to stay his soul upon God
amidst the thick gloom of the temptation, these
words of the Psalmist brought him very gracious relief: " Why art thou cast down, O my
soul? And why art thou disquieted within me?
hope in God; for I shall yet praise Him, who
is the health of my countenance and my God"
From this time he was enabled to hold the
enemy at a greater distance.   At a subsequent
period, a blessed increase of comfort was
brought to his soul by a powerful application
of the words of the prophet, " Can a woman
forget her sucking child, that she should not
have compassion on the son of her womb?
Yea, they may, yet will I not forget thee; behold, I have graven thee upon the palms of my
hands."   In his worst moments, he observed,
he had not felt the slightest doubt of his final
salvation; but he seemed scarcely capable of
finding language sufficiently strong to express
the sense which he had of his unworthiness and
unfaithfulness.   All his hope rested exclusively
on the atonement, in which he trusted and
gloried.   His whole soul appeared to find utter-

ance, while he exclaimed in the language of
Mr. Wesley,—

"I the chief of sinners am,
But Jesus died for me"

No doubt God will sanctify this most distressing
dispensation, and bring forth his servant as gold
seven times purified in the fire.   It pleased the
Father to bruise his Son Jesus; and thus make
the Captain of our salvation perfect through
sufferings; and herein my dear parent has fellowship with his Lord and Master.   O. may
his faith and patience hold out, and be stronger
and stronger to the end ! Surely it will be so,
and his final hour bring glory to his God !

Monday, 18th.—This morning early I was
sent for to attend my father, who had been taken
much worse during the night. I found him in
great bodily suffering. Since I saw him on
Wednesday, he had drunk deep of the bitter cup.
The sight was very distressing to those about
him. At ten, A M , he was seized with a con-
vulsive fit. We then thought the mortal affliction was past ; but, after lying in a state of insen-
sibility about four hours, he again awoke up in
a suffering world; but with a blessed increase
of the earnest of heaven in his soul For several
successive hours he exhibited in lively conversation all the triumph of faith. With a
countenance illuminated with holy joy, and in a
tone and emphasis not to be described, he exclaimed, " I have fought a good fight, I have
finished my course, I have kept the faith; hence-

oith there is laid up for me a crown of righte-
usness, which the Lord, the righteous Judge
hall give me in that day." Never before did I
ıear this beautiful passage quoted and applied
o appropriately and feelingly. Every clause
eemed living truth, exhibiting all the freshness
f " the tender grass springing out of the earth
y the clear shining after rain." " I speak not
oastingly," says he, " I am a sinner saved by
race,—the chief of sinners, for whom Jesus died.

'Surety, who all my debt has paid,
For all my sins atonement made,
    The Lord my righteousness;'

have no doubt, no fear, all is calm within; per-
ect love casteth out fear. I shall soon be with
esus.

'Jesus my all in all thou art;
    My rest in toil, my ease in pain;
The medicine of my broken heart;
    In war my peace, in loss my gain:
My smile beneath the tyrant's frown,
In shame my glory and my crown.'"

Ie then adverted to the assurance of faith, and
:rongly insisted on the Christian's privilege to
2tain the indubitable evidence; observing that,
God's word says, 'We know that all things
/ork together for good,' &c ; and, again, 'We
now that if our earthly house of this taber-
acle be dissolved, we have a building of God,
n house not made with hands, eternal in the
eavens; but *we hope—we trust*—but 'we
21

know.'" On a young class-leader, who was present, he urged the necessity and importance of his using every means to prevent the members of his little flock from resting short of their privileges as believers in Christ. Taking him affectionately by the hand, he said, with much meaning and emphasis, " My brother, be a spiritual guide."

To a young person who came into the room, he spoke in very affectionate and affecting terms, entreating her at once to give her heart to God ; bidding her to behold in him what religion could do ; now lying as he was on a bed of suffering and death. An aged friend taking leave of him, who, he feared, was resting short of conversion, he very urgently pressed upon her the necessity of her more earnestly seeking regeneration, and the evidence of the forgiveness of sins. Highly to our edification and joy, we now beheld the veteran Christian warrior in the bottom of the burning fiery furnace, clapping his hands amidst the flame, and triumphing and glory-ing in his great Deliverer. O, it was good to be there : I would not have been absent on any account. Truly it was a place " privileged be-yond the common walk of virtuous life,—quite in the verge of heaven." I had long seen my dear father *doing*, I now saw him *suffering*, the will of God. Whilst we knelt round his bed in prayer, we felt the presence of God in an ex-traordinary manner. Glory be to God !

Thursday, 21st.—Since Monday, my dear father has suffered much ; but his soul is more

and more humbled and purified. Yesterday
afternoon, he spoke as one who could scarcely
bear the sight of himself. He seemed to see
so many imperfections in his life, that he durst
not look at it, but at the blood of the cross alone.
"Christ," says he, "must be all in all. He
ever liveth to make intercession for us; what
should I do without this?" Feeling from
strong pain, and there being too much ground
to apprehend an increase, he begged us to pray
that his faith might not fail him. "O!" says
he, "that I had wings like a dove; for then
would I fly away, and be at rest. I would
hasten my escape from the windy storm and
tempest. But the Lord is too good to be unkind, and too wise to err. May he give me an
increase of faith!" I said, "Father, in due
season you shall reap." He instantly replied,
with much emphasis, "Yes; if I faint not."
And it may be remarked, from the general tone
of his conversation that his soul was so duly balanced on the "truth as it is in Jesus," that he
seemed equally alive to man's faithfulness and
God's free grace. Hence, when any one spoke
of his devoted life, he would eagerly introduce
the blood of the covenant; and, on the other
hand, when the great and precious promises
were held forth to him, he would carefully and
incessantly remind himself and us of the characters to whom alone they belonged.

Saturday, 23rd —I set up last night, with my
dear afflicted father. At times, his sufferings
are still very acute; but as his natural constitu-

tion is so remarkably good, though he takes little or no sustenance, his trying affliction has not yet made that inroad upon his strength which indicates a near approach of dissolution. While awake he is generally in the attitude of prayer. He is increasingly jealous, lest he should, in his extreme suffering, dishonour God by any symptoms of impatience. Faith and patience, and resignation, are graces for the increase of which he is incessantly crying to God. He manifestly aims, with the same ardour of desire, and strength of resolution, at suffering the will of God, as he formerly did at doing it. But, in suffering, he has to contend against the whole tide of his nature; whereas, in doing, he was following after, and acting in accordance with, the natural bias of his mind. Activity was ever his element; to passing sufferings he has, till now, been a comparative stranger; but, in addition to his other eminent attainments in the Divine life, his Heavenly Father now sees it meet, before he takes him to his rest, to require him to learn to suffer. O that God may graciously help him to endure hardness as a good soldier of Jesus Christ, mitigate his pains, shorten the period of his fiery trial, and honour his servant in the final hour with his special presence!

SEPTEMBER 2nd.—Since the above record, I have spent some days and nights with my father; he still remains the subject of deep affliction; nor is there any immediate prospect of his entering into that state where there is no pain. Referring to this, he observed, "I see no end;" but correcting himself, he added, "This is the language of sense, not of faith." Often, in the paroxysms of pain, he cries out, in a very affecting manner, "Precious Jesus, help thy servant!"   He is more and more given to prayer; and frequently, in a very expressive manner, begs of God to give him—

"A soul inured to pain."

No murmuring expression ever drops from his lips; he manifestly has a great abhorrence of charging God foolishly.   It is very evident, indeed, that his patience, resignation, and acquiescence in the Divine will are on the increase. These are graces, not only unconsumed, but green and flourishing, amidst the flaming fire. At different times he would say, "What a mercy, I feel no condemnation; and as to my affliction, I am thankful I brought it not upon myself; it is the lot which God has chosen for me."   The sayings of my mother, in her last severe affliction are now familiar and dear to him: On which he observed, "I wonder I have not in past years thought more of them."   I mentioned that several of his old friends at Mousehole had been very affectionately inquiring after him.   With much emotion, he said, "They are dear to me, and I suppose I am dear to them."   I read to him the last chapter of St. John's Gospel.   When I came to that part in which Christ commanded Peter to feed his sheep, he was much affected, and said, with

considerable emotion, " I have considered that
God also once gave me a particular commission
to feed his sheep; and I have felt it to be my
delight to minister to them, and help the feeble
of the flock."

Saturday, 6th.—I remained with my father
last night.   He is much the same; though his
pain is not quite so great or incessant.   But as
he takes little food or natural rest, the body is
necessarily sinking.   He breathes submission
to the Divine will, and longs earnestly for his
change.   His esteemed friend, Mr. J. Boase,
called to see him to-day.   The interview affected him a great deal.   While they talked over
past and present mercies, they seemed to mount
high in the chariot of Amminadab, and my
father was " lost in wonder, love, and praise !"
But when he thought of their long, affectionate,
and happy intercourse, connected as it now was
with the impression that he should see the face
of his beloved friend no more, his feelings for a
time overwhelmed him. While he prayed with
him, Mr. B. was deeply affected. " I felt, indeed,"
he has since observed, "the truth and force of
that fine sentiment of Young,—

' The chamber where the good man meets his fate, '
  Is privileged above the common walk
  Of virtuous life :—quite in the verge of heaven.' "

It was felt truly to be " the gate of heaven, into
which his happy spirit was then about to enter."
Two of his old and much-loved friends, from
Ponsanooth, also called to see him, and were

much affected while they beheld him on the bed
of affliction. My father also wept much, while
they stood weeping over him, and pressed his
hand very tenderly to their lips. Full of holy
animation, and abounding in hope, he gave
utterance to his feelings, by exclaiming,—

" ' My God, I am thine ! what a comfort divine ;
    What a blessing to know that my Jesus is mine !'

" Hallelujah ! I am on my journey home." I
read to him the address of the Conference, which
had just come to hand. He was much interested
with it ; and when I told him that sixty young
men had this year gone out as travelling-
preachers, he fervently prayed that the presence
of God might go with them ; and that their
labours might be made a blessing to the church
of God.

Saturday, 13th.—I spent the last night with
my father, and had much profitable conversation
with him. Truly he suffers as a Christian. His
passive graces shine more and more con-
spicuously. He greatly triumphed and rejoiced
in the application of that precious promise to his
soul, "My grace is sufficient for thee." With
many tears, he said, " I am an unprofitable servant; but, giving all the glory to God, I am
not only a witness that Jesus hath power upon
earth to forgive sin, but also that he can cleanse
from all unrighteousness." He again and
again requested, if any thing were said of him
after he was gone, great care might be taken to
ascribe nothing to him—nothing to nature. I

was very affectionately and faithfully admonished to be increasingly ardent in preaching Christ and full salvation; and his pious and affecting exhortation was mingled with many tears, and fervent ejaculations for my success in winning souls. To one of his grand-daughters, who had recently joined the society, while he held her hand, he gave the most faithful, and tender, and urgent advices; accompanied by his prayers and benedictions. The Lord has seen it meet, in his inscrutable wisdom and infinite mercy, to continue the heavy burden of his affliction; but under it He blessedly supports him, and makes him a blessing to many who approach his dying bed. According to his fervent desires, and prayers, and hopes, may God more and more strengthen him with might in the inner man!

Saturday, 20th.—My dear afflicted father is now evidently fast sinking in the outward man, but his confidence in Jehovah is steadfast, unmovable. The heat of the furnace still increases, and nothing short of an Abrahamic faith can support the " strong, commanding evidence" of God's unchanging love. But he is unburned in fire, and appears to beholders a blessed monument of the power of religion. With tears and his own indescribable emphasis, he repeated those beautiful verses,—

"Though waves and storms go o'er my head:
   Though strength, and health, and friends be gone;
Though joys be wither'd all and dead,
     And every comfort be withdrawn;
   On this my steadfast soul relies.
   Father, thy mercy never dies.

" Fix'd on this ground will I remain,
    Though my heart fail, and flesh decay ;
This anchor shall my soul sustain,
    When earth's foundations melt away ;
Mercy's full power I then shall prove,
Loved with.an everlasting love.

When I informed him I was under the necessity
of leaving him, to go to my appointment to
preach, he bid me go in the name of the Lord,
and fervently prayed that the Divine presence
might go with me, and make my testimony a
special blessing to the people.

Friday, 26th —I spent the two last days and
nights with my father ; and, blessed be God, they
have proved days and nights of no ordinary
spiritual festivity and profit. Still he suffers
much, and his flesh and strength fail him ; but
the evidence is more and more delightfully indubitable, that his soul is built on the Rock of
Ages Never, since the commencement of his
affliction, have I seen him so exceedingly far
lifted above himself. At times, for hours together, he is sustained in the highest Christian
triumph ; when no language of sacred poetry,
or of the Scriptures, appears too strong to afford
expression to the vivid feelings of his full heart.
Conscious of the abundance of his communication, and still feeling his soul borne away by
the constraining love of Christ, he often says,
' It seems as if I could not hold my tongue " In
a long and triumphantly animated conversation
early yesterday morning, the well of truth and
love within him was found overflowing with

rivers of living water. In the rich expressions
of Christian experience, which were poured
forth from his lips, during this extraordinary
confession unto salvation, two things appeared
specially conspicuous; namely, his great jea-
lousy for the honour and glory of God, in guard-
ing against every word that might have the
slightest appearance of self in it; and his eager
desire that no part of the truth of God might be
denied, of which God had made him a living
witness. He sinks low before the throne; but,
while he falls down and clings to the feet of
Jesus, by the hand of Him who rests in his love
and rejoices over him to do him good, he is lifted
up to sit in heavenly places. His heart seemed
to dance with rapture at the mention of Jesus'
charming name. At different times, and in
various ways, he expressed his ardent desire for
the increasing prosperity of the cause of God
in the earth. On its being mentioned that the
journal which he had written with so much
pains and prayers, would probably be published
after his death, he requested that if any gain
should arise from the publication, beyond the
cost of printing, it might be given to promote
the spread of the kingdom of Christ in the
world.

Oct. 13th, Monday.—This day, at half-past
eleven o'clock in the forenoon, my honoured
and dear father entered triumphantly into "the
rest that remaineth for the people of God." In
the last fortnight, though he suffered much, it
was not so acutely as in the former part of his

affliction. He gradually declined in strength, and at intervals his mind a little wandered. With fervent longing, he looked forward to his inheritance above, and often repeated,—

> " When shall I see the welcome hour
> That plants my God in me ?"

alluding, as he himself explained it, to " mortality being swallowed up of life." For some days he had dwelt with great delight on that beautiful and favourite passage of Peter, " Whom having not seen ye love ; in whom, though now ye see him not, yet believing, ye rejoice with joy unspeakable and full of glory." His mind at times appeared much occupied about the future welfare of those whom God had given him, as children in the faith: In death, as life, they were dear to him ; and, at different times, he said, with much emotion, " Now we live, if ye stand fast in the Lord." Yesterday morning he talked of his funeral very particularly, and expressed much thankfulness, as he had often done before, for the kind attention of those who had so assiduously attended on him during his long and tedious illness. And now, in strong remembrance of his character as a sinner, about to enter the presence of God, he observed, in his own peculiar manner, " I have this morning been looking about for my sins, but I cannot find any of them ; they are all gone " Towards night he sank into a lethargy and lay without speech or motion, on his left side, more than twelve hours. About eleven this morning, recollection and the power of speech again returned. He asked for my brother and being informed that he was at hand, he inquired if my sister was present; when told she was, he said something indistinctly, which it was thought was an inquiry after me; but I was absent. He now signified his wish that they should join with him in prayer. While they were kneeling round his dying bed, commending his departing spirit into the hands of his Creator and Redeemer, he was full of holy animation, and devoutly and very loudly responded to the several petitions which were offered up in his behalf. On their rising from their knees, he gave them his parting benediction, saying with fervour, " God bless you all!" And now, grateful that he had so nearly and so happily finished his work on earth, and having the heavenly crown and heavenly host full in view, with an indescribable expression of joy and triumph in his countenance, and with much of his own tone and manner when in the happiest moments of health and strength, he gave out,—

" Praise God ! from whom all blessings flow,"—

and then attempted to raise the tune. This was the more astonishing to those who stood around him, as he had not sung before during his affliction. But he could not finish his chorus on earth, for while thus in the act of praising God with his dying breath, his voice was literally lost in death, and he suddenly and sweetly,

without pain or struggle, fell asleep in Jesus.
Just after he had apparently ceased to breathe,
while one present was mentioning the circumstance of dying Christians sometimes giving a
sign with their hands when they felt great support beyond the period of utterance, he lifted up
his left hand and arm, and then let them gently
fall till they moved no more.   Thus died
William Carvosso, in the eighty-fifth year of
his age, and the sixty-fourth of his Christian
warfare.

On the Thursday following his remains were
interred in the burying-ground belonging to the
chapel at Ponsanooth, in the same grave with
the remains of my dear mother   For very
many years did he look forward with pleasure
and delight to the period when his dust should
lie mouldering in that tomb, and his spirit be
with God.   As the day was wet and unfavourable, the distance to the chapel about five miles,
and the circumstance of the funeral being known
only in a very limited degree, most of his friends
were deprived of the pleasure of attending his
body to the grave.   Yet, as it was, there was a
large concourse of people; among whom were
several travelling-preachers, and many respectable friends, from the distance of fifteen or
twenty miles or upwards.

In accordance with my father's wish, his
highly-esteemed friend, the Rev. W. Lawry,
preached his funeral sermon at Ponsanooth,
from 2 Tim. iv. 7, 8, to an immensely crowded
and deeply interested congregation.   His death

was also improved, and a sketch of his character given, from various pulpits in different parts of the district.

Mr. Lawry has kindly furnished the editor with the following judicious remarks on the character of the deceased :—

"OF few men could it be said with more propriety, than of your late venerable father, 'He walked with God.' That which many persons, of equal mental power with himself, have sought for years to understand, and have turned over many volumes to find out, he would get a full sight of at once before the throne of grace. He was eminently a man taught of the Lord; and would, therefore, learn more of the Divine nature, more of the evil of sin, more of the beauty of holiness, more of theology in general, in a few hours' earnest prayer, than many others, of the same rank and advantages, in as many years. He did not go round about to establish his own righteousness, but always took the short road, and came at once to the fountain head. He well knew the doctrine which 'speaketh on this wise, Say not, in thine heart, Who shall ascend into heaven? (that is, to bring Christ down from above:) Or, who shall descend into the deep? But what saith it? The word is nigh thee, even in thy mouth, and in thy heart: that is the word of faith which we preach.' The Bible was supreme authority with him. From its decision he appealed not. To this simplicity of aim and conversation may

ɔe attributed, in a high degree, his pre-eminent
ɪttainments in experimental and practical reli-
ɟion.   His eye was single, and his whole body
vas full of light.   He was remarkable for seiz-
ng on every opportunity of conversing with
vhomsoever he met, upon the state of their
ɔouls and the way to the kingdom.   This was
ɪis element, his forte, his special path of useful-
ɪess.   In the exercise of this talent, upon old or
young, saint or sinner, friend or stranger, at
home or abroad, with an individual or in company with many, he seemed never to faint or
be weary.   He was an evangelist, who went
from house to house, conversing freely with all
on sacred things, and generally praying before
he left the family.   In this work of faith and
labour of love he rarely gave offence; though,
sometimes, this would follow; and yet the very
person so offended would often wish to see him
again; and not unfrequently, at the second interview, the eyes which had previously be-
tokened anger would now fill with penitential
tears.   He dwelt little on speculative theology;
he was not a man of extensive reading; he
never meddled with other people's matters, or
things which did not concern him.   He kept
close to the Bible and Mr. Wesley's Works;
especially his Hymn-Book; and had a very
high esteem for the Life and Letters of Mrs. H.
A. Rogers.   To these he appealed wherever
he went; and showed their true meaning by
the light of his hallowed spirit and conversation.
I have often observed that a verse from the

hymn-book, quoted by him in the full glow of his pious remarks, would assume a freshness and a beauty not previously seen. His discourse had in it a salt which never lost its savour."

To what Mr. Lawry says of my father's walk with God, and his pre-eminent attainments in experimental religion, I wish to add a remark or two: He certainly did live in an extraordinary manner under the influence of the realizing light of faith. His interior eye was opened, and the Invisible appeared to his wondering and adoring mind. When I met in class with him his communications concerning the God "in whom we live, and move, and have our being," were very striking, and such, I think, as I have heard from no other. I can never forget the manner in which, at one time, he spoke of his awe of the majesty of God, and of his consciousness of being surrounded by the Divine presence: As if crushed beneath the weight of glory, amidst streaming tears of joy, he exclaimed, " *O what a being God is!*" In his walk it is evident God drew very near to him, and treated him with the condescension, the confidence, and the familiarity of one whom he called his "friend" This is abundantly manifest from various records in the preceding pages.

His attainments in Christian experience are justly characterized as " pre-eminent." When speaking on this subject, which is doubtless the root of the matter, he was ever at home: This is well known to tens of thousands. Our larger love-feasts furnished him with fine opportunities for pouring forth the fulness of his warm heart. Never did this favourite Methodist ordinance appear to more advantage than when he opened his mouth to witness his good confession before a thousand witnesses. The fear of man, so commonly a snare on these occasions, had here no power over him; for the love that casteth out fear appeared now his peculiar element. This gave him a door of utterance, and the whole multitude glorified God in him. In the general cast of his experience there was great simplicity and soundness, great depth and triumph. There was no art, nor appearance of art; all was natural and legitimate cause and effect. God moved on his heart; the fire kindled within him; then spake he with his tongue. Sound speech, which could not be condemned even by those who are of the contrary part, was the common dress of his thoughts concerning the kingdom within him. He was remarkably scriptural. It was evident he was no more spoiled by vain philosophy than he was the captive of wild enthusiasm. The record which God had given him concerning his Son, he believed with all his heart, and to him it was the only and sufficient rule. The wildness of speech and action which some good people have fallen into, in him stood reproved. As to the depth of his experience, by the suffrages of all, he excelled here. The honour of a professor in the deep things of God was long conceded to him. He dug deep, and brought forth treasures old and new from the unsearchable riches of Christ, dwelling in his heart by faith. He laid claim to all the great and precious promises concerning the image of God within; and when with his lips he pronounced them as descriptive of his own experience they bore the stamp and freshness of living truth. Within a few feet of the spot where I now write, I remember his standing up, above twenty years ago, before a vast concourse in a love-feast, when he described his progress into the depths of holiness under the imagery of Ezekiel's vision of the holy waters. His feeling, his voice, his action, rose with the subject till the effect was indescribable. But deep experience is not always what is termed happy experience: Some Christians drink deep into the Spirit, who are not generally remarkable for the triumph of faith. Not so my father: He felt that while he possessed a religion which brought him righteousness, it brought him also joy in the Holy Ghost. His religion made him happy. That was evident to all; and the fulness and constancy of the earnest of heaven in his breast, added much to the interest which he excited. When he visited Polperro on one occasion, the intelligent and eminent Dr. C. of that place, wrote to me soon after in New South Wales, and made some remarks on his extraordinary character. He thought him a

rue evangelist; and observed, that the solid and
:heerful happiness which he appeared habi-
ually to possess, standing, as it did, in connex-
on with age so advanced, greatly contributed
o render him a phenomenon of striking in-
erest.

———

THE story of this little volume will now be
:oncluded by a brief notice of a few of the many
)ractical and instructive lessons which it is
:alculated to teach.

1. It shows the reality and blessedness of
rue religion. Here is a man who was the
:lave of ignorance and sin, instantaneously
·oused and transformed by the call and energy
)f the Gospel ministry; and, for more than
hreescore years, the principle of fervent piety
hus implanted by the finger of God, is evinced
)y great moral rectitude, sublime mental en-
oyments, and by the continued exercise of a salu-
ary and powerful influence in promoting the
:olid happiness of those belonging to the circle
n which he moved. What has infidelity to
)ppose to this fact, or to compare with it?

2 It furnishes a commendable example of
ndustry and resolution in acquiring the know-
.edge of the useful arts, under circumstances of
;reat difficulty and discouragement. A man of
:ixty-five learns to write; and applies the valuable acquisition, very extensively, to purposes
)f great importance both to himself and to

others. Let this fact stimulate exertion in those who are in any wise similarly circumstanced.

3. It shows that a man unendowed with either distinguished talents or office, may become great in usefulness among his neighbours; so great, that it is not easy to find a parallel even among men of mind, education, and office. The subject of the foregoing pages was a man of plain understanding, without any approach to wit or humour, possessing, as we see, not the advantages of the commonest education: yet, with faith in Jesus Christ, pains and patience, he attains not only great virtues, but also great views and great energies; and last, not least, the distinguished honour of being beloved and blessed as the friend of thousands.

4. It sets before the eyes of the church an example of stability in Christian profession. Let the young professor be hereby encouraged to confide in Him who is "able to save unto the uttermost," and let "unstable souls" shed tears of penitential sorrow while they behold a man walking in the integrity of his Christian profession more than sixty years; "turning not aside, either to the right hand or to the left."

5. It speaks loudly to parents professing godliness, who have children grown to maturity; yet "without Christ, being aliens from the commonwealth of Israel." Their duty and their privilege are here set before them; Their *duty* to exercise unquenchable desire, and ardent effort for the conversion of their sons and daugh-

rs; and their high *privilege* of becoming rela-
d to them by ties more dear and tender than
1ose of flesh and blood.

6. It shows to pious persons who have re-
red from business, how happily and usefully
1ey may fill up the eve of life, provided God
as yet continued to them a measure of health
nd strength. Here is one, who, after he had
cquired a moderate competency, lays aside the
;orld as a garment: and, though now verging
)wards his "three-score years and ten," he
tarts in a new career of piety and usefulness
y which "his last days become best days,"
oth with regard to his personal peace, and to
he active benevolence of his life.

7. It shows how practicable it is for Chris-
ians to do good in their social intercourse; pro-
ided, that with a devout and spiritual mind,
hey give religion that decided prominence
vhich its infinitely momentous interests very
aturally and justly claim. To this branch of
Christian usefulness, the subject of this volume
rought no superior conversational powers, but
uch as rise spontaneously from a full heart
What he did in this way—and certainly he did
vonders—may, unquestionably, to a great ex-
ent, be accomplished by ten thousand other
overs of "the truth as it is in Jesus."

8 It shows, in the great work of saving the
oul, the corresponding and reciprocal import-
nce of the two-fold agency, human and Divine.
While most of the facts here stated clearly ma-

nifest "the power of God unto Salvation," yet are many of them so evidently made to depend on human instrumentality, as to say to our consciences, " Ye have not, because ye ask not"

9. It speaks very forcibly to those who wish to be useful in the church, and says, " Have faith in God ; for all things are possible to him that believeth." A Christian believer is here set before us, ardently desirous of saving souls from death ; faith in God through Christ is his perpetual theme; and hereby he becomes an extraordinary useful character.

10. It shows, with the force of demonstration, that the Gospel offers a free, full, and present salvation. Perhaps these three important points have seldom been more clearly established within so narrow a compass.

11. It evinces how very simple is the method of salvation by faith, and how efficacious on the heart and life is that faith, when it lays hold on the atoning blood, and the great and precious promises made to us through that sacrifice.

12. Finally, it exhibits a pleasing instance of the powerful effects of individual human influence, and the admirable economy of the Wesleyan-Methodists in bringing that influence, when right-directed, to bear on human society. Here is an humble individual in private life. He is determined on going to heaven himself; and has his heart set on the great work of moving as many thitherward as possible. With a soul filled with faith and love, he exhorts one,

and another, and another; and sets them in
motion towards the better country: He moves
from place to place, and similar effects follow.
Then he sits down in his little chamber, learns
to write, and, by his epistolary correspondence,
keeps those in motion that he had already moved.
Till shortly, by an effort, in the feebleness of
age, his pious influence is found, directly, or in-
directly, acting powerfully on the minds of
thousands, distributed in the various intermedi-
ate places between Saltash and the Land's End.
But, for his personal and relative good he was
indebted to Methodism. Although a constant
attendant at the parish church for above twenty
years, he knew nothing of religion, but lived in
utter spiritual darkness and sin, till he heard
the first sermon by a Methodist preacher. This
was the immediate instrument of an entire
change of heart and life. Inducted into the
ranks of Methodism, it was quickly perceived
he was capable of being useful; and accordingly
the subordinate, but important, office of class-
leader was assigned to him. This was his
place. In the service of sixty years, he never
rose above it, or rendered himself unworthy of
it And in conformity to the genius of Christianity, and the aggressive principle of the rules
of the body, he exhorted, reproved, or instructed
all with whom he had intercourse. Methodism is
one, in every town, in every village. Wherever
he came by the clue of friendship and impulse
of duty, his character, his office were respected;
he naturally found a wider door of usefulness

open to him; and, in the short space of a few days, he came into personal and familiar contact with hundreds of souls, hungering and thirsting after righteousness, who rejoiced in his light, and caught an increase of heavenly fire, from the Spirit of burning, which so eminently dwelt in him.

> "Much love I ought to know,
> For I have much forgiven."
> "Before the throne my Surety stands,
> My name is written on his hands."

THE END.

CONTENTS.

CHAPTER III.

CHAPTER IV.

CHAPTER V.

CHAPTER VI.

CHAPTER VII.

CHAPTER VIII.

CHAPTER IX.

Lightning Source UK Ltd.
Milton Keynes UK
UKHW022106171222
414057UK00006B/213